MODERN JAPANESE ECONOMIC THOUGHT

Since the late-19th century, Japan has made remarkable strides in industrialization. Beginning with the economic vision of Miura Baien in the 18th century, and employing a detailed comparison with the West, this book delves into the economic thought of the scholars who played a pivotal role in Japan's modernization process.

The author takes Fukuzawa Yukichi's theory of 'civilization' as the standard measure of Japan's modernization and compares it with differing visions from various critics whose research focused on rural poverty and social problems, such as Maeda Masana, early socialists, Yanagita Kunio and Kawakami Hajime. Further, the book explores new liberalism (Ishibashi Tanzan, Fukuda Tokuzo) and Marxism (Yamada Moritaro, Uno Kozo) in the 1920s and 1930s. After discussing the dilemmas faced by economists during wartime (Takata Yasuma, Ryu Shintaro, Shibata Kei), the author concludes this intellectual history with the country's post-1945 democratic reforms and their early demise.

This book is valuable reading for students and researchers of Japan's intellectual history. However, due to the book's comparative perspective, as well as the universality of the modernization experience, it will also appeal to students and researchers of the history of economic thought and modern intellectual history.

Kiichiro Yagi is Professor Emeritus at Kyoto University and Setsunan University, where he taught political economy and history of economic thought for over three decades. Thus, his research covers the theory of political economy and the history of economic thought, starting with Marxian economics and extending the scope of economic theory in the direction of evolutionary economics.

Routledge Studies in the History of Economics

Metaphors in the History of Economic Thought
Crises, Business Cycles and Equilibrium
Edited by Roberto Baranzini and Daniele Besomi

Liberalism and the Philosophy of Economics
Tsutomu Hashimoto

An Economic Philosophy of Production, Work and Consumption
A Transhistorical Framework
Rodney Edvinsson

The Early History of Economics in the United States
The Influence of the German Historical School of Economics on Teaching and Theory
Birsen Filip

Economic Methodology, History and Pluralism
Expanding Economic Thought to Meet Contemporary Challenges
Edited by Ioana Negru and Penelope Hawkins

Monetary Economics, Banking and Policy
Expanding Economic Thought to Meet Contemporary Challenges
Edited by Penelope Hawkins and Ioana Negru

Modern Japanese Economic Thought
An Intellectual History to 1950
Kiichiro Yagi

For more information about this series, please visit: *www.routledge.com/series/SE0341*

MODERN JAPANESE ECONOMIC THOUGHT

An Intellectual History to 1950

Kiichiro Yagi

Routledge
Taylor & Francis Group
LONDON AND NEW YORK

First published 2023
by Routledge
4 Park Square, Milton Park, Abingdon, Oxon OX14 4RN

and by Routledge
605 Third Avenue, New York, NY 10158

Routledge is an imprint of the Taylor & Francis Group, an informa business

British Library Cataloguing-in-Publication Data
A catalogue record for this book is available from the British Library

ISBN: 978-0-367-53293-2 (hbk)
ISBN: 978-0-367-53294-9 (pbk)
ISBN: 978-1-003-08131-9 (ebk)

DOI: 10.4324/9781003081319

Typeset in Bembo
by codeMantra

CONTENTS

FIGURES

TABLE

PREFACE

Long ago, a senior friend asked me, choosing words carefully not to offend me, to tell him the originality of Japanese economic thought if I believed its existence. He was my host professor when I did my research abroad in Germany in the year of the fall of the Berlin wall. I visited the university library there to prepare my talk on Japan and found a complete set of Collected Works of Fukuzawa Yukichi. In the days when excited people were talking about the vision of a unified European civilization, I read Fukuzawa in the guesthouse, who dared to say that civilization is the means to maintain the aim of the nation's independence. It was that time when I first thought of writing a book on the economic thought of Japan in its modernization process.

Fortunately, I could publish a Japanese book[1] on this theme after a decade in 1999. Though it had several appreciative reviews then, it remained out of print for long years, probably due to unfavorable sales. While thinking of its enlarged new edition, I received the invitation from the editor of the Routledge to publish a book on the history of Japanese economic thought, which I thankfully accepted. Since then, it has taken over two years. Now, at last, after over three decades, I can answer the question of my respectable friend with this book, though he deceased in the meantime.

It is doubtful to the variety of economic thoughts I introduced in each chapter shows the 'originality' of Japanese economic thought. I dealt with unnoticed inquiries in the age before the opening of ports, the embarrassment and excitement at the encounter with refreshing foreign ideas and with the prospect of the changing world, bifurcations in the direction of economic development, recognition of social problems, diffusion of Marxism in a generation of intellectuals, the quest for new liberalism, resistance and collaboration in the war years, and finally the reaction and disappointment in the post-war democratic reform. I would describe Japan's modernization experience as reflected in the lives and thoughts of eminent economists. I believe what I wrote was, in essence, universal to the experience of every nation despite the peculiarities that depended on the historical situation that modern Japan faced. I wouldn't say it is the 'originality.'

Out of twelve chapters of this book, the latter seven retained the outlines of my Japanese book 1999. The introductory chapter of the 1999 book described the process of introducing Western economics and the formation of academic economics from the viewpoint of 'institutionalization of the learning.' In this book, where I trace back to the origins of economic thought in the Tokugawa period and dealt with economic discussions of non-academics in the Meiji period, such an introduction is inappropriate. Another omission was the appendix, in which I discussed the features of 'developmentalism' and the mechanism of 'mobilization' of resources in the modern Japanese economy. 'Developmentalism' generally means the characteristic of a state that prioritizes economic development over the consolidation of civil rights and democracy and often uses measures of mobilization of economic resources by the authoritarian method. In that appendix, I raised whether the 'civilization' program as had been proposed by Fukuzawa was a developmentalist program or not and then discussed the modernization of Japan from this controversial perspective. However, after the long-continued stagnation of the Japanese economy since the 1990s, the developmentalist features of the Japanese economy were marginalized under financial liberalization, globalization, tertiarization of industrial structure, and rapid population aging. I now consider my appendix itself a reflection of the last intellectual boom around this concept. This is the reason for the deletion of that appendix. Still, attentive readers may notice that several chapters in this book still retain the problematics related to the 'developmentalism' debate.

The first five chapters are new. Chapter 1 is the prologue in which the endogenous growth of economic thinking in the Tokugawa period is described without details. I made it an introductory chapter, as I believe the image of the growth of Japanese economic thought before the encounter with Western economics is helpful to understanding the evolution of Japanese economic thought after the Meiji era. In Chapter 2, I chose Miura Baien as the representative of scholars in the Tokugawa period and discussed his economic idea compared to his Western contemporaries. This shows the level of economic thought a Japanese scholar could attain without knowing Western economics and suggests the institutional framework in which he had to live. Chapter 3 deals with Fukuzawa's framework with which he absorbed Western economics and conceived his development program for Japan under the heading of 'civilization.' The 1999 book had a chapter on Fukuzawa, too. But this chapter was a new rewritten version, though the main argument is not changed.

I added, this time, the divergent development programs in the Meiji Era (Chapter 4) and the early socialism and social policy (Chapter 5). The former dealt with a fundamental liberal economist Taguchi Ukichi and a nationalistic advocator of industrial promotion, Maeda Masana. The two were in the opposite position, but both represented gradualism compared with state-led industrialization under the slogan of 'Fukoku Kyōhei' (wealthy state and forceful military). While Taguchi trusted in the steady capital accumulation under a free market economy, Maeda proposed promoting indigenous industry, including agriculture and handicrafts. The chapter on early socialism and the idea of social policy (Chapter 5) is also new. It was necessary because it could provide us with the basic knowledge of these two ideas (socialism and social policy) around which every social movement, and later social scientists, should determine their positions. Combined with Fukuzawa's chapter, I hope these new chapters could considerably widen readers' perspectives on Meiji economic thought.

As I wrote, the following seven chapters retained the outlines of chapters of my 1999 book. However, I revised them based on criticism of the previous book and new literature that has emerged since then. Here, it may be helpful for the readers of this book to mention these chapters' topics briefly.

Chapter 6 discusses the 'rural economy' of Yanagita Kunio. I argue that Yanagita's works, which began with his devotion to agricultural policy, turned the Fukuzawa-type perspective of civilization upside down and expected much from the collaboration and initiatives of small producers in the countryside. Chapter 7 deals with Kawakami Hajime, focusing on his difficult path to becoming a Marxist around the years of his bestseller, *Tale of Poverty* (1917). We interpret his sway between 'self-interest' and 'altruism,' between 'production' and 'distribution' as the reflex of the split in the mind of Japanese intellectuals. In Chapter 8, we confirm the existence of a new, socially-minded liberalist Ishibashi Tanzan and follow his policy proposals that we can parallel with those of J. M. Keynes.

Then, Chapter 9 deals with Takata Yasuma's economic sociology. He could not be content with the general equilibrium theory that excluded the effect of social elements (power). His sociology led him to a fantastic idea of ethnic nationalism in the war years. Chapter 10 focuses on Yamada Moritarō, the author of the *Analysis of Japanese Capitalism* (1934). After looking into the structure of the *Analysis*, we consider the problems around the existence of 'semi-feudal' or non-capitalist agriculture under developed capitalism.

Chapter 11 discusses the collaboration and economic reform plans of two economists, Ryū Shintarō, with a Marxist background, and Shibata Kei, a modern theoretical economist. They expected reforms of the existing capitalist economy under the new order. At last, Chapter 12 tells various reactions of survived economists to Japan's surrender. This chapter is the epilogue of this book or story. Some of them were purged, and some were invited to collaborate on economic reforms and recovery. However, the 'postwar democratic reform' did not continue long. When Korean War broke out in 1950, Japan was firmly integrated into US's military strategy in the Far East.

Following chapters of this book in this way, I feel that I wrote not the history of economics *per se* but a story of a nation using the works and lives of those scholars. This nation, awakened by the encounter with Western powers, followed the course of 'civilization' to compete with them, extended its hegemony in neighboring countries, and was defeated in the long-continued war. Those who would read a more detailed description of topics and scholars concerned may be unsatisfied. I would apologize to them by saying that what interested me was the story of a nation and not the individual scholar or their works. My second apology was directed to the discontent with the too early ending. As for the history of economic thought after 1950, another volume by another author is needed.

I acknowledge the following: Routledge permitted me to use text from my old article in Chapter 11 and a table in Chapter 5 (Table 5.1). Professor Tanaka Hidetomi (Jōbu University) permitted me to use the coauthored text in Chapter 2.

The publisher of my 1999 book, Chikuma Shobō, Tokyo, noticed that I retain the full right to use its text. Similarly, Schäffer-Poeschel Verlag, Stuttgart, and Judicium Verlag, München, declared to me that I have the right to use my old text on Miura Baien and Fukuzawa Yukichi in Chapters 2 and 3, respectively.

On this occasion, I would acknowledge my sincere gratitude to my seniors and friends who encouraged my research of the history of Japanese economic thought. However, allow me to limit myself to mention only those names from whom I received their favor related directly to the topics of this book. Regrettably, I cannot show this book to those deceased seniors: Prof. Karl Brandt (Freiburg University), Prof. A. W. Coats (Duke University), Prof. Theodor Dams (Freiburg University), Prof. Peter Koslovsky (Hannover Institute for Philosophical Research), Prof. Donald Winch (Sussex University), Prof. Fukutake Tadashi (Tokyo University), Prof. Hirata Kiyoaki (Kyoto University), Prof. Mita Munesuke (Tokyo University), Prof. Morishima Michio (London School of Economics), Prof. Nishikawa Shunsaku (Keio University), Prof. Ōshima Yūichi (Nagoya University), Prof. Shionoya Yūichi (Hitotsubashi University), Prof. Sugihara Shirō (Kōnan University), Prof. Tamanoi Yoshirō (Tokyo University), and Prof. Tominaga Ken'ichi (Tokyo University). I appreciate Prof. Bertram Schefold (Frankfurt University) and Prof. Kurt Dopfer (University St. Gallen) for their encouragement related to the topic of Miura Baien (Chap. 2); Prof. Wolfgang Seifert (Heidelberg University), Prof. Komuro Masamichi (Keio University), and Prof. Ikeda Yukihiro (Keio University) related to the topic of Fukuzawa Yukichi (Chap. 3); Prof. Matsunoo Hiroshi (Ehime University) associated with the issue of Taguchi Ukichi (Chap. 4); Prof. Inoue Takutoshi (Kwansei Gakuin University) and Prof. Nishizawa Tamotsu (Hitotsubashi University) related to the topic of Fukuda Tokuzō; Prof. Negishi Takashi (Japan Academy) to the issue related to Shibata Kei; Prof. Makino Kuniaki (Keio University) related to the topics associated with Chapters 7, 8, 9, and 11; Prof. Yanagisawa Osamu (Tokyo Metropolitan University) about the issues of Chapter 11; Prof. Ikeo Aiko (Waseda University) to the topics of Chapters 11 and 12; Prof. Mizuta Hiroshi (Japan Academy) for his views on wartime and post-1945 Japan.

June 28, 2022
Yagi Kiichirō

Note on Japanese Words and Names

We use the standard Hepburn style romanization to write Japanese. We attach macrons to discern long vowels from short vowels except for internationally known names of cities and institutions. Japanese names are given in the normal Japanese order, i.e. family name first and given name next.

Note on Translated Citations

Except for those texts with the sources of translation, English citations from Japanese and other language texts are the author's translations.

Note

1 Yagi Kiichirō (1999) *Kindai Nihon no Shakai Keizaigaku* (Social Economics of Modern Japan). Tokyo: Chikuma Shobō.

1

PROLOGUE

Before Meeting Western Economic Thoughts

1.1 Social Structure of Japan in the Tokugawa Period

The Japanese term *Keizai* 経済 – in Chinese *Jīngjì* – is the abbreviation of the classical Chinese policy concept of *Keisei Saimin*経世済民, which initially meant 'governing the world and securing the life of people.' It was not the modern sense of 'economy' that signified the activities of individuals in production, distribution, consumption, and outcomes, but the moral obligation of lords and statesmen that ruled the nation. It covered the wise administration of treasuries of the central government (Shogunate in the Tokugawa period) and clans (Han) to policies that controlled and supported the people's economic activities. Still, in most cases, the arguments and judgments were constrained by the traditional ethical code of Confucianism.

However, even before the Japanese encountered Western economic thoughts, we can find many basic economic ideas and policy discussions that already utilized economic or financial analysis in the Tokugawa period. In the nearly 260 years of the Tokugawa period that succeeded the battles of warlords over a century, the economic transformation under the domestic peace (*Pax Tokugawa*) urged scholars and administrators to face new problems arising from this transformation.

When Bakufu (Shogunate) was established at the beginning of the 17th century, Tokugawa Shogunate applied the old Chinese concept of four vocational groups, *Shi*士 (warriors and officials), *Nō* 農 (farmers), *Kō*工 (artisans), *Shō*商 (merchants) in the administration of the people. Apart from the ruling status of *Shi*, the order of the other three was not hierarchical. *Nō* came second to *Shi*, as the rule of the society then was founded on the tribute from agriculture in the broader sense of the word. In familiar terms, farmers were called *Hyakushō* (hundreds of occupations) because they often performed various works in the countryside. The last two were bundled into one called *Chōnin* (town people).[1]

DOI: 10.4324/9781003081319-1

The core of this class system was the separation between ruling warriors and other classes. In particular, the separation between warriors (*Samurai* or *Bushi*) and farmers meant the disarmament of the countryside. This separation or the disarming of the country was critical to keep the rule stable. Before the reigns of Toyotomi and Tokugawa, warriors and armed farmers in the countryside were the main threat against rulers. Shogunate and clan lords forced warriors to reside in towns near the administrative headquarters or branch offices and robbed arms of farmers.

In addition to the commercial center, Osaka, and the old metropolis where the Imperial Court of *Tennō* resided, Kyoto, Edo (now Tokyo) emerged as the third-largest city in Japan, which surpassed the former two in the later Tokugawa period. Because Shogunate ordered clan lords to reside every other year in Edo, it became a gigantic consumption center that consisted of vassals of clan lords and Shogunate in addition to artisans and merchants. The treasury officials of clans sold their harvest in Osaka to support the consumption of their lords and vassals living in Edo. Merchants in Osaka distributed harvest and various products in their nationwide distribution networks.

As warriors lived separated from the land, they became dependent on the stipends given by their masters (clans and Shogunate). They generally received them in brown rice, so they needed rice dealers to change it into money. Artisans and merchants, the suppliers of daily necessities for the town life, were the primary consumers of the rice. Thus, they were symbiotic with the warriors in the town. The actual stipend payment depended on the tribute from the country (farmers including fishers) minus various expenditures of clan governments, including luxury consumption of the lord's family and constructive works ordered by the Shogunate, and it was often curtailed.

While living in town became expensive due to the general economic conditions, the living standards of warriors' households fell gradually under a general declining tendency in the actual price of rice. Wealthy merchants surpassed warriors in their economic powers, culture, and consumption. Lower or masterless warriors (*Rōnin*) had to live in poverty sustaining their lives by the piecework or various services in the town. Their distinction lay solely in the swords they wore on their sides.

The disarmed countryside was set under the self-control of village communities. Clan lords dispatched officials to villages in their territories to examine the productivity of land, impose the tributes of the harvest, and collect them. But the responsibility to deliver the tribute levied was taken collectively by the village as a unit. The village head and other village officials from upper-class farmers managed everyday village life, including delivering the imposed tribute under their joint responsibility. They sometimes bargained with clan governments in the case of difficulty such as poor harvest or on various demands of clans. As the unrest in the countryside could be a reason for the concerned clan lords' punishment by the Shogunate, clan governments had to monitor the situation in the country and nip the latent unrest by early suppression or compromise.

When the battle ceased nationwide, the 17th century marked the extension of cultivation and population increase, promoting commercial crops and side works in rural areas. Economic historians argue that it was the mid-Tokugawa period when solid farm households consisting of small families with mono-system inheritance emerged in Japan.[2] Though ordinary farmers were not allowed to have family-name, those farmers that kept their own houses in their lots of the village called each other by their house names. Farming in Japan with some side jobs has attained the stage in which the inheritance of assets and skills became significant.

The once-prevailing view of the slowdown in population and production growth in the latter half of the Tokugawa period is now in dispute among economic historians.[3] It is evident that Japan in the latter half of the Tokugawa period was marked by its intensive growth and diversification of production that leveled up the people's economic life under the market economy's penetration. It produced the possibility for not only scholars and warrior-officials but also other ordinary people, farmers, artisans, and merchants could develop a sense of economy.

Bakufu originally meant the military government of the supreme general (Shōgun).As the Tokugawa family occupied the head general of Japan since 1603, Tokugawa Shogunate could command its direct vassals and all clan lords and their subordinates indirectly, at least in principle. This political system is named the '*Baku-Han* system,' as local territories under clan lords were called *Han*. The advisors of the Shogunate recommended a loyalty-based ethical doctrine to legitimize the hierarchical structure of the ruling warriors grounded on the Neo-Confucian theory represented by Zhu Xi (1130–1200) and established a central Confucian school in Edo. It was different from the original ethical doctrines of Confucianism since the Japanese in the Tokugawa period prioritized *Chū* 忠 (loyalty to master) to *Kō* 孝 (filial duty). The classing of virtues of Confucianism was introduced into Japan with a modification suited to a hierarchically structured warriors' society.

The significance of the Shogunate's recommendation of neo-Confucianism went over its affinity to the hierarchical order of the society. Since Zhu Xi's school of Confucianism combined a rationalistic worldview with objective observation and comprehensive learning, it provided a solid ground for Japanese intellectuals to start their investigation into natural and societal areas. Since the mid-Tokugawa period, small private schools mushroomed in town and the countryside. Some used elementary summaries of neo-Confucian texts to teach reading and writing. Thus, its rationalistic traits influenced a wide range of people and loyalty-centered ethics under the rising literacy. As often suggested, it consists of one of the legacies of the Tokugawa period (Dore 1965).

1.2 Early Economic Insights[4]: From the Viewpoint of Ruling Warrior Rank

Probably the first stage of the opening of economic insights of Japanese was marked by the politico-economic discourse of warrior-scholars. Entering peace years, warriors had to question their mission to be armed. Authorized Confucian scholars taught that genuine warriors must prioritize loyalty to the master to their own life, and most warriors kept practicing *kendō* (sword fencing) and learning *hyōhō* (military tactics) without the chance of experiencing fights. Hand in hand with the challenge to the Zhu Xi orthodoxy within Confucian scholars, an accurate examination of the politico-economic situation emerged under the traditional name of *Keizai-ron* or *Keisei-ron* (discourse on politics).

Kumazawa Banzan (1619–1691) was taught by Nakae Tōjyu (1608–1648), one of the first that introduced the teaching of *Yōmeigaku* (teaching of Wang Yangming: 1472–1529), and after serving as an advisor of Okayama clan became an independent scholar. He realized the degeneration of the ruling warrior-officials and the economic misery among people. He recommended practical policies that fit people's actual attitudes affected by their financial situation. He found an irrationality in the present system where good harvests brought misery both to farmers and townspeople due to the fall in the price of rice. He saw a final solution in the return of warriors to the countryside. If warriors also cultivated the land, it could drastically reduce the tribute over farmers. As no market intervenes in production and consumption, good harvests could bring welfare to the four classes.

Though Banzan found the impracticability of the ideal rule of following ancient sacred rulers, he did not deny the ideal of *Jinsei* (a benevolent ruling). In the case of Ogyū Sorai (1666–1728) and Dazai Shundai (1680–1747), they considered the success of ruling to depend not on the benevolence of rulers but the artificially devised institutions and policies. Ogyū denied the cosmic metaphysics of Zhu Xi's philosophy and founded his school on the critical philological method to find the original views of Confucius and other ancient scholars. He interpreted sacred rulers' highly esteemed Michi (path) as an ensemble of artificial devices that ancient scholars had invented to control the people. In his *Seidan* (Political Discourses) presented to the eighth Shōgun Yoshimune in 1727, he attributed the present impoverishment of warriors to their situation like travelers without a home base and argued for their countryside returning. However, this proposal was not born from a romantic nostalgia for the community. Combined with the reform of the Shogunate that enabled its control over clans, Ogyū conceived it as an effective measure for the Shogunate to recover its hegemony in the economy from merchants. However, in the publication by his disciple, Dazai Shundai (1680–1747), which had the title of *Keizai-roku* (1729), the policy of warriors' returning to their land was no more recommended. Dazai regarded the present age as a degenerated age that needed more practical measures. Thus, he went into the policy proposal of the clan's monopoly of domestic products to acquire funds for the clan's finance and industrial growth.[5] Together with Banzan, these three scholars represented a pattern of discourse in which the classical concept of *Keizai* was applied to the socio-economic change in the mid-Tokugawa period.

Here, we must mention Sorai's rival, Arai Hakuseki (1657–1725), the scholar advisor of the 6th Shōgun Ienobu. He led the consolidation of the Shogunate's treasury which had been ill-disciplined in the era of former Shōgun Tsunayoshi rather successfully. He had a vague idea of the quantity theory of money in explaining prices and restricted the outflow of metal from Nagasaki. Seeing the reason for inflation in the successive light minting, he ordered the reminting following the standard that the first Shōgun Ieyasu fixed one century before. This reminting failed due to the shrinking of the circulating quantity of money. The deflation due to good minting stopped in the reign of Shōgun Yoshimune with the return to light minting combined with the drastic increase of copper currency. This policy resulted in prosperity during Tanuma Okitsugu's administration (1772–1786).

1.3 Deepening of Economic Insight and the Existing Order

All these scholars experienced severe life as masterless warriors (*Rōnin*), though they had occasionally served clan lords or Shōguns. Though they had to live on private teaching in the years of masterless warriors, their viewpoint remained the same as that of ruling warriors. However, as many scholars living in town began to accept disciples from non-warrior town people, they began to adapt their ideas to the life ethics of ordinary town people with their trades. Merchants in Osaka dared invite able Confucian scholars to head the school *Kaitoku-dō* that they founded in 1724. The shared learning of warriors and *Chōnin* (town people) established a unique tradition of learning in Osaka that avoided prejudice and appreciated commerce (Najita 1987). Yamagata Bantō (1748–1821), a genius merchant scholar that *Kaitoku-dō* produced, investigated the function of the rice market in Osaka that practiced futures contracts. He helped consolidate the treasury of the Sendai Clan. His warrior friend, that also showed his talent as a financial advisor of several clans, Kaiho Seiryō (1755–1817), declared the common traits of warriors' service with the principle of transaction behavior in the market.

As private teachers could not discriminate against ordinary people, they had to admit the equality of the role of the four classes. As the warriors' position was legitimized by their defense and administration service, the farmers' position was legitimized by their provision of crops and other products – the artisans' position by their refined works and the merchants' position by their service in distribution and financing.

The view of equality of the four classes could be traced back to Suzuki Shōsan (1579–1655), a Buddhist monk in the early Tokugawa period who had a warrior's prehistory. After an interval, the popular moral teaching of *Shin-gaku* (leaning of mind) appeared. Ishida Baigan (1685–1744), who came from the farmer rank and experienced merchant life, focused on the daily trade of the ordinary people and taught its sacred significance. Robert Bellah argued that this school's diffusion of trade ethics exerted the effect resembling the economic ethics of Protestantism in the West (Bellah 1957). Whether right or wrong, we can say that a functional role view of each class in society began to replace the hierarchical view of the four classes in the late Tokugawa period.

In the late phase of the Tokugawa period, the interest of administrators of clans and their advisors began to focus on the various schemes to recover the healthy treasury. They contained such measures as improving agricultural technology, promoting commercial crops and original products, introducing a clan monopoly of trade, issuing paper money whose circulation was limited in the clan territory (*Han-satsu*), etc. Some historians emphasized the emergence of the idea of common economic interest in this stage. Though their scope of 'common interest' remained in their clan territories, it could quickly develop into the concept of common national interest in the Meiji period.[6] Several authors circulated ambitious plans of trading and its expansion of united Japan before Commodore Perry arrived in 1853.

In the critical years before 1867, the main force of the rebellious Chōshū Clan consisted of irregular units recruited from non-warriors. Warriors, farmers, and town people reacted to the crisis that began during the 1863/1864 Shimonoseki War. Under the guidance of anti-Shogunate political leaders, they were led into the battle that brought forth the regime shift of the Meiji Restoration.

The obsoletion of the traditional reigns was apparent to any attentive persons. Katsu Kaishū (1823–1899) built up the Shogunate's naval force and negotiated the bloodless surrender of the Edo castle; he was a grandson of a wealthy blind masseur from the countryside that bought the warrior rank for his descendent. Ninomiya Sontoku (1787–1856) was a farmer who had experienced hardships since his youth and invented a rational method of joint saving and investment based on farmers' collaboration. He was entrusted with consolidating the administration and improving the production of several territories of minor lords and, at last, those of several domains of the Shogunate.[7] The old system then was barely maintained with such support from outsiders.

In the second chapter, we investigate economic writing of Miura Baien (1723–1789), remarkably comparing them with Western economic thought. Baien was a hidden scholar living as a local physician whose main work consisted of the universe's logical construction, including the physical and human world. His economic writings were occasional products answering the inquiry of others. We chose this scholar to represent Japanese economic thought in the Tokugawa period because we believe that Baien's recognition and analysis of the socio-economic situation reflected the top level of its understanding of Japanese then.

Baien constructed his systematic world view out of the idea of *Qì*気 in Zhu Xi's natural philosophy. However, he built the whole system by his methodology of *Hankan Gōitsu* (Reflection and integration), not by a static hierarchical order of Zhu Xi's *Lǐ* 理.[8] He eagerly collected books, including those that delivered the knowledge of Western sciences, and corresponded with scholars in Kyūshū, Osaka, and Kyoto. He visited Nagasaki to get the latest knowledge of Western science. However, he could not assimilate Western physics's atomistic or mechanical view.

Baien lived in the middle of the Tokugawa period when its basic social structure and political institutions were still stable despite the penetration of the market economy. The inapplicability of the nostalgic strategy that would resist the penetration of the market economy by returning warriors in the countryside, held by Banzan and Sorai, became apparent. However, mercantilist ideas of commercialization were not dominant yet. Thus, the period he lived in is appropriate to have a representative view of the economic situation of the Tokugawa period.

Another suitability is Baien's social position as a scholar living in the countryside. As an established physician, he was admitted to wearing swords, thus in the equal class of warriors. However, he knew well that he lived by the goodwill of his neighbor farmers in the village for his daily medical service to them. He had plenty of knowledge and experience of the economic relations between the countryside and towns and the interactions between villages and clan administrations. He was not against the contemporary political and societal institutions, but he provided several reinterpretations of traditional concepts that were more acceptable to Japan's situation in the 18th century.

However, we should not overlook another 'miracle' of a physician scholar who lived in Northern Japan's countryside, Andō Shōeki (1703–1762), who was a contemporary to Baien. He dreamt of a romantic utopia of *Shizen Kasshin no Yo* (the world of self-acting living truth), in which everyone is engaged in production equally and lives peacefully without domination. His name and ideas were long forgotten and became known widely in the mid-20th century.[9]

Through the penetration of the market economy that none could resist, a new use of the classic term *Keizai* to signify economic activity, business activity, in particular, emerged in the late Tokugawa period. Kaiho Seiryō used this term in a modern sense. Though some complained it was a misuse of the term, ordinary people, merchants, in particular, did not care about it. Thus, when Fukuzawa Yukichi (1834–1901) applied this classical term in the translation of 'economy' into Japanese, the soil for receiving the new concept of *Keizai* was already matured in Japan.[10]

Notes

1 Under these four groups, groups of discriminated people (*Eta* and *Hinin*) existed. Their discrimination survived even after the so-called 'emancipation edict' of 1871.

2 Nakamura (2000) proposed the concept of 'small-farmers' society' in which family farming occupied the majority of both agricultural production and population and argued for its development in East Asia. This proposal is in accord with the view of Japanese rural society that Hayami (2003) described using the concept of 'industrious revolution.' See also Hori and Kigoshi (2020) chap. 1.

3 According to an estimate, in the 17th century, Japan's population increased 2.6 times, arable land 1.3 times, and actual harvest 1.6 times. This growth decelerated in the next century to 1.03 in population and 1.3 in actual harvest (Nishikawa 1979: 9). Whether this slowdown means stagnation or not is one of the hot issues of economic historians. Nishikawa (1979) suggests the emergence of 'demographic transition' and the diversification of production.

4 In English, chap. 1 of Morris-Suzuki (1989) gives a basic overview of the economic thought in the Tokugawa period, while Honjō (1943) offers a detailed description of

it. Komuro (1998) is also helpful. Komuro (2003) is a research survey in the preceding two decades. Sugihara, Sakasai, Fujiwara, Fujii eds. (1990) is a convenient guidebook for modern Japanese economic thought beginning from the Tokugawa period.

5 Chap. 3 of Nishioka (2022) focuses his attention on Dazai's plan of 'Jōheisō '(public warehouse of rice to cope with famine). Nishioka further follows its development into the 'Shasō' of Nakai Chikuzan (a Kaitokudō's scholar) in chaps. 5 and 6.

6 Fujita (1998) stressed the emergence of the idea of 'Kokueki' (benefit of clan or nation). Yajima (2003) focused on the trade beyond the territories and applied the concept of 'mercantilism' to policy concepts in the late phase of the Tokugawa period.

7 See Ninomiya's biography by Tomita (1912).

8 See Mercer (1991) on Baien's cosmology.

9 Shōeki's masterpiece *Shizen Shin Ei Dō* (Andō 1753–1762?) was discovered from oblivion by Kanō Kōkichi in 1899. Kanō introduced Andō Shōeki in Kanō (1928). However, it was E. Herbert Norman (1949) that made him widely known. Now, Yasunaga (1992) provides an updated introduction of Shōeki's life and thoughts together with English translations of key texts.

10 See Mikami (1982) on this transition of 'Keizai's meaning.

References

English

Bellah, Robert N. (1957) *Tokugawa Religion: The Values of Pre-Industrial Japan*. Glencoe: Free Press.

Dore, Ronald P. (1965) *Education in Tokugawa Japan*. Berkeley: University of California Press.

Honjō, Eijirō (1943) *Economic Theory and History of Japan in the Tokugawa Period*. Tokyo: Maruzen.

Komuro, Masamichi (1998) "Trends in economic thought in the Tokugawa period." In Sugihara Shirō and Toshihiro Tanaka eds. *Economic Thought and Modernization in Japan*. Cheltenham: Edward Elgar.

Mercer, Rosemary (1991) *Deep Words: Miura Baien's System of Natural Philosophy*. London: E. J. Brill.

Morris-Suzuki, Tessa (1989) *A History of Japanese Economic Thought*. London: Routledge.

Najita, Tetsuo (1987) *Vision and Virtue in Tokugawa Japan*. Chicago: University of Chicago Press.

Nishioka, Mikio (2022) *Ideas and Economy in Japan: Innovation and Tradition*. Doshisha Economics Monographs 10. Tokyo: Yūhikaku.

Norman, E. Herbert (1949) *Ando Shoeki and the Anatomy of Japanese Feudalism*. Tokyo: Transactions of Asiatic Society of Japan.

Tomita, Kōkei (1912) *A Peasant Sage of Japan: The Life and Work of Sontoku Ninomiya*. London and New York: Longmans, Green, and co. Accessed on June 28, 2022: https://archiv.org/details/apeasantsagejap00yoshgoog/mode/2up.

Yasunaga, Toshinobu (1992) *Ando Shoeki: Social and Ecological Philosopher in Eighteenth-Century Japan*. New York and Tokyo: Weatherhill.

Japanese

Andō Shōeki (1753–1762?) *Shizen Shin Ei Dō* (The Way of the Operation of the Self-acting Truth). Included in Andō Shōeki Kenkyū-kai ed. (1982–1984) *Andō Shōeki Zenshū* (Andō Shōeki Collected Works), 31vols. Tokyo: Nōsangyoson Bunka Kyōkai.

Fujita Shōjirō (1998) *Kokueki Shisō no Keifu to Tenkai* (Lineage and Development of Kokueki Concept). Osaka: Seibundo Shuppan.

Hayami Akira (2003) *Kinsei Nihon no Keizai Shakai* (Economic Society of Japan in the Early Modern Age). Tokyo: Reitaku Daigaku Shuppan-kai.

Hori Kazuo and Kigoshi Yoshinori (2020) *Higashi Asia Keizai-shi* (Economic History of East Asia). Tokyo: Nihon Hyōron-sha.

Kanō Kōkichi (1928) "Andō Shōeki". *Iwanami Kōza Sekai Shichō* (Iwanami Lectures on World Thoughts). Vol. 3. pp. 325-350. Tokyo: Iwanami Shoten.

Komuro Masamochi (2003) "Nihon keizai shisō-shi: Edo kara Meiji he" (History of Japanese Economic Thought: From Edo to Meiji). *Keizai Gakushi Gakkai Nenpō* (Annals of the Society for the History of Economic Thought, Japan) 43. Tokyo: Keizai Gakushi Gakkai.

Mikami Ryūzō (1982) *Keizaigaku Kotohajime* (Beginning of Economics). Tokyo: Tōyō Keizai Shimpō-sha.

Nakamura Satoru (2000) *Kindai Higashi Asia-shi-zō no Saikōsei* (Reconstruction of the Historical Vision of East Asia). Tokyo: Sakurai Shoten.

Nishikawa Shunsaku (1979) *Edo-Jidai no Political Economy* (Political Economy of Edo Period). Tokyo: Nihon Hyōron-sha.

Sugihara Shirō, Sakasai Takahito, Fujiwara Akio, Fujii Takashi eds. (1990) *Nihon no Keizai Shisō 400-nen* (Japanese Economic Thoughts 400 Years). Tokyo: Nihon Keizai Hyōron-sha.

Yajima, Michifumi (2003) *Kinsei Nihon no 'Jyūshō Shugi' Shisō* ('Mercantilistic' ideas in the early modern age of Japan). Tokyo: Ochanomizu Shobō.

2

MIURA BAIEN'S *KAGEN*

In Comparison with the Contemporary European Economic Thought[1]

2.1 Reappraisal of *Kagen* in the Early 20th Century

Miura Baien (1723–1789)[2] is known as one of the most original thinkers of Japan before Meiji Restoration. Living in a province of northern Kyūshū, he established a systematic view of the world unrivaled by anyone in then Japan with his unbending investigation spirit. His logic that assumes successive stages of division and unification in every phenomenon reminds us of Hegelian philosophy's dialectics. This resemblance was first emphasized in the dark years of war by Saigusa Hiroto (1892–1963), a pioneer in Japan's history of philosophy and scientific thought. He was the first researcher to investigate Baien's natural philosophy system fully.[3] Since then, many have discussed Baien's logic and natural philosophy by comparing them with those of Western learning.[4]

Baien directed his lifelong effort toward the system of natural philosophy, culminating in his main work, *Gengo* (lit. Dark Words).[5] However, we cannot miss his economic writings: *Kagen* (lit. The Origin of Value) and *Heigo Fūji* (Propositions in 1786). The former was a reply to the question raised by a friend, Ueda Tōhaku, in 1773. The latter was the advice to the new lord of his clan. They contain Baien's penetrating views on the emerging features of the market economy and their effects on the feudal order of the society. Kawakami Hajime (1872–1946) made the first comparison of Baien's economic thought with that of Westerners. Kawakami, who became one of the most influential Marxian economists, studied Japanese economic thought in his early stage of academic life with a considerable spirit of nationalism. We can say that Baien's *Kagen*[6] was placed in the classics of Japanese economic thought by his 1905 article (Kawakami 1905), despite sporadic references preceding him.

According to Kawakami, Baien considered money a means of exchange and adopted a quantitative theory of money at the price level. He further argued

DOI: 10.4324/9781003081319-2

that Baien recognized the distinction in the concept of 'wealth' between the individual viewpoint and the national economy's viewpoint. In Baien's view, the affluence of money (gold and silver) means wealth in the former, but in the latter, not money but valuable goods (in Baien's word, 'cloth, corn, and instruments') are the true components of the 'wealth.'

After Kawakami, Fukuda Tokuzō (1874–1930) chose Pierre L. P. Boisguilbert (1646–1714) as the Western counterpart of Baien. Grounded on the knowledge of monetary economics then, Fukuda confirmed Baien's idea of the quantity theory of money but judged that Baien missed the function of money in the solution of obligation conspicuous in Boisguillebert (Fukuda 1910).[7] However, in this article, Fukuda confined his discussion only to the narrow range of ideas on money. He could not extend the comparison to the socio-economic conception of both scholars.

Kawakami was more attentive to the socio-economic aspect of Baien's thought. In Kawakami's view, Baien admitted that the expansion of the monetary economy was inevitable and aimed the prevention of the accompanying distortion of social order. Baien differed from those retrospective agriculturalists that condemned the town life of warriors and advocated their retreat into the country. He admitted that all four classes (warriors, farmers, artisans, and merchants) were indispensable to forming a healthy society. In 18th century Japan, a national network of the market economy had emerged already, and lively monetary transactions prospered in large cities. Baien envisaged contradictions in this development. He considered the rapid concentration of wealth in cities deteriorating the rural economy. The prospering cities absorbed productive resources from agriculture, and the financial exploitation impoverished farmers and warriors. In his words, "When agriculture diminishes, goods diminish. When goods diminish, the national asset is reduced" (MBCW 1: 919).

Baien discerned the egotistic profit-seeking of the individuals (*Kanbotsu*) from the guiding activities of the statesman with the ethical spirit (*Keizai*). In his view, the town was where 'playing hands' (*Yūshu*) around wealthy financiers enjoyed unproductive consumption. In contrast, the country was the economic basis on which a moral and social order was maintained. Kawakami focused his attention on this distinction. At that time, Kawakami was involved in the debate based on the national economy.[8] He interpreted Baien's criticism of luxurious consumption and financial exploitation in cities from his position in this debate as an ethical agriculturalist. During his research abroad around 1914, Kawakami had the will to introduce *Kagen* into the Western world through its German translation.[9] However, as he had to leave Berlin in haste due to the breakout of World War I, this plan came in vain. So far as is known, nothing remains in Kawakami's works directly related to this plan.

Fukuda paralleled Baien on another occasion besides Adam Smith (1723–1790) as one of the great contemporaries of the latter (Fukuda 1912). Since then, several researchers have tried to compare Baien and Smith. Among them, we would mention Nishikawa Shunsaku's analysis of the labor market (Nishikawa 1979) and

Yamasaki Masukichi's discussion on the relation between ethics and the economy in both economists (Yamasaki 1997). However, a detailed comparison between Baien's economic thought and Western economists has never been made.

2.2 Money and Currencies

In his 1905 article, Kawakami stressed that Baien stated Gresham's Law with the phrase, "If bad currency prevails, sincere gold will hide" (MBCW I: 917). However, this statement was not as original as Kawakami thought since many leading administrators and advisors of the minting policy of the Shogunate knew it already. In the years when Baien lived, the supply of the currencies was generally in shortage. It was a combined result of the limited supply of gold and silver and the rapid increase in domestic transactions. To cope with this shortage, clan lords issued paper money, '*hansatsu*,' for the occupation of their territories. The Kitsuki Clan – Baien was a physician living in the countryside of this clan – also introduced paper money, which promoted the penetration of the market into rural life.

Officially, the core part of the economic life of the four classes in the Tokugawa period was grounded on the rice distribution system. The products of clans, stipends of warriors, and the taxation over farmers were measured and determined in terms of rice crops. Since it was the basic policy of the Shogunate to maintain the separation of the country and the town, in other words, the separation of farmers and the other three classes, this rice standard system (*kokudaka-sei*) needed merchants and markets as its essential element to run. Clan lords and warriors had to sell the rice to purchase other goods for living in cities or administrative purposes. Artisans served the demand of residents in towns and farmers in the country. Thus, all three non-agricultural classes lived on the agricultural surplus.

Since the late 17th century, Shogunate's budget showed a chronic deficit, while the market had continued to suffer from the shortage of currencies. As a solution, Shogunate made a re-minting with the reduced ingredients in 1695. However, the gain from it was spent away quickly by unexpected expenditures; the former gold and silver coins flew into the hands of exchangers for melting, and the circulation of new light coins caused inflation. Gresham's law could be applied to the effect of several attempts of re-minting undertaken by the Shogunate in the Tokugawa period. This inflation brought prosperity in the Genroku era (1688–1704) among merchants and artisans in cities, while warriors with fixed stipends experienced hardships.

The reform was guided by Arai Hakuseki (1657–1725), a scholar-politician advisor of the sixth Shōgun Ienobu and the seventh Shōgun Ietsugu. To stop the inflation, Hakuseki proposed a re-basement of the coins with the idea of the quantity theory of money. Hakuseki's reform in 1714 also failed due to the Shogunate's inability to absorb the light currency from the market. From this period, the currency's instability continued to the years in which Baien wrote *Kagen*.

Hakuseki opposed the agriculturalist policy of Ogyū Sorai (1666–1728), his rival advisor of the Shogunate. Hakuseki's main concern lay in the recovery of the balance of the budget of the Shogunate and not in return to the traditional society. Still, Hakuseki shared a standard view of Confucian scholars that blamed the motive of profit-seeking and justified only the economic activities with an ethically regulated motivation. Baien's critical view of the '*Kanbotsu*' also ran in the same direction.

However, moralistic criticism against profit-seeking activity existed also in the Western intellectual tradition. In the *Zur Kritik der politischen Ökonomie* (A Contribution to the Critique of Political economy), Karl Marx reminded his readers of Aristotle's distinction between *Chremastik* and *Ökonomik*.[10] The former meant monetary transactions that aimed acquisition of profit based on unequal exchange. The latter was the exchange of necessary goods without exploitation. Baien argued, "Both – '*Kanbotsu*' 乾没and '*Keizai*' 経済 aim benefits. The former regards gains (*Ri*, in Chinese *Lì* 利) as a benefit, while the latter regards righteousness (*Gi, in Chinese Yì* 義) as a benefit" (MBCW 1: 915f.).

Behind Aristotle's distinction between '*chremasitik*' and '*oikonomik*, ' we can see the viewpoint of ancient Greek polis administrators who were concerned with the provisions of necessaries of the citizens. It is similar to Baien's distinction between '*Kanbotsu*' and '*Keizai*.' In its origin, the Japanese equivalent to 'economy' '*Keizai*' was an abbreviation of *Keisei Saimin* (lit. governing the world and saving the people) which meant a general policy of the statesman in Chinese classics. Baien's usage of '*Keizai*' retained this original meaning.

This classical position of *Keizai* had its advocator in Ogyū Sorai. He grasped 'economy' from the viewpoint of the head of the state, the *Shōgun*. In his view, the Shogun must have policy and power to secure the subordinates' life and maintain the society's ruling structure. Sorai attributed the increasing misery of the warriors to their city life. Original warriors had lived in countries with their subordinates simply. But present warriors living in cities had to purchase every necessary from merchants by their money income, thus becoming dependent upon commerce. Warriors and all residents are, therefore, unstable and vulnerable to commercial exploitation. He expressed this figuratively as 'the situation of travelers.'

> Artisans and merchants, including peddlers and day laborers, leave home and move to the capital cities yearly. The spending will be small if they realize their situation as travelers. All the residents in Edo [the old name of Tokyo] never notice it and take the traveler's life as permanent. Life in cities becomes expensive, and, thus, all the incomes of warriors are absorbed by merchants.
>
> *(Ogyū 1973: 306)*

Sorai was anxious about the deteriorative effect of city life on the 'institution' that corresponds to life with Confucian ethics.

> Institution means legislation and temperance. Under the rule of ancient saints, the institution was founded to make hierarchical order clear, prevent luxury, and thus enrich the world. A thoughtful device indeed! [...] It is the institution that settled the order in the wear, residence, and tools, or the manners of the wedding, mourning, correspondence, gift, and attendants. The institution settled all in accordance with the distinction between the noble and the mean, to the size of income and the rank of service.
>
> *(Ogyū 1973: 311)*

Sorai considered the abolition of the 'traveler's situation' and the reconstruction of the institution as the measure to prevent society from corruption. In his policy proposal, he recommended encouraging parsimony and storing rice in the hands of warriors. He intended to strengthen warriors' position in bargaining with merchants. He even approved the bankruptcy of merchants under the view that commerce was, in nature, unstable.

In contrast to Sorai's reactionary tendency, Baien took the progress of the market economy for granted. He approved the development of crafts and commerce, so long as it fit the development of agriculture and did not undermine the social order. One can assume that Baien's conditional approval of the monetary economy reflects the improved maturity of the economic society in the middle of 18th century Japan.

Boiguillebert, whom Fukuda named the Baien's Western counterpart, was a contemporary of Hakuseki and Sorai. The socio-economy of France in his age showed similarities with that of Japan in the Tokugawa period in several respects: It had a class system whose top was occupied by the nobility; the agricultural surplus that was extracted by the semi-feudal land property was the basis of the national economy; penetration of the activity of financiers caused impoverishment. Boisguillebert observed the rural economy's misery brought forth by Corbert's policy of promoting trade and industry on low grain prices. Boisguillebert suggested an alternative course of development that was supported by the growth of agriculture and was to attain 'l'opulence générale' (general welfare). In this proposal, he presented the peculiar French view of wealth that regards agricultural products as the primary products in contrast to the derivative nature of other products.

'L'opulence générale' is, in Boisguillebert's view, attained by 'natural circulation' that starts with the expenditure of landlords. Not only does the direct spending in agricultural products return to agriculture, but a part of the expenditure on industrial products is also plowed back into agriculture via the purchase of food and materials from the income of artisans. The intervention is unnecessary so long as this circulation runs smoothly.

This circulation is enabled by the function of money as means of exchange. Boisguillebert argued that due to the debasement or refinement of the spirit, modern people could not live without many sorts of goods and services and had to introduce money to expedite their transactions.

> It is, therefore, that known guarantor at most exchanges and of reciprocal tradition that was called into the world when corruption and politeness had multiplied the needs of life; from three or four species when they were in infancy up to more than two hundred where they are today, [...] and the seller of a term does not trade most often with the merchant of that which he currently needs, and for the recovery of which he divests himself of his own. The money then comes to the rescue, and the receipts, which in fact from his purchaser is him a power of attorney, with guarantee, that his intention will be carried out in proportion to what he has divested himself of the hands of the duration of which he was the owner; that is the only function of money.
>
> *(Boisguillebert 1966. 2: 985)*

In Baien's case, the introduction of money is also explained by its service as means of exchange.

> Gold and silver have their services in surrogating goods. Gold, silver, and copper coins are named as currencies. They are precious and small. Since they create mobilization among large, heavy, and not easily transportable goods, their service is paralleled with that of vehicles and vessels.
>
> *(MBCW 1: 907)*

Originally, money was only a means to purchase necessaries, but as it represented preciousness and general exchangeability, it gradually became the object of desire.

> In ancient years, when human nature was still simple and not tempted by luxury, this (six necessaries) sufficed. As the change of the world and human nature has proceeded, people have forgotten the significance of the goods that are easy to acquire and suffice their needs. They now take it essential to seek the thing that is hard to acquire and produce.
>
> *(ibid.: 906)*

> Gold and silver are noble, while six necessaries are humble. As six necessaries are humble, assets of the nation become lean.
>
> *(ibid.: 908)*

Observing the imbalances that accompanied the penetration of monetary transactions, both Baien and Boiguillebert recommended that statesmen the promotion of agriculture. But in the place of the concept of economic circulation in Boisguillebert's reflection, the logic of division and unification (*Jori*) serves as a general frame of observation in Baien's case. So, in Boisguillebert's case, the spending of the leisure class may have a positive contribution, so long as it constitutes a link in the national circulation. In Baien's case, his term 'balance' lacks the actual concept of circulation. His idea of the 'balance' consists only of a rough correspondence between the estimated amount of agricultural surplus and the size of non-agricultural classes. Thus, in Baien's thought, the possibility that luxury consumption stimulates economic industry has no place to develop.

2.3 Playing Hands and Original Vocation

After thus glancing at Baien's view of money and currencies and his dichotomy of 'Kanbotsu' and 'Keizai,' we now turn to the topic that challenged him to answer in *Kagen*. As Baien stated in its Preface, he was asked why the wage had a steep rise in the fat year, while many poor could not get jobs in the lean year. Since the food is cheap in the fat year and expensive in the lean year, many would suppose the opposite would be true. Baien's answer was the following:

> The annual surplus of food flows into the hands of wealthy merchants that transport it to the City. Therefore, the Country becomes empty. Whether it starves or not depends totally on the City. If the City becomes empty, there is no place that can supply the Country. However, the City, never being anti-famine storage, does not accumulate goods for the sake of the Country. It is just the rest of the consumption of free hands. For this reason, the Country has no provision for food, and the City has wasting worms around the accumulated food. It is easy for the grain to fill the storage and reduce it. Therefore, a fat year is enough to be plenty of food, and a lean year is enough to exhaust the Country. In the year of good harvest, having no shortage in food, the poor wish to return to their original vocations. In the year of bad harvest, because they have no food supply, the healthy poor attempt to survive by wage labor, and the weak by the begging. Leaving original vocations and moving to derivative jobs are inevitable results of the situation and are not dependent on their will. Thus, they wish to return to their original vocation as soon as they find themselves in a fat year, like those on a remote journey rejoice in the returning ship. This makes those who work for wages rare and those who perform derivative jobs idle. Therefore, all the prices rise. Then, in a year of bad harvest, as the water stream after the shower dries up soon, they desert their original vocations and run to the derivative jobs. Therefore, all the prices fall.
>
> (*ibid.: 925*)

This is the description of an early stage of the labor market, where wage laborers are not reproduced endogenously and are supplied from other sectors.

As Nishikawa (1979) pointed out, Adam Smith noticed a similar reverse movement of wages and food prices in the chapter on wages of the Wealth of Nations. He explained it by using the demand and supply model of labor.

> In years of plenty, servants frequently leave their masters and trust their subsistence to what they can make by their own industry. But the same cheapness of provisions, by increasing the fund which is destined for the maintenance of servants, encourages masters, farmers, especially, to employ a greater number. Farmers upon such occasions expect more profit from their corn by maintaining a few more laboring servants than by selling it at a low price in the market. The demand for servants increases, while the number of those who offer to supply that demand diminishes. The price of labor, therefore, frequently rises in cheap years.
>
> *(Smith 1976: 92f.)*

Since a rich surplus of corn is interpreted as a fund to employ workers, i.e. capital, demand for labor is high in the fat year and low in the lean year. On the supply side of the labor market, Smith observed that many artisans would leave their masters in the fat year with the hope that they could live independently; but in the lean year, when food price is high, poor artisans tend to lose their stock and are forced to look for employers.

> In years of scarcity, the difficulty and uncertainty of subsistence make all such people eager to return to service. But the high price of provisions, by diminishing the funds destined for the maintenance of servants, disposes of masters rather diminish than increase the number of those they have. In dear years too, poor independent workmen frequently consume the little stocks with which they had used to supply themselves with the materials of their work and are obliged to become journeymen for subsistence. More people want unemployment than can easily get it; many are willing to take it upon lower terms than ordinary, and many are willing to take it upon lower terms than ordinary, and the wages of both servants and journeymen frequently sink in dear years.
>
> *(ibid.: 93)*

Compared with Smith's explanation, Baien's differs on two points. First, Baien's explanation lacks a description of the demand side of the labor market. In Smith's case, the accumulated corn is interpreted as the fund or capital from which its owner intends to gain profit. In Baien's vision, the extra profit closely linked with monetary transactions overshadowed everyday transactions. The grain reserve in the hand of the rich is vaguely regarded as the food for employed workers. But the classical concept of capital that considers the stock of goods destined for further production as its real entity is missing. Therefore, the contrasting situation between the fat and lean years is attributed solely to the inflow and outflow of workers.

The second difference lies in the source of labor inflows. In Smith's case, 'independent workmen' are the source. Though the reproduction of the working class is not still attained, the separation of agriculture and manufacturing is already established in the Smithian world. In Baien's case, the source of labor inflow is the 'original vocation,' namely, peasants in most cases. As this is so, workers' inflow into the labor market means a kind of migration from the countryside to cities. The migrant workers retained social attachments to the 'original vocation' in the country, where they could feel at home.

The two differences above suggest that a similar view of Smith and Baien is mistaken. His counterpart in the West should be looked for among the pre-Smithian figures, to whom the process of separating the industry from agriculture was of great interest.

Baien considered the four classes system normal. The migration of peasants from the country to the city is one of his worries that might decay the system. He recommended a policy to let peasants make their own reserve of goods (cloth and corn) to avoid the ruin of the 'original vocation' in the lean years.[11] The instability of the wage level is not the matter he was worried about. He welcomed the employer's complaint about the high wages in the fat year since he regarded it as a sign that a considerable part of migrants had returned home. To him, prevention of the outflow of human resources was the best policy to stimulate agricultural production.

In addition to the migrant inflows of peasants, economic society in Baien's age had another social element that was difficult to integrate with the official four-class system. It was 'playing hands' (*Yūshu*) or 'playing population' (*Yūmin*) in the cities we already mentioned in the previous section. Baien's distinction between four classes and the 'playing population' would parallel the productive and unproductive classes in the Western political economy.[12]

> If any of the four classes are missing, the service for society cannot be performed. Therefore, endeavor to their own shared function on the ground of original jobs in the order of warriors, farmers, artisans, and merchants, is in itself the awful service for heaven. Those who stay out of this order and consume the goods of the society without any service to the people are called the 'playing population' and regarded as the evil worms of the nation.
> *(MBCW 1: 912)*

Sorai had used the term 'playing population' before Baien. 'Yūshu' is a synonym for it in Baien's usage. Kawakami interpreted it as the urban leisure class whose core consisted of wealthy merchants and financiers. However, in some cases, it was applied to vagabonds that left their home village and wandered within clans' territory. So, in a broader sense, it was used by the population that absorbed the crop reserve without offering legitimate services to society as a whole.

The term 'playing hands' reminds us of 'free hands' in James Steuart (1712–1780). He divided the population into farmers and 'free hands' exempted from the laborious burden of cultivation. In his *Principles of Political Economy*, 1767, Steuart described the course of economic development that started from the increase in the agricultural productivity, then on the grounds of agricultural surplus, made the industry of 'free hands' flourish, and finally entered the mutual stimulation process between agriculture and industry.

> One consequence of a fruitful soil, possessed by a free people, given to agriculture, and inclined to industry, will be the production of a superfluous quantity of food, over and above what is necessary to feed the farmers. Inhabitants will multiply; and, according to their increase, a certain number of the whole, proportional to such superfluity of nourishment produced, will apply themselves to industry and the applying of other wants. … From this operation produced by industry, we find the people distributed into two classes. The first is that of the farmers who produce the subsistence and who are necessarily employed in this branch of the business; the other I shall call free hands; because their occupation being to procure themselves subsistence out of the superfluity of the farmers and by labor adapted to the wants of the society, may vary according to these wants, and these again according to the spirit of the times.
>
> *(Steuart 1966: I, 42–43)*

The artisans and merchants in the four-class system in the Tokugawa period Japan correspond to the classes of 'free hands' in Steuart's classification. But the rigid hierarchy in Japan cemented their position in the social system to repress the dynamic interactions between agriculture, commerce, and industry. The 'playing hands' might be a part of the 'free hands,' but they were parasites to the system that had no productive function.

Students in the history of economic thought would mention Richard Cantillon's (c.1680–1734) concept of 'entrepreneur' as a typical Western figure liberated from the possession of the land. In his stress on the instability of the entrepreneur's situation, we see similarities with Tokugawa scholars' view of the non-agricultural population.

> All the others are Entrepreneurs, whether they establish themselves with a fund to conduct their business or are entrepreneurs of their work without any funds. They can be considered as living in uncertainty; Even beggars and thieves are contractors of this class. Finally, all the inhabitants of a state draw their subsistence and advantages from the funds of the landowners. They are dependent.
>
> *(Cantillon 1964: 54)*

However, the risk intrinsic to an 'entrepreneur' activity is not always perceived as unfavorable. "The circulation and barter of commodities and commodities, as well as their production, is conducted in Europe by Entrepreneurs, and at risk" (ibid.: 46). Entrepreneurs' risk is the other side of the coin of their freedom and initiative. The positive role of their intervention in production and distribution lies at the core of the concept.

2.4 Institution and Moral

In the pre-Smithian Western economic literature, the debate on luxury played a vital contribution to the progress of economic thinking. In the middle of the 18th century, David Hume (1711–1776)'s argument that luxury promotes the refinement of arts and tastes, at last, won the debate. Smith's emphasis on the virtue of saving presupposes Hume's victory. The capitalist's integrity of accumulative spirit should not be equaled to the archaic praise of the simple life.

In general, Baien held the opposite view of Western supporters of luxury and its diffusion. He considered that the diffusion of convenience and luxury is an evil that destroys the welfare of the people and undermines the social order.

> The cultivated land has increased since the nation's beginning, but the population also has risen considerably. Today's thrifty life would be equal to the luxurious way of life, not to say an idle and luxurious life. It's truly awful and terrible. Thus, if we aim for the welfare of the people, we should solely devote ourselves to thrift and restraint. Thrift and restraint are not in vogue because of the deficiency of institutions. Rule and guidance are a matter of institutions. Without institutions, any rules and guidance will be ineffective.
>
> *(MBCW 1: 935)*

However, he was not such a reactionary thinker that would dare to return to a simple life. In the *Kango* (Words on Morality, completed 1763), Baien discussed the place of the benefit (利*Ri*) from the viewpoint of his philosophy. He doesn't believe that the ruler or the saint can force the (Confucian) morality on the people by their will. According to Baien, the tendency to attain one's benefit belongs to the inherent nature of a man, whose mind was shaped by the transformation of the fundamental ether (気 *Ki*, *Qi*). The combined appearance of the benefit-seeking activity forms the dynamic moment, where the 'institution' device can affect the direction.

> What people like is the benefit (*Ri*), and what people dislike is the loss (*Gai*). If the ruler makes people beneficial, they become joyous and satisfied. If the ruler makes people lose, they become troublesome and dangerous. Therefore, the ruler that governs mass promotes the benefit widely. Promotion of the benefit eliminates the loss. Why are people not satisfied by it? Thus, nothing is better than bringing people benefit; nothing is worse than bringing them loss. I call the performing of the good with no benefit the wasted good; the performing evil with no loss a wasted evil.

> Tolerating waste evils of the people and providing the benefit of rescuing the mass are never waste deeds but virtues of heaven and earth.
>
> *(ibid.: 692)*

The lords in this passage resemble the enlightened princes that make the maximum welfare of the nation their obligation. However, in the phrase 'dangerous people,' we can assume a hidden memory of the large-scale peasant rebel in the Shimabara Clan (a clan in the western part of Kyūshū). This rebellion occurred in 1637 from the ruthless exploitation of the governors and provoked several unrests in the neighboring clans in Kyūshū.

In the *Kagen*, Baien distinguishes '*Kanbotsu*' and '*Keizai*' sharply by identifying them with the dichotomy of the gain and the right. But, in the following passage, the border between the contents of the 'gain' and the 'right' is very fragile: "Lords regard the virtue as the benefit; the commons regard private gains as the benefit. The benefit of the lords is wide and eternal; thus they make the right as the benefit" (ibid.: 692). Here, the difference between the benefit of lords, i.e. the right (*Gi, Yì*), and the benefit of the people lies in the degree of the width and length. Concretely, the benefit of lords means ruling the clan without severe unrest among the people. If a clan lord fails in attaining this task, the Shogunate deprives him of the clan and places another lord in his position. The factor that forced clan lords into a beneficial rule was the possibility of clans' seizure concerning the commons' unrest.

In 1786, at the age of 64, Baien was asked by the new lord about the domestic policy of the clan. It is said that Baien discussed with the lord on the ground of the previously submitted answer, *The Proposition of the Year 1786* (*Heigo Fūji*), for three days. This Proposition contains a detailed list of the necessary knowledge for the clan officials in their daily administrations and the policy proposals to attain the population's welfare. In this Proposal, Baien emphasized the communication and cooperation of clan officials with the villages, which were virtually autonomous entities with their local leaders. He even applied the term "the right of the subordinate" (Kahō no Gi) (ibid.: 875), which had been, in his view, often neglected by the arrogant clan administrators.

> The loss in the top turns out to be the gain of the bottom. The foliage prospers on the healthy root. As these represent the reason, lords must know that severe exploitation undermines the vigor of the subordinates. [...] Reflect on the revenue to be able to cover the expense by it. If it is realized, others should be left to the farmers and merchants. Under your ethical guide, the clan will naturally become prosperous.
>
> *(ibid.: 892)*

However, he never used the term 'the right' for the people in the City. Indeed, he recommended promoting handicrafts and commerce that could attract the inflow of money from other clans. But he was anxious about the commercial activity and the increase of the 'playing population' that might diminish the clan's wealth and undermine the stable social order.

Baien admitted the propensity of human nature to pursue its benefit and recognized the significance of the policy that promotes the benefits of the people. However, he didn't admit the possibility that the pursuit of individual benefits transformed itself into an ethically legitimate action.

> A small man looks only at himself and never looks at others. His mind is filled with the pursuit of self-benefit. The quest for self-benefit is to injure others. Menacing the subordinates and offending the superiors, envying and interfering with others, and the target returns to himself. It not only ruins him personally but also endangers the clan.
>
> *(ibid.: 694)*

Every economic transaction contains this trait of selfishness. But the economic activities of the 'original vocation' are integrated into the social order and would not exceed the border of toleration so far as the social order is stable. Oppositely, commercial activities and monetary transactions have no obstacle to restraining selfishness. Here appears the role of 'institution' in Baien's social philosophy.

Baien divided measures to guide the people into two categories: the first contains moral rules and teachings (*Rei*礼 and *Kyō*教) that prevent man from evil actions antecedently; the second has policing and punishments (*Sei* 政 and *Kei* 刑) that are applied after the emergence of evil acts. Baien was a moralist as much as he appreciated the former more than the latter. However, he knew well that without the general spirit of simplicity and self-restraint, moral teachings had no effective control over the action of the people. "If institutions are not stable, moral guiding has nothing to do against the evils" (ibid.: 935). In the case of Sorai, 'institution' signified basic official rules and social orders corresponding to them. The hierarchy in the family life, social status, and political order and the ways of actions corresponding to them are the core of the 'institution.' This is the canon toward which both moral teaching and policing activity are oriented. The solid existence of the 'institution' guarantees the validity of moral teachings and nourishes the spirit of simplicity and self-restraint.

A Western reader might be tempted to compare the guiding function of the 'institution' with Adam Smith's 'invisible hand.' But contrary to the latter, the former is the artificial device that the saints or saints-like politicians established (like the sacred founder of the Tokugawa reigns, Ieyasu) and cannot be maintained without careful observance of the ethical canon corresponding to it. The morals and the way of life of rulers are essential in this respect. This resembles somewhat the pre-Smithian economists' emphasis on the influence of the sovereigns and nobility over the ordinary people.

British authors from B. Mandeville to D. Hume welcomed the diffusion of luxuries for their vital functions in the tastes and arts of the people. Contrastingly,

French economists from Boisguillebert to Quesnay recognized a crisis in the nation in the excess spending on the consumption of luxury goods. But even in their case, an alternative circulation from the spending on necessaries to the productive accumulation lay behind their criticism. In Baien's case, the stress on moral influence doesn't lead us to such autonomous growth of economic society. The economy as a whole should be regulated to attain the right virtue.

In the ending paragraph of *Kagen*, he wrote:

> When the right virtue prevails, man is affected by it. Its guidance is like canalizing water to the valley. Everything is possible. Lords are molders, and subordinates are soft clays or hot irons. Whether they shape useful instruments depends solely on the hands of molders.
>
> *(ibid.: 937)*

Baien admitted the human propensity toward own benefit granted. But the liberation of the motivation of self-love was strictly rejected. The people's morality should be molded to fit the 'institution.' As the *Propositions* reveal to us, the clan then retained its military functions, through which the four-class system acquired legitimacy. In conclusion, the people in the Baien's world were not free. He seemed to stand firmly turning back on the possible transformation that J. Steuart described as "the great alterations in the affairs of Europe" (Steuart 1966, I: 24).

> The great alteration in the affairs of Europe within these three centuries, by the discovery of America and the Indies, the springing up of industry and learning, the introduction of trade and the luxurious arts, the establishment of public credit, and a general system of taxation, have entirely altered the plan of government everywhere.
>
> From feudal and military, it becomes free and commercial. I oppose freedom in government to the feudal system, to mark only that there is not found now that chain of subordination among the subjects, which made the essential part of the feudal system. The head there had little power, and the lower classes of the people little liberty. Now every industrious man, who lives in the economy, is free and independent under most forms of government.
>
> *(ibid.)*

Baien died in the year of the breakout of the Revolution in France. About half a century later, Fukuzawa Yukichi (1834–1901) was born in the neighboring Nakatsu Clan as the second son of the lowest rank family of its warriors. He avowed resolutely to be the enemy of the rank system of the Tokugawa period and became one of the first interpreters of Western economic thought in Japan. Fukuzawa's theory of 'civilization' was precisely the teaching of the conscious and accelerated catching-up process of 'the great alterations' in the West.

Notes

1 This chapter has its origin in the English manuscript coauthored with Prof. Tanaka Hidetomi (Jōbu University, Isesaki-shi) that was translated into German by Udo Wartha and published in Bertram Schefold ed. (2001). The German title was "Baien's *Kagen* in der ökonomischen Dogmengeschichte des 17. und 18. Jahrhunderts in Europa und Japan."

"The collaboration of Tanaka and Yagi began when Yagi read Tanaka's article in a journal *KAN* (Tanaka 2000) and invited Tanaka as the coauthor of the planned commentary to *Kagen*. Yagi first showed Tanaka the rough plan. Tanaka supplied Yagi the first Japanese draft of the first half. Then Yagi translated it into English and added the latter half. Yagi appreciate Prof. Tanaka for his approval to use the coauthored manuscript for this chapter.

2 Most of Baien's works were compiled in the two volumes *Collected Works*. Baien-kai (1912). Hereafter, we show the page numbers of Baien's text by this edition [MBCW].

3 Saigusa (1941) (1943). Both are now in vol. 5 of Saigusa (1972–1973). Saigusa began his historical research under the heavy influence of Marxian materialism and tried to discover the tradition of rational thought in Japan.

4 Among others, we would like to mention Yamada (1988). In Western language, see Mercer (1991).

5 Baien completed this work in 1775 after several times rewriting. It was circulated by way of transcription in the limited circle of scholars.

6 A German translation was published with commentaries (Schefold ed. 2001). The English version of the commentary by the editor, Bertram Schefold, is included in Schefold (2016: 369–393).

7 This judgment did not hinder Fukuda from distributing *Kagen* in a private printing among his acquaintances.

8 See Inoue and Yagi (1998).

9 Kawakami mentioned this plan in Kawakami (1915). See KWCW 8: 83.

10 "In Ch.9, Book 1 of his *Politics*, Aristotle sets forth the two circuits of circulation, C-M-C, and M-C-M, which he calls 'economics' and 'chremastics,' and their differences. The two forms are contrasted with each other by the Greek tragedians, especially Euripides" (Marx 1970: 137).

11 This is general advice to the lords of clans. However, in his village, he persuaded farmers to organize an association that offers aid to the severely suffering fellows in lean years. This association functioned well and continued long.

12 *Kagen*'s economics has much to do with *Guanzi*'s. *Guanzi* is a Chinese classic on political, economic, and philosophical writings written by an ancient bureaucrat Guanzhong (??-BC 645). In *Guanzi*, the author emphasized the distinction between essential activities (*Benshi*) and nonessential work (*Mozuo*), as Baien did. "It is ever so that the most pressing matter in managing a state is to be certain first of all that nonessential production and luxury and artfulness are prohibited. If nonessential production and luxury, and artfulness are prohibited, the people will have no way to make a living when wandering about. Such being the case, they must remain engaged in agriculture. When people serve in agriculture, fields will be well cultivated. If fields are well cultivated, the grain will become plentiful. If the grain is plentiful, the state will prosper. [...] Therefore, they prohibited nonessential production and put a stop to exotic arts so as to benefit agricultural activities. Now those who engaged in nonessential production and exotic arts from one day's work may obtain five days' food, while a peasant may work for an entire year and not have enough to feed himself. Hence people abandon essential activities to perform nonessential work. If this occurs, the fields will be left uncultivated, and the state will become impoverished" (Rickett 1985: 177).

References

Western Language

Boisguilbert, Pierre (1966) "Dissertation de la nature des richesses, de l'argent et des tributs, ou i'on d' écouvre la fausse idée qui règne dans le monde à l'egard de ces trois articles" (1707). *Pierre de Boisguilbert ou la naissance de l'*économie politique. 2 vols. Paris: Institut national d'études demographiques.

Cantillon, Richard (1964) *Essai sur la nature du Commerce en général*, ed. by Henry Higgs. New York: A. M. Kelley.

Inoue, Takutoshi and Yagi, Kiichirō (1998) "Two inquirers on the divide: Fukuda Tokuzō and Kawakami Hajime." In Sugihara Shirō and Tanaka Toshihiro eds. *Economic Thought and Modernization in Japan*. Cheltenham: Edward Elgar, pp. 60–77.

Marx, Karl (1970) *A Contribution to the Critique of Political Economy*, tr. by S. W. Ryazanskaya. Moscow: Progress Publishers [German original: *Zur Kritik der politischen Ökonomie*. Berlin: Verlag Franz Duncker. 1859].

Mercer, Rosemary (1991) *Deep Words: Miura Baien's System of Natural Philosophy*. London: E. J. Brill.

Rickett, W. Allen (1985) *GUANZI*,: Political, economic, and philosophical essays from early China Princeton NJ: Princeton University Press.

Schefold, Bertram ed. (2001) *Vademecum zu einem japanischen Klassiker des ökonomischen Denkens: KAGEN: Vom Ursprung des Wertes*. Düsseldorf: Verlag Wirtschhaft und Finanzen.

———. (2016) *Great Economic Thinkers from Antiquity to the Historical School*. London and New York: Routledge.

Smith, Adam (1976) *An Inquiry into the Nature and Causes of the Wealth of Nations*, ed. by E. Cannan, with a new Preface by G. J. Stigler. Chicago, IL: University of Chicago Press.

Steuart, James (1966) *An Inquiry into the Principles of Political Economy*, ed. by Andrew S. Skinner. 2 vols, Edinburgh and London: Oliver & Boyd.

Japanese

[MBCW] Baien-kai ed. (1912) *Baien Zenshū* (Baien, Collected Works). 2 vols. Tokyo: Kōdōkan.

Fukuda Tokuzō (1910) "Boiguilbert no kahei-ron to Miura Baien no kaheiron ni tsuite no guko" (A view on the concept of money in Boisguilbert and Miura Baien). *Kokka Gakkai Zasshi*, 24(6), pp. 775–791.

———. (1912) "Miura Baien-cho *Kagen* wo Dōjin ni wakatsu no jo" (Forward in the occasion of distributing Miura Baien's *Kagen* to the friends of the Society). *Hitotsubashi-kai-Zasshi*, (78).

Kawakami Hajime (1905) "Miura Baien no *Kagen* oyobi Motoori Norinaga no *Tamakushige* ni arawaretaru kahei-ron" (Ideas of money in Miura Baien's *Kagen* and Motoori Norinaga's *Tamakushige*). *Kokka Gakkai Zasshi* (University of Tokyo), 19(5), pp. 79–105.

———. (1915) *Sokoku wo Kaerimite* (Looking Back Motherland). Tokyo: Jitsugyō no Nihon-sha.

Nishikawa Shunsaku (1979) "Baien no keizai seisaku genri" (Baien's principles of economic policy). In *Edo Jidai no Political Economy* (Political Economy of the Edo Period), chap. 4. Tokyo: Nihon Hyōron-sha, pp.94–113.

Ogyū Sorai (1987) "Seidan" (Political discussions), In Ogyū *Sorai* (1973), K. Yoshikawa et al. eds. *Nihon Shisō Taikei*., Vol. 36. Tokyo: Iwanami Shoten, pp.259-445.

Saigusa Hiroto (1941) *Miura Baien no Tetsugaku* (The Philosophy of Miura Baien). Tokyo: Daiichi-shobo.

———. (1943) *Baien Tetsugaku Nyūmon* (An Introduction to Miura Baien's Philosophy). Tokyo: Daiichi-shobō.

———. (1972–1973) *Saigusa Hiroto Chosaku-shū* (Saigusa Hiroto Works). 12 vols. Tokyo: Chuō Kōron sha.

Tanaka Hidetomi (2000) "*Kagen* no economii" (Economics of *Kagen*). *KAN* (Fujiwara Shoten), 3(Autumn)., pp.220–230.

Yamada Keiji (1988) *Kuroi Gengo no Kūkan* (Space of the Dark Words). Tokyo: Chuō-kōron sha.

Yamasaki Masukichi (1997) "Miura Baien to Adam Smith – *Kagen* to *Kokufuron*" (Miura Baien and Adam Smith – *Kagen* and *The Wealth of Nations*). *Baien Gakkai-hō*, (22), pp. 26-34.

3

CIVILIZATION AND POLITICAL ECONOMY IN FUKUZAWA YUKICHI[1]

Grounds for Laws of Political Economy

3.1 Fukuzawa Meets Western Economics

Fukuzawa Yukichi (1835-1901) represents a salient case of an Asian scholar taking an active role in the diffusion and assimilation of Western ideas. His motivation for this assimilation and his creativity in this implementation is what we investigate in this chapter.

Economic thought in Japan underwent a radical turn through Fukuzawa. It was a turn away from the art of rulers, which corresponded to the original meaning of the classic word *Keizai* (*Keisei saimin*), to a social science based on a market economy. It is unlikely that Fukuzawa, born in a family that favored learning and attended a private Confucian school in his hometown, was unfamiliar with traditional economic discourse in Japan. Thus, had there not been an impressive discovery made in Western political economy that Fukuzawa could not find in the classic literature of East Asia, he would not have been so enthusiastic in his assimilation of Western political economy. He explained,

> At first, *in particular, political economy* was very difficult for me to read. However, after coming to grasp the meaning through re-reading it repeatedly, every passage startled me with novelty; fresh and fabulous arguments attracted my heart and soul so deeply as to make me forget meals. At the same time, I adopted Wayland's *Ethics* to understand ethical teachings that we cannot find in the five norms of Confucian doctrines. Around this time, I endeavored to translate Chambers's *Political Economy* and discussed its topics one by one with Mr. Obata and others. Think of my background, having grown up in a provincial samurai family with no knowledge of the world, reading only Chinese classics under the banner of loyalty. After losing the belief in Buddhism, I chose to study

DOI: 10.4324/9781003081319-3

> Western learning and been impressed by its truth, read Dutch and English literature on natural sciences, and witnessed Western society while on tours. I determined deeply to investigate its depths. I was eager to learn about human affairs, yet I had no reliable source. I knew what I should doubt and doubted it already and knew what I should believe without believing it. It is like the buds of early spring waiting for the nurturing rain. My intellect had not completely rid itself of the customs of the provincial *samurai.* As I read Western history and encountered teachings of Western economics and ethics, it was all too natural that a storm raged in my brain for a while.
>
> (*FYCW* 4: 377f.)

What element of the Western political economy impressed him so strongly? It was the concept of the 'laws' that political economy explores through social phenomena. To date, economic discourse in Japan had been that of rulers who administered the lives of the ruled. The then-current term for 'economy' in Japan, '*Keizai*,' was an abbreviation of the classic *phrase* '*keisei saimin*' or '*keikoku saimin*' (managing society or the state and rescuing the people). Within such a patronizing framework, economic laws that emerged from the people's economic activities were inconceivable.

Fukuzawa seems to have been surprised by the ideas of the Western political economy that the free competition of people in business could harmonize people's interests in determining the market's prices. However, it is essential to know that he adopted the laws of political economy or economics[2] (*Keizai no hōsoku*) not as ideology or established dogma but as similar to the study of nature in that these laws were grounded on the alert and objective investigations. Before his encounter with Western political economy, Fukuzawa was a student of natural science who had studied medicine, biochemistry, and architecture in line with Western learning during the Tokugawa period.

The first book on the Western political economy that Fukuzawa read was Chambers's *Political Economy* (Chambers's ed. 1852). When he read it, he was working as a translator of Western literature affiliated with the office of the Shogunate. In his *Autobiography*, we can read about a comical conversation he had with his senior over the term 'competition,' which appeared in the contents of *Political Economy*:

> I was reading Chambers's book on economics. When I spoke of the book to a certain high official in the treaty bureau one day, he became much interested and wanted me to show him a translation. He said that if translating the entire book was too much, he would like to see the table of contents. I began translating it (it comprised some twenty chapters) when I came upon the word 'competition,' for which there was no equivalent in Japanese, and I was obliged to use an invention of my own, *kyōsō*, literally, 'race-fight.'

When the official saw my translation, he appeared much impressed. Then he said suddenly, "Here is the word 'fight.' What does it mean? It is such an unpeaceful word."

"That is nothing new," I replied. "That is exactly what all Japanese merchants are doing, [...]."

"Yes, perhaps," went on the official. "I understand the idea, but that word 'fight' is not conducive to peace. I could not take the paper with that word to the chancellor."

I suppose he would rather have seen such phrases as "men being kind to each other" in a book on economics, or a man's loyalty to his lord, open generosity from a merchant in times of national stress, etc. But I said to him, "If you do not agree to the word 'fight,' I am afraid I shall have to erase it entirely. There is no other term that is faithful to the original."

I did delete the offending term in black ink and let him take the papers. From this little incident, one may gather the character of the other officials whom he represented in the government.

(FYCW 7: 148f.; Autobiography: 190f.)

Recognizing the Shogunate's reluctance to absorb basic concepts of Western political economics, Fukuzawa used his translation of Chambers's *Political Economy* in his commercial publication of the continuation of his bestseller, *Seiyō Jijō Gaihen* (Conditions in the West). This book is so well-written in a basic Japanese style that it may surprise today's reader to know it was, in fact, a digested translation of the Chambers' book. In what follows, we quote the book's description of the nature of the laws of political economy[3]:

> It is observed that the various phenomena of the physical world, the motions of the celestial bodies, the physiology of animals and plants, and the stratification of earth's surface are all regulated by laws attracting our wonder by their wisdom and beneficence. In political economy, we find laws of a like character — imperfect and inexplicable when viewed separately and alone, but beautiful and complete when connected together and viewed as a whole; and thus, though referring to sublunary objects, like physiology, geology, and botany, it cannot fail to elevate the mind to a contemplation of the wisdom and beneficence of Creator. Since these laws are not made by man, or capable of being altered and improved by him, it may be asked: What reason is there for his studying them? The answer is: So that he may know and obey them.
>
> *(Chambers's ed. 1852: 51)*

In the following paragraph, Fukuzawa defined the laws of political economy as those that regulate the people's material life and enable their well-being. According to the traditional conception, the economic activities of individuals did not work together to create a harmonious whole, and political economy was the art of the rulers who regulated the people. However, in this paragraph on *Political Economy*, Chambers's book denied this view. It stressed the natural or non-man-made character of the laws of political economy that govern the economy as a whole. Furthermore, it praised these laws for their beauty and completeness. According to *Political Economy*, knowing and following the laws of political economy furthers the welfare of individuals, just as understanding and following physical laws furthers industry or knowledge, and following physiologic laws furthers health maintenance.

Caution is necessary when judging Fukuzawa's view on the political economy based on his translation work.[4] Still, it is safe to say that his emphasis on the laws of economics is documented in his later works. In both *Gakumon no Susume* (An Encouragement of Learning, published in 1872–1876) and *Bunmeiron no Gairyaku* (An Outline of a Theory of Civilization, published in 1875), Fukuzawa praised the laws of economics and the founder of Western political economy, Adam Smith:

> The person who for the first time discussed the laws of economics and brought about a change in commerce was Adam Smith.
>
> *(FYCW 3: 60; On Education: 98)*

> Adam Smith discovered the laws of economics, and world commerce took on a new dimension.
>
> *(FYCW 6: 90; Outline: 107)*

Suppose the laws of economics are conceived to be natural and inherent in individual economic activities, as in the case of Chambers's textbook. In that case, the policy that fits this view must be a liberal one that is limited to protecting contracts and property and eliminating artificial obstacles that hinder the effective functioning of economic laws. As the recollection of his encounter with his senior concerning the term 'competition' suggests, Fukuzawa favored competition in the market economy. Approving the relevance of Western economics to the market economy of Japan at that point, he even attempted to circulate a popular argument for a liberal trade policy.[5]

However, Adam Smith presupposed a well-developed market economy and individuals guided independently by their plain 'self-love.' The state of society and the people of Japan at that time differed from those Adam Smith had in mind. The ordinary Japanese that Fukuzawa encountered daily were those who unquestionably obeyed feudal regulations and occasionally engaged in irrational follies. Thus, the question arises as to whether the 'laws of economics' that Fukuzawa found in the Western political economy could be valid for such people and a backward society as Japan. Could Fukuzawa maintain his conviction about the laws of economics in his later years? What remained of the 'beautiful' and 'complete' laws of economics that attracted him when he first encountered the Western political economy and applied it to explain the situation of Japan at that time? These are the questions that we address here.

3.2 Subjective Aspects of the Laws of Economics

In the middle of his career, which roughly corresponded to the 1870s, Fukuzawa published original works as an independent writer.[6] In this stage, he knew that situations of the market economy differed considerably depending on place and time; furthermore, he knew that economic outcomes rely heavily on the conditions of the actors who participated in transactions. He admitted that considerable variation existed among people in their capabilities of the competition and that, in international trade, in particular, the disparity among nations was enormously significant. Moreover, even in Western nations, he knew that a dispute between liberalism and protectionism was occurring, and every government vindicated its policy according to different principles. Thus, he recognized that the direct application of Western theory would not be appropriate for the economic policies of Japan:

> We cannot overlook the influence of this imbalance of power upon the economy of the whole country. Economic theory is very complex, extremely difficult to understand. And since conditions differ from country to country, we cannot, of course, directly apply Western economic theory to Japan.
>
> *(FYCW 4: 172; Outline: 211)*

In *Outline,* we cannot find detailed elaborations of such laws of economics that work independently from the will and knowledge of individuals. In other words, at the mid-point of his career, Fukuzawa grasped political economy from a viewpoint that emphasized the subjective elements of economic activities. Directly after the previous quotation, he continued: "Nevertheless, there are two general principles which are universal for any country at any time" (FYCW 4:172; *Outline*: 211).

> The first is that of accumulating wealth and dispersing it again. [...] the essence of economics does not lie in prohibiting expenditures. The merits or demerits of expenditures and outlays of money can only be calculated by what comes back in return. [...] The goal of economists is to make the gains outweigh the losses, and gradually enhance the wealth of the entire nation by a steady process of accumulation and expenditure.
>
> *(FYCW 4: 172f.; Outline: 211f.)*

> The second principle is that to accumulate and spend resources, there must be knowledge proportionate to the resources, and there must be knowledge proportionate to the resources and habits of handling them.
>
> *(FYCW 4: 173; Outline: 212)*

These two 'general principles' are not objective laws in the economic world but rather norms related to the consciousness or actions of economic agents. The first principle corresponds to the economic activity representing capital accumulation through transactions. The second promotes 'knowledge' and 'habit' suited to production, transaction, and accumulation. In the following pages of *Outline,* Fukuzawa applied these two principles to the situation of feudal Japan and concluded that the 'split' of knowledge between the upper and lower classes hindered Japan from prospering.

Furthermore, it is notable that Fukuzawa listed 'honesty' (*shōjiki*), 'knowledge and diligence' (*benkyō*), and 'frugality' (*kenyaku*) as the three essential elements that ground 'wealth' (FYCW 4: 52; *Outline*: 60[7]). A similar trio was repeated in *Minkan Keizairoku* (Economic Discourse for Civilians) of 1878–1880, which Fukuzawa published as the merchant's version of the *Encouragement.* At first, this trio sounds like the list of ethical virtues for merchants, but 'knowledge and diligence' combine these virtues with the 'laws of economics.'

However, we must ask ourselves whether these personal virtues are sufficient for dealing with a backward economy full of irrational customs and power imbalances. Here, we must avoid the misconception that Fukuzawa's emphasis on personal virtues should be interpreted similarly to Max Weber's emphasis on Puritan ethics in the emerging age of capitalism. On the contrary, Fukuzawa was never stoic and unwilling to force anyone to be a patient. His recommendation to those who would pursue business in unstable situations was to use the device of 'insurance,' which could guarantee a 'constant mind' in place of the traditional 'constant fortune.' On the level of the national economy, he demanded the government build a solid foundation for the rational economic activities of civilians by extending policies in the area of currency, administration, financial institutions, transportation, and public works. An economy in which the three virtues work effectively emerges via a coincidence of the efforts on both sides of civilian and government spheres.

In *Outline,* Fukuzawa interpreted the ethical virtue of 'honesty' from attaining 'profit' (*ri*). He explained how this larger target evidenced the superiority of Westerners over the Japanese in this respect:

> It would seem from this that Westerners are more honest than Japanese. However, careful consideration of the facts reveals that Westerners are not necessarily more sincere in their dispositions than Japanese. Westerners try to expand their business to gain greater profits in the long run. Because they are afraid dishonest dealings will jeopardize long-range profits, they have to be honest. Their sincerity does not come from the heart, but from wallet.
>
> *(FYCW 4: 81; Outline:159)*

In comparing the Japanese with Westerners, Fukuzawa does not hide his nationalism. He combined the rational and decisive quest for profits with ideas and customs grounded in the spirit of national independence:

> To fight for one's advantage was prohibited by the ancients, but to fight for one's advantage is a fight for principles. It is high time for our country to fight with the foreigners for its own advantage and principles.
>
> *(FYCW 4: 80; Outline: 96)*

Since this lack of concern and courage is not a natural defect but something lost as the result of custom, methods to reactivate these attitudes must also rely on custom. The only conclusion one can come to is that changing our customs is a matter of extreme importance.

(FYCW 4: 81; Outline: 96f.)

3.3 Grounds for Objective Laws

It would be hasty to conclude that Fukuzawa's objective view of the 'laws of economics' disappeared in his mid-career writings. Here, we must note that Fukuzawa embraced Western economics from the beginning as a scientific research program and not a fixed doctrine. We remember that the text of Chambers's *Political Economy* translated by Fukuzawa stated that partial and separate inquiries could not grasp the effect of the laws of economics. In Fukuzawa's view, economics required investigating these laws and their careful application according to different conditions.

Most researchers agree that *Outline* is the best of Fukuzawa's writings because it systematically conveys his thoughts. Fukuzawa dedicated this book to presenting the laws of civilization and validating them. Thus, if we consider the 'laws of economics' as a part of the more extensive laws of civilization (theory of civilization), most of the problems surrounding Fukuzawa's position on political economy are solved.[8]

Outline mentioned two methods of inquiry that apply to finding laws for human affairs dependent on variable conditions or precarious directions of the human mind. The first is a macroscopic observation, which "is to take all the human sentiments in the land en masse, compare them over a long period, and draw conclusions based on empirical observation" (FYCW 4:55; *Outline*: 63). Through this method, variation eventually diminishes, and a statistical law of a large number becomes applicable.

The second involves tracing proximate causes further to remote causes:

> The proximate are more readily visible than the remote causes. There are more of the former than of the latter. Proximate causes are apt to mislead people by their closeness, whereas remote causes, once discovered, are certain and unchanging. Therefore, the process of tracing a chain of causality is to begin from proximate causes and work back to the remote causes. The farther back the process is traced, the more the number of causes decreases, and several actions can be explained by one cause.
>
> *(FYCW 4: 57; Outline: 66)*

Fukuzawa recommended the argument of objective laws grounded on statistical inquiry. It is not a deductive method derived from infallible axioms. When Fukuzawa encountered Western economics for the first time and understood it as a 'science,' he meant that inquiry into economics is characterized by the empirical investigation that systematically identifies laws and their manifestations. Such an understanding of objective laws does not collide with his apparently relativistic understanding of economic theory cited previously.

The grand theory he established according to the two above methods is the 'theory of civilization,' which discusses "the spiritual development of the people of the nation as a whole" (FYCW 4: 3; *Outline*: 1). The people's level of knowledge and virtue reflects the level of civilization. If we call it at ease in historiography, as Fukuzawa himself did, these levels signify the general conditions of "the trend of the times" (FYCW 4: 60; *Outline*: 69). Proximate causes do not explain why Confucius and Mencius were distanced from their rulers or why Kusunoki Masashige, a hero of local samurai who fought for Emperor Godaigo, had to die in a desperate battle (e.g., the ignorance of the lords of ancient China or the misjudgment of Godaigo). From a macroscopic view of remote causes, Fukuzawa argued that the lofty ideas of Confucius and Mencius did not fit the general conditions of the people. He argued in the same way that Ashikaga Takauji, who came from a prestigious family, was more suited than Kusunoki Masashige to head the warriors who had grown up in kinship-structured societies. Generally speaking, no individual can succeed outside the effects of 'the trend of the times.'

If 'the level of knowledge and virtue of the people' determines the general trend, is it necessary for people with little knowledge and virtue to endure a despotic government and a miserable economy? In such a situation, both the people and government are caught in a vicious cycle they cannot escape. This is the definition of an uncivilized society. Fukuzawa sometimes came close to such a pessimistic vision when he criticized feudal Japan or the situations of other Asian societies, such as China and Korea. However, for the Japanese readers of *Outline*, he maintained that the level of civilization is not fixed according to destiny and that people and government share the mission to develop civilization of their nation.

> As I said before, civilization is a contract between men, and the attainment thereof is mankind's essential goal. Each and every person must carry out his function in the pursuit of that goal. The government is in charge of maintaining order and handling current affairs; scholars focus upon a wide spectrum of ideas to discover future alternatives of action; both industry and commerce manage their respective enterprises to contribute to the wealth of the nation.
>
> *(FYCW 4: 67; Outline: 78)*

Fukuzawa assumed that the fact that the human species possesses intellect and creates a society for itself implies it has the drive to pursue higher levels of civilization. He thought that each person, as well as the government, had a function in this pursuit. The economic activities of industry and commerce are indeed conditioned by the present level of knowledge and virtue of the people. However, suppose industry and commerce succeed in developing economic activities and increasing national wealth. They can contribute to progress regarding the general level of knowledge and the virtue of the people. The function of the government to provide general education and other public utilities is an essential element for the progress of civilization. To perform such tasks, the government should avoid excessive interventions.

On the other hand, the activities of scholars are worth encouraging. Their scientific inquiries are related to future possibilities. In *Minkan Keizai-roku* (Discourse on Private Economies, 1877, 1880), Fukuzawa praised scientific inquiry that is motivated by intellectual curiosity beyond economic calculation by using an old proverb: "Those who like it exceed those who know it" (FYCW 4: 349).

Economics is, to Fukuzawa, the science that aims toward 'profit' and brings 'convenience' to the life of the people. Still, the economy is only a part of civilization. Philosophical Investigations into the natural world and human society are the grounds for civilization, and civilization itself is the state that allows the human species to dominate the world or determine its level of domination. 'Science' is the modern form of that intellectual investigation. To Fukuzawa, economics is a 'science' whose mission is to 'discover future alternatives for action.' Thus, economics contributes to raising the present state of the economy as well as that of civilization.

3.4 Spatiotemporal Structure of Civilization

Through his encounter with the Western political economy, Fukuzawa knew the existence of laws in social phenomena and understood they were grounded in the competitive activities of individuals pursuing their interests. Indeed, Fukuzawa absorbed liberal and individualistic elements of Western economics, but he was never a dogmatist who applied them directly to the situation of Japan. Instead, his approach was empirical, exploring the causal relationships between socio-economic phenomena from a macroscopic perspective. Fukuzawa extended the concept of laws in human affairs that he received from Western economics to the 'theory of civilization,' which judged social phenomena from the level of civilization, that is, the level of knowledge and virtue of the people as a whole. Since economics is a part of the social phenomena as a whole, the manifestation of the laws of economics must also be modified by the level of civilization.

We cannot judge precisely how mature Fukuzawa's view of civilization was before reading F. Guizot's *General History of Civilization in Europe* and H. T. Buckle's *History of Civilization in England*. However, the concept of civilization had certainly been familiar to him ever since he translated Chambers's *Political Economy*.

Chambers's *Political Economy* distinguished between the 'barbarous state' and 'civilized state' of the human species and asserted that history showed the progress of nations from the former to the latter. Since inferior passions of men flourish and moral virtue develops weakly in the 'barbarous' or 'savage' state, Chambers maintained that trust among the people is missing and no institution that enhances general welfare can appear. In contrast, inferior passions are mitigated in the civilized state, and institutions for general interest are established. Some may imagine that primitive people live in freedom. However, their freedom is only the freedom to starve or pursue despotism and crime. It is never similar to the freedom allowed under the laws of the 'civilized' state.[9]

The progress of civilization, however, does not proceed uniformly. The view of civilization in Chambers's *Political Economy* retained a spatial structure that ordered nations according to their level of civilization. In the present, there are still tribes that remain in the 'savage' stage of human development. They live in a primitive state without any effective rules or government. That said, not all nations that have governments are fully civilized. China is equipped with institutions and morals, many of which, such as the custom of foot binding among women, go against the nature of the human species, according to Chambers's *Political Economy*. Thus, China is ranked the stage of the 'half-civilized' state. This corresponds with the second stage, the 'semi-civilized state,' of the three stages in *Outline*. Chambers's textbook also added that, even in a civilized nation, many uneducated people are similar to 'savages' and, in some regions, such people comprise the majority of the inhabitants. Thus, even in a civilized nation, there are social or regional disparities in the level of civilization.

In Chambers's *Political Economy*, such disparities are mentioned rather indifferently. However, to Fukuzawa, who made a hemispherical tour from feudal Japan before the Restoration to Europe, the world appeared to have a geographical structure in which the 'savage' or 'semi-civilized' nations in Asia and Africa were dominated by the Western 'civilized' nations. The Western 'civilized' nations who entered the Eastern 'semi-civilized' region exerted their advantage over Asian nations that maintained outdated traditions. They extended their colonial rule in all port towns where Fukuzawa's ship was harbored. The distance between the levels of civilization created a relationship of domination and subjection. In Fukuzawa's later work, he wrote, "when some countries are more advanced than others, it is natural for the advanced to control the less advanced and the less advanced to be controlled by the advanced" (FYCW 4: 183; *Outline*: 225).

In Asia, 'civilized nations' controlled the 'semi-civilized.' Fukuzawa's concern was to propose a way for the Japanese to rise from the 'half-civilized state' and enter the 'civilized state.'

What difference is between the 'civilized' and the 'semi-civilized' state? In the second chapter of *Outline,* Fukuzawa illustrated the three stages of the development of the human species: the primitive stage, the semi-civilized stage, and the civilized stage. We cite his description of the second stage below:

> Secondly, there is the stage of civilization wherein daily necessities are not lacking since agriculture has been started on a large scale. Men build houses, form communities, and create the outward semblance of a state. But within this façade, there remain very many defects. Though book learning flourishes, there are few who devote themselves to practical learning (*jitsugaku*). Though in human relations sentiments of suspicion and envy run deep, when it comes to discussing the nature of things men lack the courage to raise doubts and ask questions. Men are adept at imitative craftsmanship, but there is a dearth of original production. They know how to cultivate the old, but not how to improve it. There are accepted rules governing society, but slaves of custom that they are, they could never form rules in the true sense. This is called the semi-developed stage. It is not yet civilization in the full sense.
>
> *(FYCW 4: 17; Outline: 18)*

Fukuzawa surely imagined China, Korea, and Japan before the Restoration in writing this paragraph. He wrote ironically, "since these designations are essentially relative, there is nothing to prevent someone who has not seen civilization from thinking that semi-development is the summit of man's development" (FYCW 4: 17f.; *Outline*: 19).

To enter the civilized stage that was represented by Western nations at that time, Fukuzawa recommended that societies first take up the difficult task of nourishing the 'inner spirit' of civilization than beginning with the 'visible exterior' of Western civilization, such as constructions, machines, meals, clothes, and institutions. Below we can see Fukuzawa's description of the third 'civilized' stage in *Outline*:

> Their spirits enjoy free play and are not credulous of old customs. They act autonomously and do not have to depend upon arbitrary favors of others. They cultivate their own virtue and refine their own knowledge. They neither yearn for the old nor become complacent about the present. Not resting with small gains, they plan great accomplishments for the future and commit themselves wholeheartedly to their realization. Their path of learning is not vacuous; it has, indeed, invented the principle of invention itself. Their industrial and business ventures prosper day by day to increase the sources of human welfare. Today's wisdom overflows to create the plans of tomorrow.
>
> *(FYCW 4: 17; Outline: 18f.)*

Fukuzawa thus concluded that what the old Japan lacked was true scientific exploration (*kyūri no gaku*) and a sense of independence (*dokuritu-shin*). In the situation where the latecomer Japan confronts the mighty Westerners, nourishment of the 'spirit' of civilization must be accompanied by an awakening of the nation. The political changes of the Restoration abolished the old imbalances of power, creating space for rapid civilization. With the government's efforts to construct and consolidate modern bureaucratic administration, Fukuzawa endeavored to introduce modernization in education and industry through his school and publications. He wished to create a 'middle class' equipped with education and an innovative spirit. However, considering the vast base of 'semi-civilized' people and regions, those involved in this grand project of civilization, at least in the early stage of the project, occupied only a tiny percentage of the total population. Thus, their efforts created a dual structure: on one side, the elites and middle class were affiliated with the project of civilization; on the other, most people continued to live in the same situation as before. This combination highlighted the spatial aspect of Japan's civilization.

Moreover, it indicated the temporal aspect of progress toward civilization. Fukuzawa viewed catching up with advanced Western nations as his goal. The progress of civilization presents itself as the temporal aspect of civilization. Figure 3.1 depicts the spatiotemporal structure of civilization as Fukuzawa conceived it.

In this structure, world nations of various levels of development are arranged in an order representing relationships of domination and subordination. Furthermore, this structure shows the groups affiliated with the project of civilization and those representing the majority of people living in those regions. In international trade and finance, the constellation of interest differs according to the region Japan occupied in relation to other nations. The urgent task in this area is the maintenance of independence in the rivalry of nations.

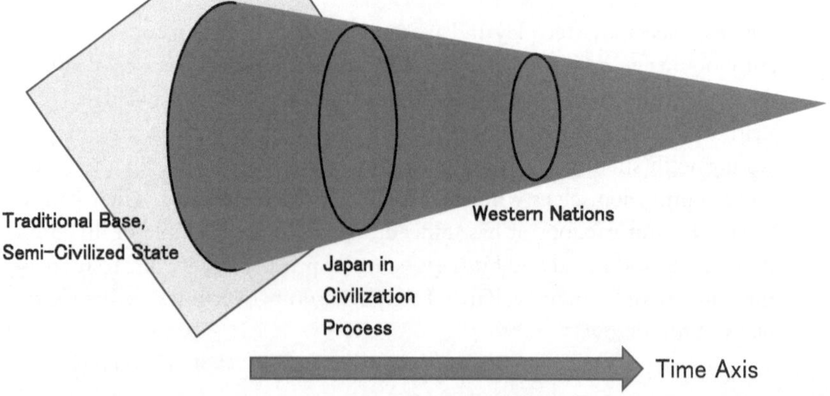

FIGURE 3.1 Spatiotemporal structure of civilization
Source: Yagi (2015) p. 211, modified

In domestic policy, competition is desirable in principle, but the general conditions of the people's knowledge and virtue must be considered. Thus, the direct application of liberal economic policies that presuppose a fully 'civilized state' is inappropriate. Measures of protectionism are of use where they are better suited to the conditions of the process of civilization.

Fukuzawa rejected the traditional Confucian concept that the civilization of an ideal society is attained through a harmonious reign of virtuous rulers and instead adopted Western ideas that rely on freedom of the people and rational inquiry. According to his understanding, civilization is a universal process, and Western nations were only one step ahead of the Japanese.

Nonetheless, the spatiotemporal structure shown in Figure 3.1 invokes the question of which laws control the relationships between nations with different levels of civilization. In *Outline,* Fukuzawa urged his readers to consciously absorb Western civilization to maintain national independence. This was his recommendation to help the backward nation of Japan cope with more advanced nations. In contrast to the universal nature of civilization, this reversed the order of the relationship between ends and means. According to the natural order, domestic governance and national independence are the results of civilization. Still, given the perils of foreign control, Fukuzawa maintained that the value of civilization should be subordinate and act as the means to the end of national independence:

> Someone may say that mankind's conditions do not allow us to make national independence our only goal; we must, in addition set our sights on more lasting, more noble values. This is true [...] However, as things are in the world today, there is still no place in international relations for talking about lofty things, and anyone who would talk about them would be branded as a stupid and fanciful dreamer.
>
> *(FYCW 4: 207f.; Outline: 254)*

We can easily see the recommendations this reversal might produce regarding the relationships between a slightly advanced country and those that are behind.

3.5 Fukuzawa on Economic Policy

What puzzles those who regard Fukuzawa as a liberalist is his strong opposition to the liberation of inland trade by foreign merchants. From 1873 to the following year, ministers of Western states demanded Japan the freedom of traveling and direct trade with their citizens, and some Japanese scholars such as Nishi Amane (1829–1897) supported it. Fukuzawa opposed it on his view that the foreign trade since the opening of ports brought loss to Japan in contrast with the gain on the side of Western nations. He borrowed the metaphor of the trade of pumpkin Nishi had used and described the current situation as "having bought pumpkins under the high pressure of grocers and continued to eat so much that the originally harmless pumpkin induced diarrhea and weakened the vigor of Japan seriously"

(FYCW 19: 543). He mentioned three evils that the current free trade caused to Japan: losing the gain of industry and its skill due to the contrast of import of industrial goods and export of raw products; the outflow of an enormous amount of gold and silver due to substantial negative balance of trade; and the inability of the prevention of the rule of Western merchants over Japanese.

Fukuzawa did not deny the mutual gain of international trade. When both production skills and commercial talent of the Japanese were far behind the Westerners, in addition to the inadequate public administration, he had to say "refrain from the use of drug cautiously and to increase it only gradually." As Japan then hadn't tariff autonomy due to the treaties of 1858, Fukuzawa would not lose the barrier for the protection of domestic industry.

During these years, Fukuzawa worried about the old-fashioned state of Japanese business people seriously. Thus, he published the textbook of Western accounting, recommended the graduates of his school to enter the business, and supported the business school (Shōhō Kōshū-jo) that Mori Arinori (1847–1889) had founded and deserted in the middle. Further, realizing the evil of ineffective imitation of Western-style, he wrote and published two volumes of *Minkan Keizai-roku* that we cited above. In this easy reading, so to say, a businessman version of his bestseller *Gakumon no Susume* (An encouragement of learning), he surmised a rational view of the market economy and necessary morals for businesspeople.

Fukuzawa refused *the laissez-faire* doctrine and supported the government's promotion policies in the area of industry and commerce. He believed as government must work outward to prevent the control of advanced nations over latecomers, business people of the latter must protect themselves inwardly to countervail the advanced forerunners.

> This is the measure to awaken the sleeping people and save them from paralysis. In this respect, the government of Japan differs from that of Western nations. It has a private task in addition to its original public task. Thus, those who blame the various intervention of government under the empty phrase of laissez-faire, importing Westerners' view without observing the situation of their nations, are only arguing on paper.
>
> *(FYCW 4: 268)*

On the other hand, Fukuzawa kept doubt on the effect of promotion policy driven by the government's authority since 'civilization' in his view, depends not on government but on the level of knowledge and virtue of the people. His unpublished criticism of the industry promotion policy led by Ōkubo Toshimichi (1830–1878) coincides with the theory of civilization in the *Outline* more than his public support. It might be the agony of Fukuzawa that he had to support government leadership beyond the limit of his theory of civilization.

> Looking at the government's works up to Meiji 10 (1877), those inappropriate in nature were rare. Schooling for agriculture, commerce, and

> science or opening exhibitions was not wrong in itself. The evil consists solely in that the government manages them. The domestic exhibition held this year in Ueno was similar. Suppose Lord Okubo should stay among the people and prepare the exhibition by calling comrades to people. In that case, it could show the actual level of civilization and effectively promote the industry. Since the knowledge of both Okubo and his subordinate was not enough to perform the task without the government's authority, the result was a forced frame-up. It's like an occasional construction by an emotional head of a house driven by his temporary desire. Who anticipates the prosperity of the house, seeing its hasty construction?
>
> *(FYCW 7: 684)*

According to Fujiwara (1988), Fukuzawa emphasized foreign trade from the beginning to the end of his life, but the focus shifted stepwise. Around 1880, he maintained export promotion by improving traditional products like silk, tea, and mineral products. He recommended farmers change rice fields to mulberry fields and promote silk production. He supported the commercialization of agriculture and opposed the agrarian policy centered on rice production. However, exporting traditional products grounded in domestic resources had limitations on production capacity and accompanied the evils of losing skills in growing industries. Thus, it was only in the nineties, when modern industries like spinning using cheap raw overseas cotton began to grow, that Fukuzawa could argue for the development strategy grounded on commerce and industry. Fukuzawa compared the profitability of the Japanese cotton industry with that of the Indian and British cotton industries and concluded Japan's competitiveness compared the two. The real labor cost in Japan was well below that of the Indian cotton industry; Japan could export its cotton product at a lower price than Britain. In 1893, he openly declared that he supported 'free trade.' He believed that Japanese industry finally attained the stage where the promotion or protection by the government became unnecessary.

As seen above, though Fukuzawa did not exclude the necessity of the promotion of industry by the government, he was principally against the government's intervention in the private sector. In his view, the government's main task is to provide and maintain the institutions that support the private economic activity and, if necessary, manage public work in the area of transportation and communication. From his view of the division of agenda between the government and the private, the first issue that appears in the front is that of currency, as it serves all private entities as the value standard, means of exchange, and formation of funds.

The situation of currencies in Japan in the early years of Meiji was quite confusing. Despite the proclamation of the mew monetary ordinance of 1871 that adopted the gold coin standard, silver trade coins were used in port towns, while paper money of the government and notes of admitted national banks circulated in other areas. Banknotes that had initially been convertible turned out inconvertible due to the lack of reserves. Under the inconvertibility, the value of currencies declines if they should increase. However, prices kept stable just before Fukuzawa published his first *Tsūka-ron* (Discourse on Currency, 1878). In this book, Fukuzawa preached trust in government. However, he admitted the difficulty for the government to control the quantity of circulating currency to fit the nation's population and the condition of commercial activity.

However, after its publication, the accumulation of inconvertible currency with which the government paid the military expenditure to suppress the Satsuma Rebellion ignited the inflation in 1881. In the middle of the inflation, the head of public finance changed from Ōkuma Shigenobu to Matsukata Masayoshi. Now, Fukuzawa published the sequel of *Tsūka-ron* in the editorial of the daily *Jiji Shimpō* (newspaper Fukuzawa started in 1882) and urged Matsukata to restore the value of notes to that of gold and silver coins as soon as possible.

Fukuzawa's idea in his first *Tsūka-ron* deviated considerably from the classical notion of the gold standard. Fukuzawa regarded the essence of currency as 'a bill of commodity' and preferred paper money to gold and silver. As evidence for the circulation of paper money without convertibility, he mentioned the experience of his native Nakatsu Clan before the Restoration. In his view, the problem to be solved was to find the appropriate level of the quantity of currency that does not disturb the real economy. The peculiar difficulty that had not existed in the case of the Nakatsu Clan in the Tokugawa period was the compatibility of domestic currency circulation with foreign trade, which was performed in the term of gold and silver money. The inconvertible domestic currency might differ from the currency's value for foreign exchange, while under the gold standard, the circulation of convertible banknotes automatically fluctuates to balance the international trade.

The concept that Fukuzawa proposed was an introduction of an administrative device to control the domestic circulation of currencies. He thought if the government carefully watched the possible deviation between the purchasing power of notes and gold and silver coins in their domestic circulation and controlled the circulation of notes to erase the difference, domestic and international trade compatibility would be possible. Nishikawa (1985) called Fukuzawa "an early advocate of the managed currency." While the fiscal administration under Matsukata Masayoshi in the 1880s caused severe deflation, Fukuzawa believed it could be avoided. As for the recovery of the convertibility of paper money to stabilize its value, Fukuzawa admitted foreign loans on the conviction that the economy's recovery would make its redemption easier.

The second policy problem was taxation. What is impressive to us is Fukuzawa's persistent opposition to the demand for land tax reduction. As is well known, the Meiji government consolidated its fiscal base through the land tax reform started in 1873, according to which the land owners were taxed yearly at 3 percents of land value in cash. Though this rate was curtailed to 2.5 percent in 1887, reducing this tax rate and the registered land price became one of the main demands of opposition parties representing the local and agricultural interests. Fukuzawa gave sharp criticism in his editorials of *Jiji Shimpō* in April and May 1892.

Fukuzawa argued that the gains from the reduction fell in the hands of landowners, not producers (farmers). The reduction of land tax would result in an increase of landowners and a hike in land prices, thus promoting their aspiration for land acquisition. Fukuzawa didn't deny the gain of farmers that cultivate their land; however, he was afraid of the increasing risk of losing their land due to the distress caused by the leveling up of their consumption standard.

> Land tax reduction promoted land acquisition and landed farmers diminished. If someone may ask my judgment on the nation's state, I must say the misery of the economy. Most landowners don't perform the services of the brain nor that of hands and legs. They monopolize the profit from the lending of heavenly-given resources to others. As the population grows and the scarcity of land becomes felt, the rent must rise accordingly, as the interest rate increases from the shortage of funds in commerce. By what means can farmers maintain their livelihood? I cannot do but deplore such an outcome.
>
> *(FYCW 6: 133)*

As we can see from this citation, Fukuzawa's attitude against landowners is black and white evident. Fukuzawa went so far as to say that recognizing the private ownership of the land itself was a failure. If the trade of land remained prohibited as it had been in the Tokugawa period, the deprivation of farmers' land and the domination of landowners over them would not occur. Though 'nationalization' of land would be impossible, "total absorption of rent in the hands of landowners by way of a heavy land tax would be the good policy" (FYCW 6: 118). The heavy land tax would promote intensive land use, and the government could abolish or reduce other taxation. Fukuzawa would be stimulated by land nationalization or single land tax proposals.

Indeed, theoretically, nationalization of land or total confiscation of land rent is possible under the market economy. It is the extreme policy that rationalism on bourgeoisie (or capitalists) could imagine. However, as Karl Marx noted, the attack on the noblest property must lead to the attack on private property in general. In reality, as the interest of landowners depends on economic development, which would provide them with leisure and prestige, landowners would be the source of the ruling stratum. A bourgeois state without a landed class is not realistic. In Japan, local landowners that once appeared as the base of opposition parties in the Meiji era were soon integrated into the ruling system of Japan.

Further, the possibility that land nationalization or confiscation of rent could support the total public finance is limited only to the stage where agriculture occupies a large share of the national economy. The land tax share in the Meiji government's total revenue declined gradually. Though land tax could contribute to Japan's economy's development as the government's solid revenue, its significance would diminish if Fukuzawa's ideal, 'lead of commerce and industry,' should realize. Generally, the agricultural sector of advanced national economies becomes a sector that absorbs subvention to survive.

The third economic issue that Fukuzawa faced was the growing disparity between the rich and the poor, accompanying industry development. When he used the translation of Chambers' textbook in his guide, he omitted the text that dealt with criticism of capitalism or socialism coming from the social problems that capitalism brought forth.

In the middle of the Meiji era, when labor or social problems began to appear, he had to deal with these problems. In the editorial, *Hinpu-ron* (On Poverty and Wealth) of *Jiji Shinpō* in 1884, he was still optimistic that social problems could be mitigated by the philanthropy of the rich and the provision of recreations for the ordinary people. At this stage, he regarded the emergence of social problems as not a real problem but a manifestation of the discrepancy between rising aspiration and the lagging affluence of the people. However, after seven years, he must warn the public about the neglected disparity between rich and poor.

> In the words of those who talk about the economy, wealth and poverty depend on the person's knowledge. If one does not learn, he remains ignorant. Ignorant people stay in poverty. Education is the fund to become rich. – Thus, they attributed the reason for the poverty and the wealth solely to the intellectual level of the people.
>
> *(FYCW 13: 69)*

Did most of his contemporaries learn so from Fukuzawa's *Encouragement*?

> This is not at all false. Indeed the poor generally are, taking the average of the mass of the poor, ignorant, but taking both of the reason and the outcome and looking into the details of the society, in not rare cases we can say that the poor today are poor not because they are ignorant. Still, they are ignorant because they are poor.
>
> *(FYCW 13: 69)*

Against the vicious circle of ignorance due to poverty and that of poverty due to ignorance, Fukuzawa's economic discourse has nothing to do with it. As the economic development proceeds on a sustained path, the chance for the poor to become wealthy on their effort or fortune would diminish. At the same time, the rich would concentrate their wealth by using the acquired knowledge and capital more effectively. So far as it is legal, the rich have no reason to be blamed. However, if the rich, relying on the justification of their wealth, are cold to the poor, the desperation of the poor would bring a critical situation of the 'outbreak of conflict' (FYCW 13: 94).

However, even in this stage, Fukuzawa feared the subjective deprivation of the 'ex-warrior students' and 'poor scholars,' etc., more than the mass poverty of workers and farmers. Thus, the remedies Fukuzawa recommended were no more than stopgap measures such as promoting philanthropy and public works, encouragement of religion, the constraint of excess education, and overseas emigration.

Fukuzawa did not approve the factory legislation and social policies. The low wage and long working day that sustained the competitiveness of Japanese industry seemed to be consciously eliminated out of his sight. Probably he thought that the main risk that might deviate Japan from the path of civilization lay more in the outbreak of discontent of those who entered the course of civilization promotion incompletely rather than the resistance of workers and farmers at the bottom of civilization.

3.6 Conclusion

Fukuzawa deeply absorbed the ideas of Western economics. However, he did not receive Western economics as a valid system for any conditions. He considered the 'law' of economics as it is situated in the people as a total. Thus, his economics was integrated into his theory of 'civilization.' His deviation from classical liberalism in economics could be interpreted as his conscious application of the law of economics to Japan in its peculiar place in his spatiotemporal view of the 'civilization.'

The policy stance that admits the limitation on the free economic transaction and democracy is called 'developmentalism.' Fukuzawa, who approved the promotion policy and currency control by the government and advocated coordination between government and private sector, was not alien to 'developmentalism' perfectly. However, as he believed in the private initiative in the economy and rejected the concentration of knowledge and power to the government, we can set him outside of 'developmentalism.'

Fukuzawa's view of the spatiotemporal structured civilization made him a pragmatist. He continued to publish his teachings and policy proposals following his strategy of 'civilization' of Japan. However, compared with the reality of the modern history of Japan, there remained many that were not in Fukuzawa's sight. For example, despite his realistic insight into the labor relations in modern industry, such as cotton spinning, he did not combine it with the emergence of social problems. Though he recommended farmers plant mulberry, raise silkworms, and go into the silk industry combined with export, he supplied no consistent vision that could consolidate a sound development of agriculture. What Fukuzawa focused on and placed his hopes are the middle class in the process of civilization, not farmers and workers at the bottom.

Notes

1 This chapter uses the English text of Yagi (2015) partly. The Japanese text of Yagi (2006) contains more detailed descriptions of Fukuzawa's view of Japanese society and his economic policies. See also Fujiwara (1998).
2 In this chapter, we use 'economics' as a synonym for 'political economy.'

3 The original text retained some expressions from the author's (J. H. Burton's) deistic view of the world. Fukuzawa translated them into Japanese skillfully using conventional vocabularies that aroused no antipathy among ordinary Japanese readers. See Craig (1984) and (2009: 65–69).

4 See Sugiyama (1986, 1994). Sugiyama described Fukuzawa's political economics as "a miserable system of contradictions" (Sugiyama 1986: 151). See also Sugiyama (1994).

5 In 1865, Fukuzawa wrote an essay *Tōjin Ōrai* (Interactions with Foreigners), to persuade opponents to open the ports. He circulated it in the form of handwritten copies.

6 *Gakumon no Susume* (An Encouragement of Learning) that Fukuzawa published in pamphlet series (Fukuzawa 1872–1876) diffused all over Japan and made him 'the teacher of the nation.' *Bunmei-ron no Gairyaku* (An Outline of a Theory of Civilization), in which Fukuzawa revealed his general view systematically, was considered his masterpiece. (See Maruyama 1986). English translation of the former is provided in Fukuzawa (1985) and that of the latter in Fukuzawa (2008).

7 The translator of *Outline* adopted 'diligence' in place of the original Japanese '*benkyō*.' However, I adopt 'knowledge' because Fukuzawa restated this trio in *Minkan Keizai Roku* (Economic Discourse for Civilians), published in 1877–1880, like 'knowledge' (*Chie*), 'honesty,' and 'frugality' (FYCW 4: 313).

8 It was at a symposium in Heidelberg in February 2011 on the topic 'historical context of globalization in East Asia' that the author first showed Figure 3.1. When the author stressed that Fukuzawa received Western political economy not as dogma but as scientific inquiry, Prof. Sasagawa Tadakatsu (Meiji University) asked him whether he would consider Fukuzawa's stage theory of civilization as 'scientific' as well. Through this question, the author realized that an extension of laws with a perspective as grand as the 'theory of civilization' stands on the border between science and ideology. Thus, Prof. Sasagawa taught him that the classification of countries into the 'primitive' or 'semi-civilized' stages, which was the prevalent ideology at that time, implied the right of 'civilized' nations to make backward countries their clients. This suggestion coincides with the author's view on the spatiotemporal structure of the world that Fukuzawa held in his middle and later writings. Fukuzawa was probably aware of this crossing of borders when he stressed national independence over the values of civilization (see Section 3.4).

9 Craig (2009) has attentively studied the origin of the stages of the theory of civilization that Fukuzawa adopted.

References

English

Chambers's ed. (1852) *Chambers's Educational Course*, ed. by W. and R. Chambers. [Written by John Hill Burton]. *Political Economy for Use in Schools, and for Private Instruction.* Edinburgh: Chambers. [Referred to as *Chambers's Political Economy*].

Craig, Albert M. (1984) "John Hill Burton and Fukuzawa Yukichi." *Kindai Nihon Kenkyū* 1. Tokyo: Keio Gijyuku Daigaku Fukuzawa Center, pp.218–238.

———. (2009) *Civilization and Enlightenment: The Early Thought of Fukuzawa Yukichi.* Cambridge, MA and London: Harvard University Press.

Fukuzawa, Yukichi (1966) *The Autobiography of Yukichi Fukuzawa*. Revised translation of *Fukuō Jiden* by Eiichi Kiyokawa. New York: Columbia University Press. [Referred to as *Autobiography*].

———. (1985) *Fukuzawa Yukichi on Education. Selected Works*, tr. and ed. by Nakayama Kazuyoshi. Tokyo: University of Tokyo Press [Referred as *On Education*].

———. (2008) *An Outline of a Theory of Civilization*. Revised translation of *Bunmeiron no Gairyaku* by David A. Dilworth and G. Cameron Hurst, III. Tokyo: Keio University Press. [Referred as *Outline*].

Sugiyama, Chuhei (1994) *Origins of Economic Thought in Modern Japan*. London: Routledge.

Yagi, Kiichiro (2015) "The reception of Western economics by Fukuzawa Yukichi in the context of 19th century globalization." In Zachmann, Urs Matthias and Uhl, Christian eds. *JAPAN und das Problem der Moderne: Wolfgang Seifert zu Ehren*. Munich: iudicium, pp.197–213.

Japanese

Fujiwara Akio (1998) *Fukuzawa Yukichi no Nihon Keizai-ron* (Fukuzawa Yukichi on Japanese Economy). Tokyo: Nihon Keizai Hyōron-sha.

Fukuzawa Yukichi (1872–1876) *Gakumon no Susume* (An Encouragement of Learning). 1–17. Tokyo: Fukuzawa Yukichi, etc. [FYCW 3].

———. (1875) *Bunmei-ron no Gairyaku* (An Outline of a Theory of Civilization). Tokyo: Fukuzawa Yukichi. [FYCW 4].

———. (1877–1880) *Minkan Keizai-roku* (Economic Discourse for Civilians). 1st, 1877; 2nd, 1880. Tokyo: Fukuzawa Yukichi. [FYCW 4].

———. [FYCW] (1969–1971) *Fukuzawa Yukichi Zenshū* (Fukuzawa Yukichi Collected Works). 22 vols. Tokyo: Iwanami.

Maruyama Masao (1986) *Bunmeiron no Gairyaku wo yomu* (Reading *An Outline of a Theory of Civilization*, Iwanami Shinsho. 3 vols. Tokyo: Iwanami Shoten.

Nishikawa Shunsaku (1985) *Fukuzawa Yukichi to Sannin no Kōshin-tachi* (Fukuzawa Yukichi and Three followers). Tokyo: Nihon Hyōron-sha.

Sugiyama Chūhei (1986) *Meiji Keimō-ki no Keizai Shisō* (Economic Thought in the Enlightenment Years of Meiji Japan). Tokyo: Hosei Daigaku Shuppan-kyoku.

4

ECONOMIC LIBERALISM AND INDUSTRIAL PROMOTION IN THE MEIJI ERA

Taguchi Ukichi and Maeda Masana

4.1 Taguchi and Maeda before Their Emergence

The reason why we introduce Taguchi Ukichi (1855–1905) and Maeda Masana (1850–1921) in the next chapter after Fukuzawa Yukichi's chapter is that both of the two showed peculiar deviation from the course that Fukuzawa had designed under his spatiotemporal view of civilization, despite the common aspiration of economic nationalism.[1] Taguchi and Maeda belonged to the generation who began their public activity a decade after the political change of the Meiji Restoration. At that time, Fukuzawa (1835–1901), of the same generation as the prominent political leaders of the new government, such as Ōkubo Toshimichi (1830–1878), Kido Takayoshi (1833–1877), and Ōkuma Shigenobu (1838–1922), had established his reputation and influence in the intellectual world of Japan. Taguchi challenged Fukuzawa with his fundamental conviction on the economic advantage of free trade. At the same time, Maeda quested to promote domestic industry and agriculture based on the regional aptitudes that had been out of Fukuzawa's sight. Indeed, we cannot identify Fukuzawa's position in economic policy with that of the Meiji government. Still, despite his constant criticisms and disaccords with the government, Fukuzawa legitimized the government's policy stance generally with his view of a harmonic division of the agenda between the government and the private. Comparing Fukuzawa's position with Taguchi and Maeda, we can understand the range of economic thought in the early Meiji era.

4.1.1 Taguchi's Experience before the Foundation of Tokyo Keizai Zasshi

Taguchi Ukichi was born in 1855 in Edo (Tokyo) in a family of low-ranked warriors serving Tokugawas directly. Though he lost his father early, he was proud to have famous Confucian scholar Satō Issai (1772–1859) in his ancestors.

DOI: 10.4324/9781003081319-4

He attended the Confucian school of the Shogunate and kept close relations with Otsukotsu Tarōotsu (1842–1922), a teacher of English at the Kaiseijo school[2] of the Shogunate. The political change in the years around the Restoration hit hard to such families as Taguchi's. Taguchi's brother-in-law that had joined the rebel of remaining Tokugawa loyal warriors, had to hide, deserting his family in a disaster. However, young Ukichi did not lose vigor despite experiencing street vendor and caddie boy of an American missionary in his refugee life in Yokohama. With Otsukotsu, who became a teacher at the school in Shizuoka, where vassals of Tokugawa assembled around the ex-Shōgun Tokugawa Yoshinobu confining there, Taguchi stayed a few years in Shizuoka studying medicine.

At the end of the fourth year of Meiji (1871), Taguchi could return to Edo, which was renamed Tokyo. After entering Kyōritsu School that Seki Shinpachi (1839–1886) founded at Ryōgoku in Tokyo, he moved to the trainee school of the translating section of the Ministry of Finance (MOF), following Seki's appointment as its head (1872). When this short-lived trainee school was abolished, Taguchi worked in the currency section of the Ministry as a translator at first (1874), then as a lower official. During these years, Taguchi became familiar with Western economic literature and acquired professional knowledge in trade and finance. Belonging to the Ministry from May 1875, he anonymously began contributing his opinion to journals. Taguchi dealt with the drain of gold and attributed its cause to the plethora of currencies caused by issuing paper money. His contributions implied criticism against the policy of the section he served. He felt restrictions of his position in the Ministry and, at last, in 1878, decided to live on his pen. Those who once served Tokugawa – Taguchi was one – could not occupy the influential policy-making position in the Ministry, despite some respect for their practical knowledge.

January 1879, *Tokyo Keizai Zasshi* (Tokyo Economist)[3] emerged under Taguchi's editorship. Taguchi revealed his ambition in the first number of this journal:

> I was acquainted with Mr. Shand [Alexander A. Shand 1844–1930], the authority of banking in Britain. One day, as I saw *The Economist* on his desk, I talked to him, "Japan, too, must have such a journal." With a smile, he answered me, "I'm afraid to say that the wealth of Japan hasn't attained the level to have a journal alike." Of course, this is chattering, but alas, I felt like an iron pin stuck to my chest in depth. I promised Mr. Shand I'd show him a comparable Japanese journal by founding it with my hand.
>
> *(Nr. 1, Tokyo Keizai Zasshi, January 29, 1879)*

Together with several close friends, Taguchi established its publisher, Keizai Zasshi-sha. The leader of modern banking in Japan, Shibusawa Eiichi (1840–1931), appreciated Taguchi's ambition and prepared the aid from his bankers' club for this journal.[4] However, after two years, Taguchi declined this aid and made this journal independent.

Compared with Fukuzawa and Maeda, who had traveled in Western countries and had rich experience in the reality of Western capitalism, Taguchi's ideas in economics kept the feature of idealistic fundamentalism that emerged from the direct application of fundamental theorems of Western liberal economics. As he owed much to Otsukotsu and Seki – they were the colleagues of Fukuzawa at the translation bureau of the Shogunate – Taguchi was a product of Japanese language learning and translation activity since the closing years of the Tokugawa period. However, we must not depreciate his experience in the MOF. The lack of direct experience in Western society may reflect in Taguchi's monotone manner of economic liberalism that he conserved to the end of his life. Some researchers argued that his reception of economic liberalism reflected the universal principle 理 (Ri, Lǐ) in the ZuXhi philosophy – the orthodoxy Taguchi had learned before the Restoration.[5]

4.1.2 Maeda's Stay in France

Though Maeda was five years senior to Taguchi, due to his long stay in France, his career as a policy-maker of the industrial promotion policy of the Meiji government started in the same period as Taguchi's start as a leading journalist. Born in 1850 as a son of a physician in Kagoshima (Satsuma Clan) of the warrior class, he had been involved in the political enthusiasm of the youth of this clan. However, he had cherished the wish to study abroad since 1865 when Satsuma Clan sent 15 youths to Britain. He was out of the selection but received the order to learn English in Nagasaki at a private language school managed by a famous foreign language interpreter, Ga Noriyuki (1840–1923). As a study abroad was publicly permitted in 1866, Maeda, with his elder brother and friends, planned to fund it by publishing an improved version of the English-Japanese dictionary they had used, which had been very scarce and expensive in Japan then.[6] Consuming two years, Maeda's group accomplished this project, though they had to rely on a printing house in Shanghai. When Maeda returned from Shanghai with some copies of it, the government had changed already after the Restoration. Impressed by Maeda's ardor to study abroad, Ōkubo Toshimichi, the head of the Satsuma clique in the new government, ordered Maeda to be accompanied by Count Charles de Montblanc (1833–1894). This French had served as an advisor of the Satsuma Clan and the new government for several years and was going to return home to be the delegate Japanese consul general in Paris. Maeda was to serve him as his Japanese assistant.

Maeda's stay in France continued for seven years long. Count Montblanc let the young Maeda live in his residence and advised Maeda to attend school. Maeda and Count Montblanc exchanged language lectures in addition to the ordinary tasks of the Consulate, which seemed to have been not much. However, Maeda seems so depressed by the tremendous gap between Japan and the West that he couldn't establish any study plan himself. The imperialistic features of the expansion of Western powers he had witnessed on his tour to Paris strengthened both his nationalistic conviction and desperation. After observing the confusion resulting from the Franco-Prussian War and Paris Commune (1870), he could recover the hope of Japan's catching up to the West.

After receiving encouragement from Ōkubo, who visited Europe as the vice of the government missionary headed by Iwakura Tomomi (1825–1883), at the Kagoshima students' gathering in Paris (March 1873), Maeda decided to devote himself to the research of policies and praxis of promotion of industry and agriculture in Western countries. Maeda visited Eugēne Tisserand (1830–1925) at the French Ministry of Agriculture and learned basic knowledge of agronomics and the administration in agriculture and related industries. The protectionist position in agriculture and the focus on regional suitability grounded on the firsthand survey was what Maeda inherited from this agronomist administrator.

When Maeda acquired the information that France would hold the third Paris Universal Exposition in 1878 to promote commerce and industry and demonstrate her recovery from the confusion after its defeat, Maeda finally discovered his mission with which he could contribute to the development of Japan. While getting a job in the preparation office of the Exposition to learn the know-how, he persuaded the Japanese government to participate in this Exposition. He prepared to return to Japan to lead the Japanese exhibition at Paris Expo in his hand and accumulated plants, seeds, and other agricultural products of France to bring to Japan with him.

Ōkubo, who guided the first Domestic Exposition for Promotion of Industry held at Ueno in 1877, was pleased to adopt Maeda's proposal. For the seeds and agricultural products that Maeda brought with him, Mita Breeding Station headed by Maeda was established. Maeda was entrusted with preparing a Japanese exhibition at the Paris Expo as the secretary of the Japanese mission in Paris. In this Expo, Maeda showed his organizing talent and brought success to the Japanese exhibition.[7] However, he had to receive the sad news of Ōkubo's assassination (May 1878) during the days of the Paris Expo. Still, after two years in Europe devoted to the research of the industrial promotion policies of European nations, Maeda received the appointment to the department of commerce of the MOF and returned to Japan. To Ōkubo Shigenobu, the then Minister of Finance, Maeda could present his *Chokusetu Bōeki Iken Ippan* (An Opinion on Direct Trading) in October 1789. Thus, after a decade of staying abroad, Maeda joined the Japanese administration and economic policies as a promising ideologue of industrial promotion policy in the line of Ōkubo and Ōkuma. However, we can see Maeda's peculiarity that reflected his sympathy with the French specific ideas of the harmonious development of three sectors of the national economy: agriculture, industry, and commerce.

4.2 Taguchi's Genuine Economic Liberalism

Taguchi's fundamental liberalism was clear from the years of his debut while serving in the Ministry. Against the worry over the outflow of gold due to the appreciation of silver coins expressed in the journal article, Taguchi, using a pseudonym, contributed his criticism. He negated this worry on the ground that the outflow of gold was a natural outcome of the free trade that moved toward an equilibrium. He argued that the affluent inconvertible paper money was the true origin of the confusion. In another contribution, he criticized the ban on private melting of money as an artificial intervention and an infringement of private property.

In 1877, the first part of the *Nihon Kaika Shōshi* (Short History of Japan's Enlightenment, 1877–1882) was published. Taguchi interpreted the history of Japan from the ancient years to the end of the Tokugawa period from his view of enlightenment (*Kaika*) in the sense of the progress of the human mind, knowledge, and material apparatus. In contrast with the academic historians that focused their attention on governments and politics, Taguchi's view that interpreted literature and material apparatus both as the certificates of the progress of enlightenment was novel. The affinity with Fukuzawa's view of civilization (*Bunmei*) is apparent. Still, Taguchi admitted that Japan had its progress of enlightenment in its history and believed in its future without emphasizing the need for artificial intervention.[8]

Next year, he published *Jiyū-Kōeki Nihon Keizai-ron* (Free Trade and the Japanese Economy, 1878). The book's primary purpose is the advantage of free trade and the criticism of protectionism. Taguchi began this book in the first chapter with the argument that the cause of economic science based on the trade in the world of a developed division of labor vindicates the doctrine of free trade. He declared that free men depend more on the economy than government and called himself a "free citizen of the economic world."

> So long as being a man, beware the reality of the society and see that what affects our life most is not the government but the demand of the economic world. … The need of the economic world is the origin of our trade and the guarantee of its continuity. Once it should change, we lose our trade. As we are free citizens of the economic world, we should know that our fortune depends more on the economic world than on the government.
>
> *(Taguchi 1878: 31f.)*

Taguchi believed that so long as no artificial intervention should influence the economic exchange, the interest of individuals coincides with that of the economic world as a whole. Further, Taguchi did not restrict the principle of free trade in economic exchange and extended it to the intellectual area[9]:

> Some Western economists excluded intellectual phenomena from economics, saying they cannot be included in the concept of wealth. What a stupid saying! How does the teacher's lesson differ from a weaver's provision of clothes to me? What differs my accumulation of knowledge from that of goods? What is the difference between the demand for learning

> by students and the demand for goods? Production of goods is impossible without knowledge. Knowledge cannot be obtained without goods. They are two wheels of cargo.
>
> *(ibid.: 28f.)*

After preaching the benefit of international trade, Taguchi refuted the argument for protectionism:

> 1 Protective tariff may make the trade protected thrive, but it cannot increase the nation's wealth.
> 2 Protective tariff gives the monopoly of sales to domestic merchants and shifts labor and capital to the protected goods. This degree of concentration causes harm to the nation.
> 3 Government is not legitimized to give the gain of a person to another.
> 4 It is meaningless to argue for a protective tariff to rescue the ex-warriors.
>
> (ibid.: items in 51–66)

Tokyo Keizai Zasshi became the representative journal of economic liberalism. As for the repeal of the ban on the domestic trade of foreign merchants, which Fukuzawa opposed, Taguchi supported this repeal definitely and demanded further to abolish the foreign settlement in Yokohama and Kobe. A year and a half after Taguchi's journal, a competitive journal of protectionist camp, *Tōkai Keizai Zasshi* (East Sea Economic Journal), edited by Inukai Tsuyoshi (1855–1932), appeared. The hot debate of two journals attracted the public and propagated economic ideas in Japan.

However, while Inukai turned his primary interest to politics, Taguchi kept his journal to extend his educational activity. He invited scholars of different opinions to contribute to his journal and kept the objective quality of reports on economic policies, trade, finance, and commerce. Thus, *Tōkyo Keizai Zasshi* became Japan's first successful economic journal in the Meiji era.[10]

Taguchi showed his talent as an organizer and publisher, too. He formed a society of journal subscribers in Tokyo and other local towns to hold numerous open lectures. The protocols of lectures and autodidactic textbooks were distributed by his publisher, in which the first Japanese translation of *Wealth of Nations* emerged in 1884–1888 (Smith 1884, 1885, 1888).[11] Often, he was called 'Adam Smith in Japan.' However, Taguchi corrected it and declared himself a disciple of Richard Cobden's Manchester School. As his antipathy to D. Ricardo and J. St. Mill showed, Taguchi assimilated economic liberalism, not from the theoretical system of classical economics. In theory, he confessed his affinity with the subjective value theory of Henry Dunning Macleaod (1821–1901), whose *Principles of Economic Philosophy* (1872–1875) he had translated into Japanese in abridgment in 1878. In Taguchi's definition, economics was 'a mental science,' and 'demand' that results from the universal human nature was the commanding principle of economics.

Of the various topics[12] on which Taguchi's journal and the Inukai's quarreled, we choose the topic of railroad construction because it showed Taguchi's deviation from Fukuzawa's direction toward the coordination between the public and the private clearly.[13] In the editorial of the first issue of *Tōkai Keizai Shimpō*, Inukai declared the protectionist position of the journal and added an urgent topic of transportation. Inukai studied at Keio Gijuku and represented Fukuzawa's nationalist aspect in economic policies. Inukai raised the construction of domestic transportation because Fukuzawa had stressed in his *Minkan Keizairoku Nihen* (Two Discourses on Private Economy, 1880) that the construction of railways was an urgent task that was appropriate to use the public fund.

Thus, Taguchi's attack on Inukai's journal began with a critique of Fukuzawa's view on railway construction. Taguchi criticized Fukuzawa's misleading stress on the future benefit of the railway construction and revealed its gap with the sober observation of Fukuzawa himself of the scarcity of available resources. Further, Taguchi stressed the distress of the people that would lose the existing trades by the railway. Finally, he showed the enormous gap in the construction cost between public works and private firms. Clearly, Taguchi adhered to the priority of the private economy and chose gradualism in constructing the railway.

Tōkai Keizai Shimpō published several articles to criticize Taguchi and his journal. Inukai found the solution to the construction fund by mobilizing the local private fund by establishing a private construction company that could sell its share under the government protection and subsidy. The government protection was given to ensure small private investors the safety of their investment and to nourish their public spirit.

Nihon Tetsudō Kaisha (Japan Railway Company) was founded in 1881, relying mainly on the investment of nobility families. The wave of investment boom among the wealthy in the countryside, as Inukai had anticipated, did not occur. In reality, it was a semi-public company aided in every aspect by the government. Out of the original ambitious four nationwide plans, the plan from Tokyo to Takasaki and Aomori became the immediate task. Taguchi examined this plan in detail and concluded that except for the line Tokyo – Takasaki, the extension far to Aomori (the north end of Honshū) was unrealistic. As Takasaki was the entrance of the region of the silk-spinning industry, Tokyo-Takasaki might be economically sustainable. The extension far to Aomori would lack rentability and require enormous construction costs. Taguchi was not foreign to the benefit of the railway. In the late 1880s, he became one of the initiators of a private railway in this silk industry region. This area was the 'Manchester' to him, and his railway should bring the silk to Takasaki and then to Tokyo and Yokohama. Taguchi was dismissed from its head, probably due to the conflict with investors, and returned to scholarly life.

In contrast to Fukuzawa and Inukai, Taguchi preferred gradualism in constructing the railway. Such a construction project that might change the business environment deeply had to be accomplished under a private initiative backed by those people that would be affected. Taguchi proposed temporarily building a wooden highway for wagons until the iron railway could replace it. In Taguchi's view, the benefit of the private as a whole should support and promote such construction.

As Taguchi believed sincerely in the private initiative, he supported the political movement to open the Diet and joined its small fraction. For several years, he collaborated with the journal of the *Jiyū-tō* (Liberal Party). However, he did not support the demand for depreciation of land tax by opposition parties, which was combined with the hike of taxation rate over the business earnings in cities. Thus, he made the distance from the opposition parties and remained an economic expert representing the interest of the urban businessmen in the City Council of Tokyo and the Diet (1894–1905).

4.3 Maeda's Program of the Promotion of Indigenous Development

In the *Opinion* that Maeda submitted to the MOF after his return from Paris (1879), he argued that the recovery of trade hegemony from foreign merchants by way of the promotion of direct export of Japanese fabricants to overseas markets was the critical agenda of the trade policy of Japan. Further, on the side of producers, he stressed the improvement of domestic products and the effort to guarantee their qualities to get recognition in the overseas market. To facilitate direct trades, Maeda made three proposals. In contrast to Taguchi, that believed in the universal principle, Maeda put the fitness with the actual conditions of the indigenous people before the abstract theory. Maeda's *Opinion* of 1879 began with the following sentence:

> I am dissatisfied with the prevailing policy discourse full of empty theories that deviate from the actual conditions of the private. I am willing to establish laws that fit the actual conditions and the mind of the people and practice them.
>
> *(Maeda 1881: 1)*

Grounded on the view that the vast chronic trade deficit was the cause of the outflow of gold, depreciation of the paper currency, and inflation, Maeda fixed the recovery of trade hegemony from foreign merchants to the aim. He stressed the promotion of the direct export of Japanese producers as the critical agenda to cope with this trade imbalance.

> What is the most urgent task for the nation? In my view, it is the opening of the direct trade, the recovery of the hegemony in the business that enables the conservation of gold and silver, the stability of the paper currency, and then the recovery of the nation's forces.
>
> *(ibid.: 2)*

To make the direct export succeed, it needed the improvement of products and the effort to guarantee their qualities to acquire recognition in the overseas market on the side of fabricants and merchants in Japan. As the government's policies, Maeda proposed the following three in a set: establishing an imperial bank for financing the trade, founding trading companies, and promoting combinations of fabricants. The imperial bank supplies documentary bills on the export commodities and protects the advance bills in Japan. Trading companies should open overseas branches and sell Japanese products worldwide. Lastly, associations of fabricants and dealers should be responsible for improving and guaranteeing their products.

Maeda's proposals were in the policy line of Ōkubo and his successor Ōkuma, who would cope with the trade deficit by promoting export. The first of Maeda's three proposals was realized as the establishment of Yokohama Specie Bank (1880). Societies of direct trade were protected, and the financial subsidy for cargo bills was created. However, these measures could not bring out a remarkable result in the trade balance. Ōkuma's rival, Matsukata Masayoshi (1835–1924), preferred fiscal consolidation and the liquidation of paper currencies to spending money to promote the industry. His policy fit more than Ōkuma's expansion policy in the years when everyone felt the pressure of inflation. In 1881, when Ōkubo was expelled from the government (political change of the fourteenth year of Meiji) and Matsukata replaced him, the promotion policy lost its most prominent supporter within the government.

Maeda was put in a distant position and received the order to research abroad on the economic and industrial conditions in Europe as an official of the newly founded Ministry of Agriculture and Commerce (MAC). After his return in 1883, he conceived integrated regional research to promote agriculture and domestic industry. After acquiring approval from his seniors, Maeda drafted the plan and pushed forward with this research. He led a team in the Ministry, collected available statistics on Japan's regions, and added the guidelines to promote and develop agriculture, industry, and commerce. The draft of this research report, *Kōgyō Iken* (Advice for Promotion of Industry), was completed in the summer of 1884 and distributed within the government in small numbers (Nōshōmushō 1884a). However, as it contained many criticisms against Matsukata's financial policy, this draft was withdrawn soon and went under severe censorship by the MOF. The official version (Nōshōmushō 1884b) was published with many omissions and corrections from the government's printing office at the end of the year.[14]

As this report collected a wide range of statistics available then, it was like an economic census of the nation, so far as we see its official version.[15] However, the original report was more ambitious. It was a development program for agriculture, commerce, and industry in Japan based on the regional level. Of course, Maeda was not such a conservative that would sustain the traditional pattern of cultivation and handicraft. He wished for the improvement and cooperation of the people in the region under the government's guidance and the leadership of indigenous farmers, fabricants, and merchants. Through the collection of product statistics and local interviews, he would find what was suited and worth promoting and what was not in each region to establish the direction of regulations and practical measures to make most of the local advantage of the area. As Soda Osamu maintained, *Kōgyō Iken* took the position of "gradual modernization that starts from the indigenous industry" (Soda 1973: 99).

In the first summary volume, *Kōgyō Iken* surmised its fundamental policy stance, called 'spirit,' as follows:

> In the section called 'spirit,' we have discussed the idea that it is spirit/willingness will make the best possible use of capital, laws, and institutions. We agree that the progress of agriculture, industry, and commerce is greatly dependent on the amount of capital, and that in reality the protection of people by laws, regulations, and benefits arising from development institutions and facilities will contribute considerably to the growth of agriculture, industry, and commerce. Nevertheless, we argue that these two factors will prove usefulness only when there is a spirit/willingness in our people so that these elements can be utilized effectively.
>
> *(Inukai 2003: 126f.)*

In the part of the 'Spirit' (volume 11), we can see that a gradual but clearly visible development was recommended for local economies with several principles as followings:

> Any enterprise must be promoted in conformity with specific local conditions.
>
> *(ibid.: 286)*

> Enterprise must be promoted in conformity with the capital available.
>
> *(ibid.: 287)*

> We should make visible progress year by year.
>
> *(ibid.: 288)*

> Substantial, not superficial, progress must be secured.
>
> *(ibid.: 288)*

This gradualism contained the criticism of the current modernization policy of the government that aimed at Fukoku Kyōhei (wealth and military strength). The construction of ports, roads, and railways was stressed from the viewpoint of national unity and army expediency. The industrial promotion policy under Ōkubo and Ōkuma focused on introducing advanced industry and public works at first in large cities. Under the consolidation policy, model plants of the government were sold to the private, primarily to merchants that kept close relationships with politicians. Whether having roots in the Tokugawa period, Mitsui and Sumitomo, or not, Mitsubishi, Fujita, Furukawa, etc., mighty business concerns emerged under the protégée of the government. Still, the public revenue was supported mainly by the land tax, and most exporting goods were indigenous products such as silk and tea. The surplus from the indigenous industry, including agriculture, supported the modern style of industrialization. The recursive investment in the indigenous sector was neglected. Maeda sided another gradual industrialization based on harmonized progress of agriculture, commerce, and industry.

Maeda would support this gradual development by creating Kōgyō Ginkō (Industrial Promotion Bank) under the MAC. However, this plan collided with the plan of the MOF directly. While Maeda would establish the network of industrial promotion funds from regions to the center to provide the necessary support to local entrepreneurship, MOF would make regions share the burden of the national project of Fukoku Kyōhei by this new bank. At last, the plan of Kōgyō Ginkō was postponed after the economic recovery and virtually abandoned. Thus, to secure the farmers and artisans in regions that suffered from the deflation Matsukata's consolidation policy brought about and to promote regional development without any effective means, MAC had nothing to rely on than the thrift and saving of farmers, artisans, and merchants in the local area. Maeda, who was sent to such a spiritualistic campaign around regions, contributed to the diffusion of his image as a conservative spiritualist.[16]

With the shelving of Kogyō Ginkō's plan, Maeda was put out of the office at the end of 1885, and his group dissolved. It took a few years before he could return to MAC. When he returned to MAC in 1889, he resumed the nation-level and prefecture-level research and started bringing his program into concrete plans. They contained the method of organizing Nōkai (Agricultural Association) at the prefectural and the national level and establishing local promotion banks specialized in agriculture. It seems as if Maeda's program would realize MAC's official policy since he ascended to its vice-minister in the next year. However, Maeda was discharged from the office by the new minister, Mutsu Munemitsu (1844–1897), who detested Maeda's arbitrary style. Maeda's reluctance was great, as Mutsu had been one of his old classmates at Nagasaki.

Recovering his energy, Maeda determined to practice his program on private initiatives by gathering comrades in various regions and industries. He started his campaign (local pilgrimage on foot) to organize associations of farmers and fabricants – at first, that of tea producers – in 1892 and started the journal *Sangyō* (Industry) in the next year. His selfless devotion and passionate talk attracted many people. He succeeded in establishing national associations of producers of tea, handicrafts, match, coal, silk spinners, traders, and so on. He further organized the national association of agriculture. In the mid-1890s, Maeda's effort ignited the tide for forming trade-based associations all over Japan.

The government did not obstruct Maeda's campaign since the practical objectives of Maeda's movement were agreeable to the government so far as they should not bring an extra burden on it. Further, the extension of the movement of business matters that were not affiliated with oppositional political parties was welcome to the government that was annoyed by the high wave of opposition at the regional and national levels. On Maeda's side, he made most of those associations press the government and the Diet to adopt their proposals. That troublesome plan of establishing a local promotion bank was ratified at the Diet in 1985. They said 'a private MAC' existed around Maeda, 'the Minister in commoner's clothes.'

In March 1897, even Matsukata, the then Prime Minister, conceived the idea of appointing Maeda as the Minister of Agriculture and Commerce in his cabinet. However, just at this moment, a very critical comment on the incoming Minister appeared on *Jiji-Simpō* under the name of Fukuzawa Yukichi. Without mentioning the candidate's name, Fukuzawa described him as "a commonplace spiritualist with no knowledge and learning, missing both the idea of civilization and commonsense. He knows nothing of the reason and the recent tide of development of trade and business and believes in the success of artificial protection and intervention measures" and declared that he would demand the abolishment of MAC if the government should appoint such a spiritualist as its Minister on behalf of the interest of the business.[17] None know the influence of this criticism on Matsukata, but Maeda's last chance to return to the head of promotion policy in the government went in vain.

Maeda's confidence and stubbornness brought many quarrels in and out of the movement. In addition, his endeavors to create bases by which he could finance his campaigns were not successful. Most of the associations he contributed to their creation left his hand. He kept close ties up to his death with GoNi kai (Five and Two Society), which covered seven indigenous craft trades (textile, pottery, copperware, lacquerware, paperware, curving, and rugs). However, the weight of indigenous trades, particularly those of GoNi Kai, which were based on manual craftmanship, was considerably diminished in domestic life and foreign export.

4.4 Gradualism and Civilization

Compared with Fukuzawa's strong demand in his *Outlines* for the Japanese nation to take the course of Western-style civilization, Taguchi's optimistic trust in the progress of the Japanese nation after the Meiji in his *Enlightenment* is conspicuous. While Fukuzawa approved the role of the government to guide the private sector and opposed the free activity of foreign merchants, Taguchi supported fundamental liberalism in economic affairs and demanded the government not to intervene in the economic affairs except for jurisprudence and currencies. Fukuzawa encouraged his students to enter the business. His school provided core personnel in renovating old merchant capital (Mitsui, Sumitomo, etc.) and the formation of the emerging business concerns (Mitsubishi, Furukawa, Fujita, etc.). Taguchi appealed to the metropolitan and local middle classes that looked for new businesses and investment opportunities in economic development. Thus, as seen in the discussion around the construction of the railroad network, Taguchi took a gradualist approach that corresponded to the accumulation of private capital.

Fukuzawa's choice of Western-style civilization combined the economic nationalism that admitted several sorts of mercantilist policies. Following his priority of national interest (independence) to the ideal of universalism, Fukuzawa's view on economic policies and foreign policies contained elements of real politics, which present researchers have often critically discussed. On the other hand, Taguchi seems to have been somewhat naïve about the problems that accompanied the international expansion of the economic interests of Japan. He approved using military power to protect the business interest of Japanese merchants. He supported the Sino-Japan war in 1894 and the Russo-Japan war in 1904. However, he was against annexing territories and keeping armed forces oversea. To him, national interest is realized more by the prosperity of free trade rather than by military power's acquisition of special interests. Taguchi dreamt of a great free trade area in the Far East in which Japan occupied the center. Some researchers classified Taguchi's vision as a variation of 'free trade imperialism'[18] in which the state could afford influential armed forces to protect the trade and investment of Japanese capital overseas without imposing a heavy burden on the national economy.

Maeda represented another sort of gradualism that was based on indigenous industries. However, he was not so optimistic that he could believe in the spontaneous progress in the enlightenment of the people. As we saw in his career, he belonged to the government officials in charge of promoting industries, even in years when he was out of the government. As an ardent nationalist, Maeda was not a liberal but an enthusiastic interventionist. However, as Maeda learned thorough empiricism from his witness in Europe and his mentor Tisserand, he could place the voluntarism of farmers, communities, and trade organizations in his vision of promotion policy.

Maeda's recommendation of the organization of producers and traders to guarantee/enhance the quality of traditional exporting goods (silk, tea, porcelains, etc.) fitted the trade situation in the early years of the Meiji. In the MAC, Maeda extended his vision of renovation of indigenous industries, including agriculture as a whole, to the level of local units. However, when the promotion of indigenous industries needed money from the government's budget, the priority of the spending taken was not favorable to Maeda's direction. The promotion activities without necessary funds degenerated into a spiritual recommendation of thrift and investigation.

Maeda was against such a uniform style agricultural policy to order rice planting in every village. He learned in Europe that many areas have their aptitude for plants and crafts and that the in-place investigation is inevitable to judge the appropriate plants and industry to develop there. Maeda's gradualism came from this empiricism. In the progress of agriculture of Meiji Japan, neither scholars nor politicians but the innovative farmers (Rōnō) that devised improvements from their investigation occupied the leading role. Maeda knew it. In his pilot project of agriculture development in a newly irrigated village, he invited a group of them to be a model for the native farmers in agriculture and daily behavior.

Under free trade, manufacturing could develop relatively independently from the local economy on the ground of overseas demand. Commerce could also flourish even from transit trade. When we remind here the spatiotemporal structure of civilization in Fukuzawa's chapter, introducing advanced Western technology and finding its market overseas is the step of climbing upward. On the other hand, gradualism is an inevitable feature when a nation chooses harmonious development of manufacturing and agriculture as its development strategy. As Takahashi Korekiyu, Maeda's close collaborator in the 1880s, recollected, Maeda was a man that had been unsuccessful in every project to which he had devoted himself.

Contrary to Fukuzawa and Taguchi, Maeda rejected any economics theory and adhered to his intuition and naïve empiricism. In this respect, as Fukuzawa judged him, he was a man of 'no idea of civilization.' However, his life reminds us of the possibility of this gradual course of development or the latent reality of this path in the growth of modern Japan.[19]

Notes

1 Yoshikawa Kōbunkan (Tokyo) published the biographies of both of the two in its biograph series (Taguchi 2000 and Soda 1973). For non-Japanese readers, Kumagai (1998) is a guide to Taguchi and Crawcour (1997) and Inukai (1979, 2003) to Maeda. Inukai (2003) contains selected translations from *Kōgyō Iken* (1884).

2 Kaiseijo is the school that the Tokugawa Shogunate opened in 1863 to educate youth with the knowledge of Western learnings. Its forerunner was the translation bureau to which Fukuzawa had once belonged. This school was closed with the dissolution of the Shogunate. However, it was rebuilt in 1868 under the new government. Together with the medical school, this school became the origin of the Imperial University when the government decided to establish it in the line of Western learning.

3 *Tokyo Keizai Zasshi* (1879–1923) is now available in the reprinted edition. On this journal and Taguchi, see Sugihara (1969), Sugihara and Okada eds. (1995) and Matsunoo (1996).

4 Shibusawa Eiichi (1840–1931), too, was an ex-vassal of the Tokugawa Shogunate. Though he was not a scholar, his activities in introducing Western-style economic administration and business made him a figure worth discussing independently in the history of modern Japanese economic thought. Born in a farmer's family in the suburbs of Kanto (now Saitama Pref.) that exercised the indigo production and its trade as a side job, his talent for entrepreneurship and accounting was appreciated when he served Hitotsubashi Yoshinobu (later the last Shōgun of Tokugawa). Yoshinobu trusted him so deeply to order him to be accompanied to his brother Tokugawa Akitake's study in Paris in 1867. Akitake's study was interrupted soon by the demise of the Tokugawa Shogunate. Still, Shibusawa learned much about the Western business and finance system from this relatively short stay in Paris. After a service to ex-Shogun Yoshinobu confined in Shizuoka, the new government ordered Shibusawa to serve it as an expert in finance, banking, and currencies. He established the main structure of the administration in the area of public finance and international trade during his

service from 1869 to 1873. When Taguchi started *Tokyo Keizai Zasshi*, Shibusawa was a leading figure of the modern bankers in Japan. As he participated in the foundation and the management of various firms and business organizations, he was often called the 'father of capitalism in Japan.' His motto was the "harmony of morality and economy," as is shown in his publication *Rongo to Soroban* (1927) (Confucius' *Annalects* and Abacus). See Friedenson and Kikkawa (2017).

5 Kumagai (1998, 2006).
6 It was called Satsuma Dictionary.
7 On Japan's participation in Paris Expo 1878, see Teramoto (2017).
8 As the two books appeared nearly same time, Taguchi was both historian and economist. As a historian, he not only founded a journal in history in 1891 (*Shikai*: Sea of History) but also contributed to the systematic collection of basic literature in history. In this chapter, we cannot deal with Taguchi's work as a historian.
9 It is natural that Uchida Yoshihiko, the representative scholar of the post-1945 theory of 'civil society,' appreciated Taguchi as the forerunner of the concept of civil society in Japan, which is based on the free exchange of individuals on an equal level. See Uchida (2002).
10 Taguchi's writings are collected in Taguchi (1927–1928). On Taguchi's wide-range activities centering on *Tokyo Keizai Zasshi*, see Sugihara and Okada eds. (1995) and Matsunoo (1996). *Zasshi* itself was reprinted by Nihon Keizai Hyōron-sha (1981–1987).
11 Ishikawa Eisaku started the translation of Smith's *Wealth of Nations* in 1880 and published two volumes before his early death in 1886. Saga Shōsaku continued Ishikawa's work and completed the full translation in 1888.
12 One of the most discussed problems was currencies and their consolidation on an appropriate monetary standard. Taguchi sided bimetallism on the ground of relative affluence of silver in Eastern countries. He maintained bimetallism till 1897, when the new money law that adopted the gold standard passed the Diet.
13 On this matter, we rely much on Kawasaki (2017a, 2017b, 2018).
14 Inukai Ichirō published his research into *Kōgyō Iken* and its significance for development economics in English (Inukai 1979, 2003). Inukai (2003) contained selected translations from *Kōgyō Iken*.
15 Before the original version of *Kōgyō Iken* was discovered and became accessible to researchers, it had been known only fragmentarily from the recollections of Maeda and others.
16 Takahashi Korekiyo (1854–1936) was a loyal Maeda's man then. He vindicated Maeda's plan for the Industry Promotion Bank against that of MOF and shared the defeat with Maeda (Smethurst 2007: chap. 5). But Maeda's group lost its back during the temporary retreat of Shinagawa Yajirō (1843–1900). Though Chō (1969) and Soda (1973) are sympathetic to Maeda's group, Miyachi (2004) was skeptical of the feasibility of Maeda group's 'all round' promotion plan and focused his attention on the formation of another policy group in MAC.
17 "Nōshōmu-shō no daikaikaku" (A large reform of Ministry of Agriculture and Commerce), *Jiji Shimpō*, March 28, 1897.
18 Kijima (1999). Kumagai (2006).
19 See Chō (1969), Soda (1973), Inukai (2003) on Maeda's reappraisal.

References

English

Crawcour, Sydney (1997) "*Kōgyō iken*: Maeda Masana and his view of Meiji economic development." *The Journal of Japanese Studies*, 23(1), pp. 69–104.

Friedenson, Patrick and Kikkawa Takeo (2017) *Ethical Capitalism: Shibusawa Eiichi and Business Leadership in Global Perspective*. Toronto: University of Toronto Press.

Inukai, Ichirō (1979) "*Kōgyō Iken*: Japan's ten year plan, 1884." *KSU Economic and Business Review*, 6, p. 1–100.

———. (2003) *Japan's First Strategy for Economic Development: With selected translation of Kōgyō Iken*. Niigata: International University of Japan – International Development Program (IDP) Press.

Kumagai, Jirō (1998) "Enlightenment and economic thought in Meiji Japan: Yukichi Fukuzawa and Ukichi Taguchi." In Sugihara Shirō and Tanaka Toshihiro eds. *Economic Thought and Modernization in Japan*. Cheltenham: Edward Elgar, pp. 23–43.

Smethurst, Richard J. (2007) *From Foot Soldier to Finance Minister: Takahashi Korekiyo, Japan's Keynes*. Cambridge, MA: Harvard University Press.

Teramoto, Noriko (2017) "Struggle of a non-European country in the World Fair: The case of Japan." *Journal of Environment Studies*, 60, pp. 25–53.

Japanese

Chō Yukio (1969) "Nationalism to *Sangyō* undō – Maeda Masana no Shisō to Katsudō" (Nationalism and *Sangyō* movement: Ideas and activities of Maeda Masana). In Chō Yukio and Sumiya Kazuhiko eds. *Kindai Nihon Keizai Shisō-shi 1*. Tokyo: Yūhikaku, pp. 85–133.

Fukuzawa Yukichi (1880) *Minkan Keizai-roku Ni-hen* (Two Discourses on Private Economy). Tokyo: Keio Gijuku Shuppansha.

Kawasaki Masaru (2017a) "Fukuzawa Yukichi no testudō ron" (Fukuzawa Yukichi's view of railroad construction) *Kindai Nihon Kenkyū* (Bulletin of Modern Japanese Studies), 34. Tokyo: Keio Gijyuku Daigaku Fukuzawa Center, pp. 101–145.

———. (2017b) "Taguchi Ukichi no tetsudō ron" (Taguchi Ukichi's view of railroad construction). *Musashino Daigaku Seiji-Keizai Kenkyūusho Nenpō*, 15, pp. 229–262.

———. (2018) "Taguchi Unkichi no *Jiji Shinpō* hihan" (Taguchi Ukichi's criticism on *Jiji Shimpō*). *Musashino Daigaku Seiji-Keizai Kenkyuusho Nenpō*, 16, pp. 111–141.

Kijima Kumi (1997) "Taguchi Ukichi ni okeru jiyūshugi: shisō no tokushitsu to sono tenkai" (Features of Taguchi Ukichi's liberalism and its development). *Keizai Ronkyū* (Kyūshū University), 99, pp. 1–20.

Kumagai Jirō (2006) "Taguchi Ukichi -Shakai no 'dairi' to Keizai-gaku." In Ōmori Ikuo ed. *Nihon no Keizai Shisō 1*. Tokyo: Nihon Keizai Hyōron-sha, pp. 43–82.

Maeda Masana (1881) *Chokusetsu Bōeki Iken Ippan* (Opinion on Direct Trading). [Written in 1879]. Tokyo: Hakubun-sha.

———. (1971) *Kōgyō Iken: Hoka Maeda Masana Kankei Shiryō* (Advice for the Promotion of Industry and other Materials related to Maeda Masana), ed. by Andō Yoshio and Yamamoto Hirofumi. Tokyo; Kōsei-kan.

Matsunoo Hiroshi (1996) *Taguchi Ukichi to Keizaigaku Kyōkai – Keimō Jidai no Keizai-gaku* (Taguchi Ukichi and Economics Association: Economics of Enlightenment Age). Tokyo: Nihon Keizai Hyōron-sha.

Miyachi Hidetoshi (2004) "Shoki nōshōmu-shō no seisaku tairitsu" (Economic policy confrontation in the Ministry of Agriculture and Commerce in the early years). *Rekishi to Keizai*, 183. pp. 38–51.

Nōshōmu-shō (1884a) *Kōgyō Iken* [Miteikō] (Advice for the Promotion of Industry [Draft]). 26 vols. Nōshōmu-shō.

———. (1884b) *Kōgyō Iken*, Dai 1-kai (Advice for the Promotion of Industry, 1). 31 vols. Nōshōmu-shō.

Shibusawa Eiichi (1927) *Rongo to Soroban* (Confucius's Analects and Abacus). Tokyo: Chūsei-dō.

Smith, Adam (1884, 1885, 1888) *Fukoku-ron* (On Wealthy Nation) (Japanese translation of *Wealth of Nations* by Ishikawa Eisaku and Saga Shōsaku). 3 vols. Tokyo: Keizaigaku Kōshū-kai.

Soda Osamu (1973) *Maeda Masana*. Tokyo: Yoshikawa Kōbunkan.

Sugihara Shirō (1969) "Koten-ha keizai-gaku to *Tokyo Keizai Zasshi*" (Classical economics and Tokyo economist). In Chō Yukio and Sumiya Kazuhiko eds. *Kindai Nihon Keizai Shisō-shi 1*. Tokyo: Yūikaku, pp. 223–239.

Sugihara Shirō and Okada Kazuki eds. (1995) *Taguchi Ukichi to Tokyo Keizai Zasshi* (Taguchi Ukichi and Tokyo Economist). Tokyo: Nihon Keizai Hyōron-sha.

Taguchi Chikashi (2000) *Taguchi Ukichi*. Tokyo: Yoshikawa Kōbun-kan.

Taguchi Ukichi (1877–1882) *Nihon Kaika Shōshi* (Short History of Japan's Enlightenment). Tokyo: Keizai Zasshi-sha. [Included in TUCW 2].

———. (1878) *Jiyū Bōeki Nihon Keizai-ron* (Free Trade and Japan's Economy). Tokyo: Keizai Zasshi-sha. [Included in TUCW 3].

———. (1927–1928) *Teiken Taguchi Ukichi Zenshū* (Teiken Takuchi Ukichi Collected Works). 8 vols. Reprinted in 1990 by Tokyo: Yoshikawa Kōbun-kan.

Tokyo Keizai Zasshi (Tokyo Economist) (1879–1923). Reprinted in 1981–1987 by Nihon Keizai Hyōron-sha, Tokyo.

Uchida Yoshihiko (2002) *Nihon Shihon-shugi no Shisō-zō* (Vision of Japanese Capitalism). Included in *Uchida Yoshihiko Chosakushū*. Vol. 5. Tokyo: Iwanami Shoten.

5

EARLY SOCIALISM AND SOCIAL POLICY FROM THE 1900S TO 1920S

Turn, Split, and Rivalry

5.1 The First Social Democratic Party of 1901

On May 18, 1901, the year when Fukuzawa died, a political party named Shakai Minshu-tō (Social Democratic Party) was founded.[1] Founders printed its declaration in the special issue of the journal close to them, *Rōdō Sekai* (World of Labor), and sent it to presses asking to report it. Ministry of Interior, on May 20, soon after receiving the notice of its foundation, ordered its dissolution. Several newspapers wrote about this party and its declaration despite the ban on reporting. This news made the Japanese realize that socialism and the social problems it addressed, which had been regarded so far as overseas matters, really emerged in Japan. Since then, throughout the 20th century, socialism continued to be one of the main pillars of political ideas around which most social and political movements had to decide their position.

The founders of this party were six: in the order of their age, Katayama Sen (1859–1933), Abe Isoo (1865–1949), Kinoshita Naoe (1869–1937), Kōtoku Shūsui (1871–1911), Kawakami Kiyoshi (1873–1949), and Nishikawa Mitsujirō (1876–1940). In April, they held several meetings to adopt the name, rules, and the party's declaration. Drafting the declaration was entrusted to Abe. Abe,[2] then a lecturer at Tokyo Senmon Gakkō (later Waseda University), had sufficient knowledge of socialism in Western countries from his study abroad and had published a popular guidebook on social problems and socialism, *Shakai Mondai Kaishakuhō* (Understanding Social Problems: Abe 1901a, and 2008), just before this foundation. Katayama and Kinoshita, who represented the practical activity in this group's social and political movement, assumed the party's secretary.

Katayama[3] then was a Christian social worker who returned to Japan in 1896 after his long stay in the United States. He extended his social service to support the early unionization of urban factory workers. He was the chief editor of *Rōdō Sekai*, which printed the declaration of the newborn party in its special issue.

DOI: 10.4324/9781003081319-5

Kinoshita was a journalist that came from the radical people's rights movement that demanded universal suffrage. Before entering the *Mainichi Shimbun*, he had experienced 16 months-long imprisonment due to his criticism of local administrators. After 1901, he became a well-known author thanks to his pacifist and socialist-themed novels.[4] He left the movement of socialism after 1906 but remained an active humanist until his death.

Out of the remaining three, we cannot miss Kōtoku,[5] then a journalist of the *Yorozu Chōhō*, already known as a fine writer, was a disciple of Nakae Chōmin (1847–1901), a famous scholar called 'J. J. Rousseau in Japan' due to his well-read translation of *Contrat Social*. Together with the *Mainichi Shimbun*, the *Yorozu Chōhō* reported the party's foundation in full and received punishment – confiscation and fines – from this reporting. We'll discuss the unique development of Kōtoku's thoughts together with that of Katayama and Abe soon.

Kawakami studied social problems and socialism widely and entered the *Yorozu Chōhō*. After the Social Democratic Party dissolved, he left Japan to study in the United States, where he lived as a freelance journalist until his death.[6] Nishikawa then was a collaborator of Katayama in publishing *Rōdō Sekai*. In the movement of socialism after 1901, Nishikawa advocated the 'parliamentarian strategy' near Katayama and opposed Kōtoku, who showed sympathy for the 'direct action' of workers. In 1910, Nishikawa declared his conversion from socialism and lived his later life as an ethical moralist.[7]

Given a glance at this party's founders, we can notice two distinctive features of the early socialism in Japan. The first is the influence of social Christianism. Of the six founders, except for Kōtoku, five were Christians. Even Kōtoku, who later wrote the denial of Jesus Christ,[8] was in accord with the idealism and humanism of Christian Socialists at this stage. After the advent of Marxism in Japan still, we can find many Christians in the social movements of Japan. For many non-Christians, even those who professed themselves as materialists, Christian preaches of fraternity often worked as an impact that guided them into a social movement. Convictions in the universal fraternity of Christianism remained one of the vital components of the movement of socialism in Japan since then.

Another finding in the composition of the six founders is the overwhelming weight of journalists among them. Neither workers nor scholars occupied the majority. Around this age, presses and journals were the main arenas where political confrontation was fought. On the other hand, the government endeavored to monitor and control presses and journals with the Press Ordinance since the 1880s when the early Jiyū Minken Undō (people's rights movement) spread all over Japan.

The border between political activists and journalists was not clear then. In addition to their natural interests in social problems, journalists were susceptible to the new movements and their leading ideas, including those overseas. Naturally, most of the early socialists in Japan around the turn of the century came from journalists or freelance authors. It was only after the movement of

Taishō Democracy around 1920 that academic scholars and university graduates joined the direction of socialism together with the full-scale introduction of Marxism.

Despite Katayama and Abe's Western experience before this foundation, the 1901 party was not the result of the caprice of Westernized intellectuals. A researcher of this 1901 party suggests that this party was born when three streams, the study of socialism, early unionization, and the movement for universal suffrage, met.[9] Katayama was the key person to this triple linkage. With the wish to develop Christian social service in Japan, he opened an urban settlement hall, Kingsley House at Kanda, in the mid of Tokyo. Influenced by the idea of Christian socialism, he extended his interest in urban social problems and supported the early unionization of workers in collaboration with Takano Fusatarō (1869–1904)[10] and others. When Rōdō-kumiai Kiseikai (Society for the Promotion of Labor Unions) founded a journal for workers, *Rōdō Sekai*, in 1898, Katayama became its chief editor. On the other hand, he joined several study groups on social problems and socialism. One of them was Shakaishugi Kenkyūkai (Society for the Study of Socialism), founded in the same year. In this Society, Katayama met not only Abe but also Kawakami and Kōtoku. This society was reorganized in the early 1900 to Shakaishugi Kyōkai (Socialists Association) to go into public enlightenment for socialism and social problems. At this stage, Kinoshita and Nishikawa joined it. Thus, this society was the forerunner of the party of 1901, all of whose six founders belonged.

The third stream of the demand for universal suffrage consisted of the primary stimulus for the foundation of a political party. The repressive Security Policing Law of 1900 made union organizers recognize the necessity of universal suffrage and the political party to repeal repressive laws and represent the interest of the majority of workers in the Diet. They joined the movement for universal suffrage and organized a mass campaign for social legislation and the voting right of workers. Members of Shakaishugi Kyōkai participated in the open speeches for workers. On April 3, 1901, over 20,000 workers assembled at the Great Banquet of Workers to demonstrate their presence in the new age. It was just after the success of this mass meeting that Katayama was informed that ca. 1,000 workers of the union of Nihon Tetsudō (Japan Railroad Co.) were willing to join the planned new socialist party. This information pushed Katayama and others finally to the foundation of the party.

The Ministry prosecuted editors and presses of those media in charge of offending the Press Ordinance. The not-guilty verdict of the first court was overturned to be guilty in the upper court. The repeated attempt to acquire legal registration under a different party name failed, too. Founders of the party had to return to the previous style of research and enlightenment of socialism under the reorganized Shakaishugi Kyōkai. However, as they did not refrain from public propaganda of socialism, they succeeded in preserving the ground for the growth of socialist ideas in the following years. The bold pacifist claim against the Russo-Japanese War was one of its conspicuous results.[11]

The emergence of legal socialist parties was postponed considerably. In 1906 when the cabinet of Duke Saionji seemed to relax its control, socialists in Japan succeeded in having a legal party, Nihon Shakaitō (Japan Socialist Party), for one year. After this, the repression of socialists culminated in the large-scale suppression at the High Treason Incident of 1910. The so-called 'winter age' followed it. It was only after the introduction of universal male suffrage in 1925 that Japanese workers could have mass political parties. However, the Peace Preservation Law enacted in the same year proclaimed the party that aimed to abolish private property together with the change of national polity (i.e., the sovereign of the emperor) illegal. Thus, these proletarian parties could not raise the socialist claim to abolish private property in their program. Therefore, the movement of revolutionary socialism was unlawful. The formation and activity of the Japanese Communist Party (JCP) had to remain underground. This legal/illegal discrepancy accompanied the leftist movements of Japan up to 1945.

5.2 The Declaration and Its Repercussions

The declaration of the 1901 Party began with the following statement that called for the change of focus from political equality to the underlying problem of economic inequality.

> How to break the cleavage between the rich and the poor has emerged as a big problem in the 20th century. Although the idea of liberalism and democracy that had originated in the late 18th century France and transferred to Europeans and Americans contributed much to realizing the equality in politics, however, the enormous material progress since then replaced the old class system of nobilities and laypeople with a more formidable system of the rich and the poor. Saying generally, the equality of the economy is the base, while that of the politics is its derivative. Thus, so far as the inequality in the economy is not eliminated, even if politics should follow the constitution and the participation in government should be allocated equally, misfortunes of the majority of the people would continue. This is the reason why our party focuses its attention on economic problems in dealing with political problems.
>
> *(Shakai Minshu-tō Hyakunen Shiryō Kankōkai ed. 2001: 268)*

After suggesting the complete hegemony of the rich both in government organs and existing political parties, the declaration stresses the need for a political party representing the majority of the people, standing on socialism, democracy, and pacifism.

> Existing political parties that are totally under the control of the rich cannot represent the will of the majority of people. The rich may neglect the majority of the people on the ground of the ignorance and illiteracy of

> the workers and tenant farmers. However, it goes without saying that they should occupy a significant position in the future society due to the fact that they are the real producers of goods and wealth. Giving them their proper place thus enhances the welfare of the whole society. Our party is born here to represent the joy and sorrow of the majority of the people. However, it is not so narrow-minded to regard the rich as an enemy to protect the poor. Despite our will to promote the wealth and strength of our nation, we avoid the national egoism that makes foreign nations our victims. Saying the wish of our party directly, recognizing the world as a whole and trend of the economy, grounding on genuine socialism and democracy, our party wishes to eliminate the division between the rich and the poor and establish the victory of pacifism in the global world.
>
> *(ibid.: 269f.)*

Then, it raised eight ideal goals and twenty-eight practical demands. While the formers were very lofty, the latter covered sensible reforms from public service and urban residential policy, taxation, free compulsory education, labor legislation, protection of tenant farmers, general referendum, curtailment of the armed forces, abolition of oppressive police law, and Press Ordinance. The ideal goals were the following:

1 Developing the idea of the universal fraternity of human beings despite the difference in ethnicities and polities.
2 Total abolition of arms for the sake of world peace
3 Total elimination of the class system
4 Transfer of all capital and land necessary for production to public ownership
5 Transfer of all transportation facilities, railroads, ships, canals, bridges, etc. to public ownership
6 Equalization of the distribution of goods and wealth
7 Making people participate in the government equally
8 Making people receive education equally on the total cost-bearing by the government

(*ibid.*: 270)

A clear universal and international aspect is seen in this foundation declaration. It is incorporated into the ideals of democracy and pacifism. True, it reflected Abe's Christian view on socialism and social problems. However, the name, as well as the dualism of an ideal program and the practical demands, was taken from the model of the German Social Democratic Party. All of the six founders approved it unanimously. We can consider this document as the starting point of modern socialism in Japan.

Two months after the foundation and dissolution of the Social Democratic Party, senior professors of the Shakai Seisaku Gakkai (Association for the Study of Social Policy) moved to release a statement to discern social policies from socialism strictly under the name of the Society. This statement was called the 'plea' of this Association. It reflected the basic view of the Association very clearly.

> We oppose *laissez-faire*. Its reason is that the extreme exercise of self-interest and uncontrolled free competition would result in an excessive gulf between rich and poor. We also oppose socialism. The reason is that the destruction of the existing economic structure and the abolition of capitalists would harm the progress of national destiny. Our beliefs are as follows: we support the existing economic system of private property and wish, within this system, to prevent class conflict and promote social harmony through both individual action and the authority of the state.
>
> *(Shakai Seisaku Gakkai 1901)*

This 'plea' counted free competition and private property as the two fundaments of the present economy and regarded socialism that intends to eliminate both as the enemy to economic progress. However, it legitimized the state's intervention from the viewpoint of the public interest and the nation's needs.

> It is clear that a range of interventions exists to solve social problems keeping the present social organization based on free competition and private property untouched. Factory legislation for the protection of children and women, workers union that guarantees the interests and welfare of workers, mutual aids that stabilize the living of workers, insurance for working life, consumer cooperatives that promote thrift and saving of the small people, and so on. Social policies such as these are not incompatible with the present economic organization. The degree of their effect is already apparent in European countries. We aim to solve social problems gradually through such policies.
>
> *(ibid.)*

Abe took his pen against this statement and published an "Inquiry to the members of the Shakai Seisaku Gakkai" (Abe 1901b). From the viewpoint that socialism and social policy are in the same direction to deal with social problems, he used a simile of two passengers starting from Tokyo to reach Kyoto and Kobe. Indeed, the passenger aiming for Kobe (socialism) goes further than another aiming for Kyoto (social policy); they take the same train. As the train on the Tōkaidō line stops at Kyoto before Kobe, socialists accept social policies as the necessary provisional measures and promote their effects to go further to the solution of social problems. Thus, Abe demanded members of the Shakai Seisaku Gakkai be open-minded against socialism.

This debate stimulated Taguchi Ukichi, a classical liberalist we discussed in Chapter 4, to reveal his view on social policy in his *Tokyo Keizai Zasshi* (Taguchi

1902). He agreed with Abe regarding the common direction of socialism and social policy and directed his criticism on the basic ideas of supporters of social policy.

The first point is on the condemnation of 'extreme exercise of the self-interest.' Regarding employment relations, Taguchi argued that 'the extreme exercise of the self-interest' does not occur in the normal contractual situation under free competition. It occurs in his view instead of in the case of artificial intervention grounded on legislations, such as in the case of judicial approval of slave labor for the interest of employers on the one hand, and in the case of restriction on the employment attempting high wages and the reduction of the working hour for the interest of employed workers on the other hand.

Taguchi further raised his objection to the 'harmony between labor and capital' as the aim of social policy. Quoting the example of the cotton spinning industry in the Osaka area, where the shortage of spinners brought forth the improvement in their wages, Taguchi maintained: "Labor and capital under the free competition are harmonized already. I cannot understand why you deny this to add legislative intervention."

Finally, Taguchi complained about the combination of private property and *laissez-faire*. In the case of urban infrastructure such as tram rails, he declared that he approved the raise of public tribute of private rails. As we saw in the former chapter, Taguchi supported the land tax hike to support public finance. He was against the extra profit from the monopoly and against rent from the land as monopolized private property.

5.3 Growth and Split of Socialism in the Early 20th Century

To Abe, the difference between social policy and socialism was that of degree in the goals toward the same direction. There is no contradiction for a socialist to support social policies. Distancing from radicalism after the High Treason Incident, he kept the position of legal gradualism and widened the scope of socialism to the daily life of commoners' families as well as leisure and sports.[12] Abe was welcomed in the age of legal proletarian parties as a moderate leader that was acceptable even to the middle class. He assumed the presidency of its moderate wing parties: Shakai Minshū-tō (Social People's Party) in 1926, then Shakai Taishū-tō (Social Mass Party) in 1932. Probably of the six founders of the 1901 party, he was the most stable figure that retained the spirit of its declaration.

Katayama became critical of the collaboration of capital and labor and withdrew from the organizations that stood in such direction. However, from his evolutionary view toward socialism, he didn't deny the progress of social policies in industrial relations as well as in the life of people. He regarded varieties of measures in social policy as the manifestation of emerging socialism. In particular, he focused his attention on the public ownership and management of the urban social infrastructure. He named it 'urban socialism' and poured his energy into demanding its extension and democratic management (Katayama 1903a, 1903b).

At the end of 1903, he left Japan to consolidate the economic foundation of his social activity in the United States. He attended the sixth Amsterdam Congress of the Socialist International in August 1904. Shaking hands with the Russian delegate, Georgy Plekhanov, he called for a protest against the Russo-Japanese War. Since then, he has become an internationally known representative of Japanese socialism.

Returning from the United States in 1906, he collaborated with Abe and Nishikawa in the one-year lived Nihon Shakaitō (Japan Social Party). In this age, Katayama and Nishikawa's legal 'parliamentarian strategy' was in sharp conflict with the appraisal of 'direct action' advocated by the wing led by Kōtoku. After the dissolution of the 1906 party, Katayama was in disaccord with Nishikawa and led a small group in a short period with Tazoe Tetsuji (1875–1908) to practice the 'parliamentary strategy.' Despite his legal strategy, he was arrested in early 1912 in charge of agitating tram workers of Tokyo City to go on strike. He stayed in prison till receiving the pardon at the beginning of the new Taishō Era.

Facing distress and isolation in Japan, he left Japan in 1914 to support the movement from overseas. He endeavored to continue his Japanese journal in San Francisco in vain. In 1916, he moved to New York to join the leftist group from which the American Communist Party was founded. In 1921, Katayama, then a complete Moscow loyal communist, was requested to move to Moscow to organize an assembly of the workers of the Far East. Since then, he stayed in Moscow as an executive member of the Communist International until he died in 1933. For Japanese Marxists in these years, the old Katayama in Moscow was a symbolic figure that combined Moscow and Japan.

Katayama was neither theoretician nor an ideologue. In contrast to Katayama, who reached socialism empirically from his activity at the grassroots level, Kōtoku was a native fine writer who quested for the world's most advanced intellectual tide. It was Kōtoku that showed remarkable progress and transformation in the decade after 1901, which caused tumults and tragedies in the camp of Japanese socialists. In the same year of the foundation of Shakai Minshutō his book on imperialism, *Nijyū-Seiki no Kaibutsu Teikoku-shugi* (Imperialism: Monster ear of the 20th century) (Kōtoku 1901) that preceded J. A. Hobson's *Imperialism* (1902) one year, Lenin's *Imperialism* (1917) 16 years, characterized imperialism as the amalgam of militarism and economic egoism that manipulated jingoism for the interest of oligarchy.[13] Under the overwhelming atmosphere in favor of imperialistic expansion policies in the years toward the Russo-Japanese War, the publication of such criticism was a brave act that supported the anti-war position of critical journalists and socialists.

In his next book on socialism, *Shakaishugi Shinzui* (Quintessence of Socialism) (Kotoku 1903), Kōtoku introduced doctrines of socialism depending heavily on Karl Marx's *Communist Manifesto* and Friedrich Engels's *From Utopia to Science.* This was one of the first guides of socialism from a Marxian perspective in Japan.[14] When *the Yorozu Chōhō* switched its pacifistic stance to a pro-war direction, Kōtoku, together with Sakai Toshihiko (1871–1933), left it to establish a new press, the *Heimin Shimbun* (The Commoners News). This press published the first Japanese translation of the *Communist Manifesto* in its November 13, 1904 issue, anticipating receiving the sales ban.

However, under the subsequent repression of socialists and labor movements, Kōtoku became skeptical of the effect of the legal and parliament strategy that focused on the introduction of 'universal' (though men only) suffrage. During his stay in the United States from 1905 to 1906, he initially aimed to recover the mental health damaged by the repeated imprisonment; he got acquainted with radical anarchists living in the San-Francisco area. Further, he witnessed the voluntary collaboration that emerged among the people during the San Francisco earthquake (April 1906) and was impressed by the vision of spontaneous collaboration without authority. Thus, he returned to Japan as a convinced anarcho-communist that favored P. A. Kropotkin before Marx.

In the February 9 issue of the *Heimin Shimbun*, Kōtoku declared the change of his thought public. "A true social revolution is never accomplished by that way of universal suffrage nor parliamentary strategy. To attain the goal of socialism, no other way exists than the direct action of the united workers" (Kōtoku 1907). Mentioning the degeneration of the radical Jiyū-tō (Liberal Party) in the 1880s to a bourgeois party and the stagnation of European socialist parties despite their participation in the election, Kōtoku concluded that the parliament strategy instead degenerates revolutionary movement than strengthens it. He was caught by the myth of 'direct action' of united workers that should culminate into a 'general strike.'[15] The co-publisher of the *Heimin Shimbun*, Sakai, did not abandon the parliament strategy but expressed his sympathy for Kōtoku's radicalism. Heiminsha, under Kōtoku and Sakai, was a cradle of the radical wing of Japanese socialism that differentiated from moderate gradualism that took the parliamentarian strategy.

After the dissolution of Heimin-sha, Kōtoku was relatively isolated from his old friends. In 1909, he tried to start a new journal *Jiyū Shisō* (Free Thought) but received the order of prohibition. Around him, a group of disgruntled radicals gathered, to which his common-law wife Kanno Suga (1881–1911) belonged. In June 1910, Kōtoku was arrested with Kanno under the charge of planning terror against the emperor. Kōtoku himself was not involved in this conspiracy. However, the police made most of this conspiracy to abolish 'dangerous ideas' and 'dangerous persons.' Hundreds of socialists and anarchists were arrested, and 26 of them were indicted. Of them, 24 were sentenced to death in January 1911, and 12 of them, including Kōtoku, were executed in the same month. It was said that only those socialists who had been detained in prison for other charges could survive when this large-scale frame-up was designed. Details of this High Treason Incident of 1910 were strictly concealed within the top circle of government and judicial officials. However, to those who acquired some of the fragmented information about this incident, it was shocking to know that the government of Japan behaved so determinately to abolish new ideas of socialism.[16]

As F. G. Notehelfer (1971) convincingly argued, Kōtoku retained the spirit of a Confucian moralist that appreciated the purity of the mind before the external procedure. Though his book on imperialism was a pioneering work on this matter, the dominant tone of the criticism was that of a moralist. In the case of his reception of socialism, he did not receive it from the experience or observation of social problems, but he found his affinity in the ideal of socialism and in the purity of the devotion of revolutionaries, which guided him later to anarcho-communism. To him, the consideration of practical measures and tactics was foreign. He stressed the 'direct action' or 'general strike' in the age when the actor, 'united workers,' did not exist. Since he retained the traditional belief that nothing significant could accomplish without the devotion of convicted individuals (Shishi), the emergence of the convicted workers, even if few, is more important than acquiring voters in large numbers. This sense that sought purity of mind in the political action stimulated Kōtoku's move to radicalism. It accompanied the repercussion that pushed dissatisfied activists around him to imagine the fancy of terrorism.

5.4 Renovation of the Concept of Social Policy

Shakai Seisaku Gakkai, which released its 'repeal' against socialism in 1901, had its origin in an informal study group of university professors that had started in 1896.[17] The original intention was to study social policies in Germany and to prepare their introduction to Japan. In the following year, it adopted the name Shakai Seisaku Gakkai and reorganized into an academic society with the model of the German Society for Social Policy (*Verein für Sozialpolitik*). The paragraph of its 1901 Plea, which we quoted before, was taken from the Prospectus that this Association stipulated before a few years (Shakai Seisaku Gakkai 1899).

Main members in its formation stage were Kuwada Kumazō (1868–1932), Yamzsaki Kakujirō (1869–1945), Onozuka Kiheiji (1871–1944), Takano Iwasaburō (1871–1949), Kanai Noburu (1865–1933), Tajima Kinji (1867–1934), Wadagaki Kenzō (1860–1919), and others. Sakuma Teiichi (1846–1898) an enlightened entrepreneur who supported the factory legislations in Japan, and Takano Fusatarō, a moderate union organizer, joined this Association. As this Association kept close relations with ministerial officials in charge of industrial relations and social welfare, it could organize an open academic meeting in October 1898 to discuss the draft of factory legislation, to which Katayama also served as one of its speakers. In the case of Katayama's entry to the Association, a concern for his deviation from the harmonic view of capital and labor existed in the founders' circle. On the side of Katayama, he felt incongruity at adopting the Prospectus 1898 and began to keep his distance from the Association.

The Association developed into the first established academic society in the area of economics and social policy. It had an annual assembly with a particular topic in social policies from 1907 to 1924. The list of topics (Table 5.1) tells us the interest of economists and policymakers of this Association in these years.

TABLE 5.1 Topics of Assembly Discussion of the Association for the Study of Social Policy

	Year	*Topic*
1	1907	Factory legislations
2	1908	Custom problems seen from the viewpoint of social policy
3	1909	Immigration problems
4	1910	Municipal enterprise
5	1911	Workers insurance
6	1912	Problems of living costs
7	1913	Labor disputes
8	1914	Protection of small farmers
9	1915	Taxation problems seen from the viewpoint of social policy
10	1916	Public enterprises and protected companies
11	1917	Problems of small scale manufacturers
12	1918	Problems of women workers
13	1919	Labor unions
14	1920	Problems of intermediate classes
15	1921	Institutions of wage and profit-sharing
16	1922	Tenant problems in Japan
17	1923	Not held due to the earthquake?
18	1924	Problems of labor union law

Source: Yagi 2017: 100.

The member increased year by year. While it was ca. 20 in 1898, it surpassed 200 in the early years of the 1920s. Having a chance to present at its assembly was the 'gateway' to being recognized as a scholar.

The problem of the demarcation between social policy and socialism caused tension within the Association once more in 1919, when the Association approved the entry of Asō Hisashi (1891–1940), then the general secretary of Rōdō Sōdōmei (General Labor Federation). At the banquet after the assembly, Fukuda Tokuzō (1874–1930) raised the question of whether the Association could have a socialist as its member. This question touched not only on Asō's entry but also on Kawakami Hajime (1879–1946) and other members known as socialists. The tension at the banquet hall that emerged from Fukuda's question was erased when Takano Iwasaburō admonished Fukuda and Fukuda followed him. According to Ōuchi Hyōe (1888–1980)'s recollection, Takano talked to Fukuda that it was possible and likely that socialists should emerge in the Association in accord with the change of time and added that the Association should admit that socialists, too, could advocate social policy. Takano's talk correctly reflected the situation in and out of the Association at this time.[18]

This happening imposed on Fukuda the task of consolidating the theoretical foundation for social policy that could compete with theories of socialists, in particular, that of Marxism. The étatist view of social policy and the credo of the conformity of capital and labor became obsolete in the years of the 'Taishō

Democracy' when varieties of social and cultural movements emerged along with the high tide of the demand for universal suffrage. Labor disputes, as well as disputes on tenant land, became commonplace in the urban area and countryside, respectively. Under the Russian Revolution's impact, Marxism, which stressed class struggle as the moving force of history, gained popularity.

From the beginning, Fukuda was critical of Marxism and social democracy. He studied in Germany from 1898 to 1901 and acquired his doctorate under Lujo Brentano in Munich. Following his mentor's left-liberal position that appreciated the growth of labor unions as independent voluntary organizations, Fukuda supported labor movements grounded on the voluntary base of individuals. Thus, he was against the étatist view of social policy *á la* Adolf Wagner, which had been held by his senior generation that had advocated state intervention to make workers dependent on the state and to promote their loyalty to the state. On the other hand, he opposed social democracy for the reason of its giving priority to the interest of the working class. In his view, social democracy lacks the essential universality that the term 'democracy' must equip.

Questing for an alternative to the ćtatist concept of social policy, Fukuda replaced 'state' with 'society' and defined social policy as 'the policy of the society by the society for the society.' But what is the core of this newly discovered subject of social policy? Under the guidance of Anton Menger's criticism of bourgeois law and his conceptualization of the 'right to work,' Fukuda found in the concept of 'right to life' the transcendental idea that can guide social policy. In his view, the social policy that is driven by the idea of the 'right to live' should occupy the central position in the economy in parallel with the democracy in politics. In his view, social policy with the guiding idea of the 'right to live' was not classified in the direction of 'distributive policy' but in that of 'productive policy' because it would promote the production and productivity of the society.

Next, what about Fukuda's rejection of socialism and Marxism? As the 'right to live' is a universal idea, Fukuda's new concept of social policy is exempted from such partiality as Fukuda saw in social democracy. In this respect, Fukuda need not rely on socialism in his design of the social policy. However, against Marxism, which gained plausibility in interpreting social and economic unrest in the nineteen-twenties of Japan by its stress of class struggle and the prospect of the collapse of capitalism, Fukuda had to provide an alternative interpretation of class struggles and labor dispute.

To Fukuda, who could read the literature of and on Marxism in the original language and knew the trends of contemporary economics, writing criticism on Marxism was a relatively easy task. In the early stage of the introduction of Marx in Japan, he was indeed counted as an authority both in the knowledge of Marxian economics and its criticism. Fukuda refuted both the necessity of the collapse of capitalism and the coming of a classless society under socialism.

What attracted Fukuda was the concept of 'welfare economics' in contrast with the prevailing economics based on prices. In his view, class struggles were fought not solely for the gains (profit and wages) of fighting classes but contained the element of the demand for approval of the independent personality of the lower class. As the approval of personality is in itself the core element of the 'right to live,' it contains an extra element that was not dealt with by usual economics, which Fukuda called 'price economics.' As the employer must treat the employee as an independent counterpart in the case of individual labor disputes, the labor movement demands the approval of the personality of the working class as the oppositive part to the class of employer in the society. This effect of class struggle would diffuse to other areas by encouraging varieties of social movements there.

In the preface of the *Shakai Seisaku to Kaikyū Tōsō* (Social Policy and Class Struggle) of 1922, he wrote:

> I would briefly summarize the outline of my thought that integrates the whole of this book. Community life is inevitably needed to fulfill our unlimited wants through our feeble individual capability. As the community life develops, classes emerge from it, and their struggles begin. The present class struggle is fought between the capital owners' class and the wage earners'. The former uses the power of employment, and the latter uses labor disputes. Socialism, social policy, and everything that had the adjective 'social' in the name deal with the struggle in this form.
>
> *(Fukuda 1922: 5)*

Then, Fukuda regarded Socialists and Marxists as optimists who foresaw class struggle extinction too easily.

> They [socialists and Marxists: YK] maintain that because capitalism is destined to collapse, class struggles inevitably disappear with capitalism. Social policy, as I understand, does not take such optimism. ... If we leave things untouched, the movement of capital accumulation gains power more and more to result in a situation where the true welfare of human life is infringed by it. Thus, we advocate that we should countervail this overwhelming move with artificial policies. This is the *raisonne d'etre* of social policy.
>
> *(ibid.: 6)*

Fukuda's social policies as 'artificial policies' are not state-led policies. The driving force of these countervailing policies is the class struggle itself. In Fukuda's view, the labor movement that fights against the domination of the employers class occupied a leading position in various social movements. It should establish the independent personality of workers and fight to enhance their welfare. In correspondence with the Preface, the final paragraph of this book suggests the close tie between the labor movement and social policy.

> The course of social development demands the labor movement that has accumulated lots of experience to recognize its true mission and exert its full power to perform it. This true mission is not other than to acknowledge the essence of the labor movement as a welfare movement and that of labor dispute as a welfare struggle. Awakening its mission is not different from that the labor movement recognizes the significance of the realization of welfare by its movement. Thus, the *raisonne d'etre* of the science of social policy consists in that it shows the true consequences [of class struggles: YK] for the sake of the elimination of this fundamental contradiction [of capitalism] and for the sake of the labor movement to serve this end, liberating from the erroneous view of the materialistic view of the history.
>
> *(ibid.: 313f.)*

In the last years of his life, he aimed to establish welfare economics that could serve the social policies he conceived. He explored contemporary inquiries, including A. C. Pigou's welfare economics, but he could not find theories that fit his scheme. In the Preface of his last book, *Kōsei Keizaigaku Kenkyū* (Studies in Welfare Economics) (Fukuda 1930), he confessed to the immaturity of his scheme. His welfare economics remained as a torso due to his abrupt death in 1930.

It is said that Fukuda's idea of the 'right to live' was adopted in the 1947 Constitution of Japan. Further, we can find the affinity of Fukuda's vision with recent discussions on welfare and personality. For example, Amartya Sen's concept of 'capability' (Sen 1992) seems to fit well with Fukuda's scheme. However, in this chapter, we confine ourselves to describing his foundation of social policy distinctive to socialism in Fukuda.

Fukuda was often counted in the line of social liberalists in the early decades of the 20th century in Japan. Fukuda, who was the co-founder of the Reimei-kai (The Society of Dawn, 1918–1920), together with Yoshino Sakuzō (1878–1933), was one of the leading figures of the enlightenment movement of 'Taishō Democracy.' He represented it in the area of economy and social policy with his idea of 'approval of personality' and 'right to live.' The former lies in the core of the conviction of liberalism, and the latter could also be acceptable to a liberal if (s)he would understand the former in its substantial context. Then, what is the difference between Fukuda and Taguchi, the representative figure of classical liberalism in Japan?

First, Fukuda approved and supported social policies and the labor movement. The latter, whose essence lay in the combination of workers, deviates from classical liberalism based on genuine individualism. Like his mentor Lujo Brentano, Fukuda would give liberalism a more comprehensive social scope by recognizing combinations (labor unions) as the essential element of economic society and introducing necessary legislation to regulate conflicts between capital and labor. Both Fukuda and Brentano admitted the development of trade unions as the crucial progress of the modern economic society.

However, classical liberalist like Taguchi could maintain that the liberal market economy could solve the conflict by the coordination between demand and supply under the condition of free competition. Then the difference between social policy and classical liberalism consists of whether we can trust in the working of the market mechanism. Here Fukuda found the limitation of the prevailing theory of economics. The overall economics grounded on the price mechanism analysis is not fitted to explain the effect of class struggles and labor disputes on the advance of society. This finding led Fukuda to the vision of 'welfare economics' in distinction with 'price economics' (Fukuda 1930).

Notes

1 We wrote the 'first Social Democratic Party' since several political parties of the same name, Shakai Minshu-to, existed (and the one exists at present) in the political history of Japan. Shakai Minshutō 100 Years Shiryō Kankōkai ed. (2001), whose chief editor was Yamaizumi Susumu, provides basic information about this 1901 party.

2 See Powles (1961). In the 1930s, Abe prevailed to preside over moderate proletarian parties. He was equipped with the sense to integrate the working class's family life and leisure need into his vision.

3 Katayama's name was firmly combined with the communist movement in Japan, as he later joined the international communism in the United States and lived in Moscow to death as a symbol of Asian communism. However, Kublin (1964) followed Katayama's life attentively from his youth. Sumiya (1960) focused on Katayama's empiricist approach in his activities in Japan before his leave for the United States in 1914.

4 Kinoshita's first novel, *Hi no Hashira* (Pillar of Fire) (Kinoshita 1904), has an English translation by Kenneth Strong (Kinoshita 1972).

5 Kōtoku's unique combination of Western socialism and his traditional mentality led him to a pathetic radicalism that ignored the actual progress of the movement. See Elison (1967) and Notehelfer (1971).

6 On Kawakami, see Gavin (2016).

7 On Nishikawa, see Tanaka (1990).

8 In the short prison days before the execution, Kōtoku wrote a note that denies the existence and teachings of Jesus Christ (Kōtoku 1911). Most researchers are perplexed by Kōtoku's intention to choose this topic for his final writing. In our view, he thought a liberation from the idea of god is essential for the liberation of ideas of individuals.

9 Ota (2001: 37).

10 Takano Fusatarō joined the labor movement during his long stay in the United States. He was an ardent follower of Samuel Gompers and was nominated by him as AFL's union organizer in charge of Japan. He was the elder brother of Takano Iwasaburō. See Kublin (1959).

11 On the relation of pacifism in Japan to Christianity and socialism, see Bamba and Howes eds. (1978).

12 At Waseda University, Abe served its athletic clubs as University's chief consultant. In particular, his name was combined with the academic league baseball. See Gavin (2013) on Abe's extension of social democratic scope to the life and leisure of future citizens.

13 Robert Thomas Tierney published its translation together with his full-length introduction to Kōtoku and the early anti-imperialist movement in Japan then (Tierney 2015).

14 Kirkup (1888) and Ely (1894) were the main sources of the early introduction of socialism in Japan.

15 Kōtoku's ideas were inherited by a new generation of anarcho-syndicalists when a similar conflict in the labor movements occurred between 'anarchists' and 'Bolschevists.' The representant of the former, Ōsugi Sakae (1885–1923), was also killed by the military police in the occasion of the Great Kantō Earthquake of 1923.
16 See Gavin and Middleton eds. (2013) on the repercussion of this Incident 1910.
17 For this Association, see Fujii (1998) and Morris-Suzuki (1989) chap. 2. On Fukuda Tokuzō, see Inoue and Yagi (1998).
18 Ōuchi (1961: 19f).

References

English

Bamba, Nobuya and Howes, John F. eds. (1978) *Pacifism in Japan: The Christian and Socialist Tradition*. Kyoto: Minerva Press.

Elison, George (1967) "Kōtoku Shūsui: 'The Change in Thought.'" *Monumenta Nipponica*, 22(3–4), pp. 437–467.

Ely, Richard T. (1894) *Socialism and Social Reform*. New York: T. Y. Crowell & Co.

Kinoshita Naoe (1972) *Pillar of Fire: Hi no Hashira*, tr. by Kenneth Strong. London: Allen & Unwin.

Fujii, Takashi (1998) "The Japanese Social Policy School: its formation and breakup." In Sugihara, Shirō and Tanaka. Toshihiko eds. *Economic Thought and Modernization in Japan*. Cheltenham: Edward Elgar.

Gavin, Masako (2013) "Abe Isoo's social democratic commitments to future citizens after the high treason incident." In Gavin, Masako, and Middleton, Ben eds. *Japan and the High Treason Incident*. London and New York: Routledge.

———. (2016) "A Meiji Christian socialist becomes a spokesperson for Japan: Kawakami Kiyoshi's pilgrimage in the sacred land of liberty." *East Asia: An Intellectual Quarterly*, 33(5), pp. 175–196.

Gavin, Masako and Middleton, Ben eds. (2013) *Japan and the High Treason Incident*. London and New York: Routledge.

Inoue, Takutoshi and Yagi, Kiichiro (1998) "Two inquirers on the divide: Tokuzō Fukuda and Hajime Kawakami." In Sugihara, Shirō and Tanaka Toshihiro eds. *Economic Thought and Modernization in Japan*. Cheltenham: Edward Elgar, pp. 60–77.

Kinoshita, Naoe (1972) *Pillar of Fire: Hi no Hashira*, tr. by Kenneth Strong. London: Allen & Unwin.

Kirkup, Thomas (1888) *An Inquiry into Socialism*. London: Longmans, Green.

Kublin, Hyman (1959) "Takano Fusataro: A study in early Japanese trade-unionism." American Philosophical Society, Proceedings, CIII (no. 4).

———. (1964) *Asian Revolutionary: The Life of Katayama Sen*. Princeton NJ: Princeton University Press.

Morris-Suzuki, Tessa (1989) *A History of Japanese Economic Thought*. London and New York: Routledge.

Notehelfer, Fred G. (1971) *Kōtoku Shūsui: Portrait of a Japanese Radical*. London and New York: Cambridge University Press.

Powles, Cyril H. (1961) "Abe Isoo and the Role of Christians in the Founding of the Japanese Socialist Movement: 1895–1905." Paper on Japan (East Asian Research Center, Harvard University), 1.

Sen, Amartya (1992) *Inequality Reexamined*. Oxford: Oxford University Press.

Tierney, Robert Thomas (2015) *Monster of the Twentieth Century: Kōtoku Shūsui and Japan's First Anti-Imperialist Movement*. Oakland: University of California Press.

Yagi, Kiichiro (2017) "The diffusion of Western economics in Japan." In Malcolm Warner ed. *The Diffusion of Western Economic Ideas in East Asia*. London and New York: Routledge, pp. 94–116.

Japanese

Abe Isoo (1901a) *Shakai Mondai Kaishaku-hō* (Understanding Social Problems). Tokyo: Tokyo Senmon Gakkō Shuppan-bu.

———. (1901b) "Shakai seisaku gakkai kaiin ni shitsusu" (Questioning the members of the Association for the Study of Social Policy). *Mainichi Shimbun* (July 12).

———. (2008) *Shakai Mondai Kaishakuhō. Shakai Minshu-tō no Sengen* (Understanding Social Problems. Declaration of Social Democratic Party). Tokyo: Gakujutsu Shuppankai.

Fukuda Tokuzō (1922) *Shakai Seisaku to Kaikyū Tōsō* (Social Policy and Class Struggle). Tokyo: Ōkura Shoten.

———. (1930)*Kōsei Keizai Kenkyū* (Studies on Welfare Economics). 2 vols. Tokyo: Tōkō Shoin.

Katayama Sen (1903a) *Toshi Shakai-shugi* (Urban Socialism). Tokyo: Shakai-shugi Tosho-bu.

———. (1903b) *Waga Shakai-shugi* (My Socialism). Tokyo: Shakai-shugi Tosho-bu.

Kinoshita Naoe (1904) *Hi no Hashira* (Pillar of Fire). Tokyo: Heimin-sha.

Kōtoku Shūsui (1901) *Teikoku-shugi: Nijyū-Seiki no Kaibutsu* (Imperialism: Monster of the Twentieth Century). Tokyo: Keisei-sha.

———. (1903) *Shakai-shugi Shinzui* (Essence of Socialism). Tokyo: Chōhō-sha.

———. (1907) "Yoga shisō no henka (Futsū senkyo nit tsuite)" (The change of my thought – on general suffrage). *Heimin Shimbun*, 16 (February 5).

———. (1911) *Kirisuto Massatsu-ron* (On the Denial of Christ). Tokyo: Heigo Shuppan-sha.

Ota Masao (2001) "Shakai Minshu-tō no tanjō" (Birth of the Social democratic Party). In Shakai Minshu-tō Hyakunen Shiryō Kankō-kai ed. *Shakaishugi no Tanjō*, Tokyo: Ronsō-sha, pp. 1–90.

Ōuchi Hyōe (1961) "Shakai seisaku gakkai to Takano sensei" (The association for the study of social policy and Prof. Takano). In Takano Iwasaburo ed. *Kappa no He: Iko-shū* (A Fart of Kappa: Posthumous Fragments). Tokyo: Hosei Daigaku Shuppan-kyoku, pp. 1–35.

Shakai Minshu-tō Hyakunen Shiryō Kankōkai ed. (2001) *Shakaishugi no Tanjō – Shakai Minshutō 100 Nen* (The Birth of Socialism – Social Democratic Party 100 Years). Tokyo: Ronsō-sha.

Shakai Seisaku Gakkai (1899) "Shakai seisaku gakkai shuisho" (Prospectus of the association for the study of social policy). *Kokka Gakkai Zasshi*, 13 (no. 150, August 1899) pp. 105–106.

———. (1901) "Shakai Seisaku to Shakai-shugi" (Socialism and social policy [Socalled Plea of the Association for the Study of Social Policy]). In: Shakai Seisaku Gakkai Shiryō Shūsei Henshū Iinkai ed. (1978) *Shakai Seisaku Gakkai Shiryō* (Historical Documents of the Association for the Study of Social Policy). Tokyo: Ochanomizu Shobō, pp. 62–65.

Sumiya Mikio (1960) *Katayama Sen*. Tokyo: Tokyo Daigaku Shuppankai.

Taguchi Ukichi (1902) "Shakai seisaku gakkai no benmei-sho wo yomu" (Reading the plea of the association of the study of social policy). *Tokyo Keizai Zasshi*, (1114) (January 25, 1902), pp. 4–8.

Tanaka Hideo (1990) *Nishikawa Kōjirō Shōden – Shakai-shugi kara no Ridatsu* (Nishikawa Kōjirō Biography: Exodus from Socialism). Tokyo: Misuzu Shobō.

6

YANAGITA KUNIO'S RURAL ECONOMY

Investigation into the Nationality of Japan

6.1 Backgrounds

Viewing it from the industrial structure and the composition of the population, Japan in the Meiji Era (1868–1912) was an overwhelmingly agricultural society. Despite the rapid growth of metropolitan areas and the emergence of new towns, people living in rural areas occupied the majority of the nation. However, we cannot find an intrinsic view of the local agricultural society in such enlightenment scholars as Fukuzawa Yukichi and Taguchi Ukichi. As descendants of the warrior families in the Tokugawa period, they had no experience living in an agricultural society. Warriors in the Tokugawa period had lived in town in separation from agricultural villages and viewed peasants as the source of tributes on which they lived.[1] Such stance seems to have continued among urban citizens in modern Japan who had no real experience in rural life or, even though they had it, had deserted it after entering the urban life.

In the article on land taxation (Fukuzawa 1892), Fukuzawa criticized the demand of the opposition parties for its reduction on the ground that land tax would not harm agriculture so far as its portion did not exceed the rent from the land concerned. He argued that the land tax reduction would increase landowners' revenue only, with no gains for cultivating farmers. As we saw in the previous chapter, Taguchi was also against this reduction and favored its rise.

Indeed, the demand for land taxation reduction reflected landowners' interest, especially in the age when the tenant system was spreading with the increase of impoverished farmers. However, the direct application of the teaching of the classical economy to Japan did not hit the reality that capitalistic farming, with its clear distinction of the landowner, tenant farmer, and wage laborer, did not exist. Further, the new government could not exert its administration effectively without integrating the agrarian interest in the countryside. Even before the

DOI: 10.4324/9781003081319-6

opening of the Diet, the government had to introduce local councils with limited elections to complement the centralized local administration. It is no coincidence that the systematic organization of agrarian societies (Nō-kai) at each level of the prefecture, county, and municipality (village and town) was established at the turn of centuries (1900). In these years, the integration of opposition parties originated in the democratic movement into the parliament (Diet) with limited suffrage was completed with the euphoria of the victory over China.

As we saw in the previous chapter, the significance of promoting endogenous industry, including agriculture, fishery, and forestry, was first stressed by a group in the Ministry of Agriculture and Commerce (MAC) around Maeda Masana. Though Maeda's untimely effort failed, he could stimulate the move to trade-wise associations through his independent campaign. He actively organized agricultural societies, but he had to leave them, as his wish of keeping their autonomy was not accepted by the government.

The pauperization of Japanese farmers in the Meiji era became the concern of two German invited experts: Paul Mayet (1846–1920) and Udo Eggert (1848–1893). They worried over the intensified misery and land expropriation in the agriculture sector and submitted policy recommendations to the government. Some of them were published in Japanese translation and contributed to awakening the public interest in agricultural problems. Contrary to the American advisors that taught the merits of large-scale farming, German experts preferred the conservation of landed farmers and recommended agricultural credit associations to prevent the downfall of farmers.[2]

Their recommendations were in accord with the German orientation of a group of bureaucrats-politicians headed by Yamagata Aritomo (1838–1922). Shinagawa Yajirō (1843–1900), who was once Maeda's superior at the Ministry of Agriculture, and Hirata Tōsuke (1849–1925) found in the growth of local cooperatives in Germany (Schulze-Delitzsch type credit associations and Raiffeisen type cooperatives) the measure to mitigate the difficulties of the farmers under the rapid change of industrialization. They believed that the easy way to agricultural finance could aid aspiring farmers and those in distress. However, in their case, the interest in the public order prevailed over that of the activation of producers.[3] The agricultural policies and policies of domestic control were intermingled in the mind of politicians and administrators.

The systematically organized Agrarian Societies (Keitō Nōkai) themselves remained only as formal institutions supported by the public subvention. For renovating its agricultural policies, MAC would apply the more practically oriented production unions (Sangyō Kumiai), whose bill passed the Diet in 1900.

6.2 Yanagita on Agricultural Policy

This year 1900, Yanagita Kunio (1875-1962),[4] a fresh Imperial University graduate who studied agricultural policy, entered MAC. The Ministry immediately placed him in the front department of the new policy whose center the introduction of production unions occupied. During a few years in this department and following, he made many tours to explain the nature and function of production unions in agriculture and conduct on-the-spot research. He published an introductory guidebook of the agricultural production union (Yanagita 1902) and accepted the request for lecture courses on agricultural policy at several universities. He was one of the few experts that knew the actual conditions of farmers of Japan then.

Furthermore, Yanagita was equipped with a precious sense to perceive the mind of people living in the country and the literary talent to sublimate them into attractive prose. In his student years, he had been one of the most promising young poets in line with Shimazaki Tōson (1872–1943) before he devoted himself to the study of agricultural policy. After leaving the public service, he became the founder of folklore studies in Japan. A disaccord exists among Yanagita researchers on the unified interpretation of his agricultural policies and folklore studies. While some would find continuities between both, R. A. Morse, in the preface of the Japanese edition of his Yanagita study, rejected this continuity thesis, saying that Yanagita's view on agricultural problems is 'more scientific' while that of his folklore studies is near to 'literature' (Morse 1977: 8). Indeed, Yanagita's wording of his folklore studies (Minzoku-gaku) with the term 'rural economy' (YKCW 30: 335–337) would support the continuity thesis. Still, Morse's intuition suggests that the term 'rural economy' in Yanagita represents a different meaning from the prevailing word of 'economy.' It connotes a broader sociocultural perspective that supersedes the usual sense of 'economy' thanks to his poetic mind and imagination.

As an expert on the government's agriculture policy that focused its attention on local administration belatedly, Yanagita felt the naïve wonder of small producers.

> In the age of a closed, self-sufficient economy, such a wonder as "why I am poor?" might be a stupid question. Except for the damage of natural disasters, every effort had corresponding rewards. At present, however, even a hard worker may fall into poverty. Thus, this wonder has become a very plausible, severe, and important question.
>
> *(YKCW 16: 13)*

For such a question, the enlightenment scholars such as Fukuzawa remained to give an indifferent answer as 'learning is possible even while being involved with rice farming.' Contrastingly, Yanagita thought, "to understand how such miseries of life or such disaccord and troubles came to appear, we should know the most significant contract we have, namely the relationship between our land, our group, and ourselves deeply." Thus, the learning that was needed was "the learning to find ourselves in the land and groups of the nation." (YKCW 25: 89) Yanagita liked to call this 'Shin Kokugaku' (new national studies) that stood in contrast with the learnings from foreign origins.

Fukuzawa expected much from the development of modern industry and commerce and relatively little from agriculture. It means that an essential part of the nationality of modern Japan is missing in his cone-like scheme of modernization (Figure 3.1), which is ordered along the temporal axis of civilization. A spatial dimension that can contain the life of the majority of the nation at the base is missing. Our view is that we can interpret Yanagita's move from agricultural policy to folklore studies as the recovery of the spatial structure of the nationality that has been under the rapid change of modernization. Yanagita paraphrased 'rural economy' into 'chronicle of rural life' and added that it 'describes how common man is living' (YKCW 30: 335–337).

A different sense was needed to fill the missing spatial structure in the 'civilization' view. It was Yanagita that supplemented Fukuzawa by placing a spatial dimension that can contain the basic sense of the 'common man.'

He wrote the guidebook on production unions during his service as an official of the Ministry, *Saishin Sangyō Kumiai Tsūkai* (New Guidebook of Production Unions: Yanagita 1902), which contained his initial view on the living conditions of the people. In the preface, he revealed his general view of Japan then, which showed a clear contrast to Fukuzawa's optimistic vision of civilization.

> The conditions of the market in the new age always affected adversely to the small-sized producers. Despite ever-improving credit institutions and traffic facilities, their benefits are monopolized by large firms. What small-sized producers receive from the society is simply distress that becomes a grudge against the disparity of the society. Small farmers, in particular, that generally live in provinces, are affected severely by their bad conditions to observe the change of the tide and adapt themselves to it. On the one hand, their products are severely threatened by domestic and foreign competition. On the other, in many cases, their income, including all side jobs, does not reach even half of the wage of ordinary workers in the town. Under this situation, the ambitious youth hurry to leave their native community for cities or overseas. However, they are not guaranteed to have a pleasant life after decades. It's scarce that those who left their native community return home with their assets to revive the native community. This trend gains the speed, especially in these years. It hinders the progress of the local economy and undermines national power. Looking at families, we know that this emigration results in the decline of ethics and rituals of family. As the weakening of morality of the nation, we cannot mention all the deplorable effects of such a situation.
>
> *(YKCW 28: 3f.)*

The general framework of this passage written by a young ministry official is the problem of national pauperization that advanced with the progress of the market economy and created the spatial division between the urban area and rural area. Yanagita learned the viewpoint of social policy from his mentor Matsuzaki

Kuranosuke (1866–1919). From this viewpoint, the problem of the poverty of small-sized producers ranged from agriculture, fishery, forestry, handicrafts, transporters, and rural pauperization in general. It was a far more vast and severe problem than the labor problem that began attracting the concerns of scholars and journalists of Japan then.

The pauperization in the countryside resulted from the ongoing commercialization's impact on small-sized producers with their unfavorable location and insufficient knowledge. Under the given structural disparity between the urban and rural areas, the urban exodus of ambitious youth from the countryside was unavoidable. Metropolitan regions that absorbed capital and population thrived on animated commerce and industry. Under this situation, agricultural protectionism that prioritized agriculture before industry and commerce considerably influenced scholars,[5] bureaucrats, and representatives of agrarian interest.

Yanagita was critical to the discourse of pro-agriculture protectionism because he believed that what was needed was not the protection but the provision of the conditions on which farmers could exert their initiatives on the ground of voluntary collaboration. In Yanagita's view, the poverty of Japanese farmers originated not from the lack of protection but its lilliput size of farming with poor capital equipment and insufficient adaptation capability. The protection of agriculture and the authoritarian control of farming might hinder the possibility of the breakthrough of these barriers by farmers' initiative.[6] The production unions that Yanagita promoted during his service under the Ministry should occupy a central role in activating farmers' initiatives.

> Philanthropists often call that small people are waiting for salvation. In my view, this is a disdaining phrase for the people. I would ask them, why you won't make the people help themselves? Self-help, Progress, and Collaboration with Mutual Assistance. These are indeed the main objects of production unions.
>
> *(YKCW 28: 130)*

However, the mainline of the agricultural policy then was an authoritarian introduction of a uniform farming style aiming to increase rice and wheat production. Most of the agricultural societies and production unions were oriented to the interest of landowners and did not represent the interest of cultivating farmers. Yanagita further recommended the commutation of the rent to promote the initiatives of the producers. However, his stress on farmers' initiative caused considerable suspicion from several persons that kept influencing the agricultural policy then. It is guessed that it might be the cause of his removal from the front position of the agricultural policy to the Legislation Section of the Cabinet.[7]

Yanagita's vision of the development of Japanese agriculture differed considerably from the leading tone of agricultural policy then. What Yanagita imagined as the goal of agriculture policy was the consolidation of viable middle-scale farming that could respond to the new development of the market. The production unions Yanagita drew in his guidebook should support and assist sound farmers with provisions of credit and functional collaboration in production and distribution. To him, even the emergence of quitting farmers was welcome, as it provided the possibility of scaling up the remaining farmers.

In the countryside, while labor was abundant, land and capital were scarce. Yanagita recommended the scaling-up of farming by releasing the excess labor force and enriching working capital through the credit supplied by the production unions. This may sound like a commonplace vision of the modernization of agriculture. However, Yanagita would not welcome the penetration of urban style individualism in the countryside. In his view, rural villages are the homes that cumulated experience and wisdom of the community life of the long antecedent years. He believed that reviving them in the modern way of collaboration was the key to recovering prosperity in rural life.

Taking the land-use problem, Yanagita's view of the farming right differed considerably from propagators of the modernization of agriculture. While the latter wished to guarantee the tenant the redemption right of the investment on land (land improvement) as fully as possible, Yanagita opposed it.

> Good or bad, the invisible solidarity of the direct cultivators of land for long years has created the present condition. If it is approved that those who quit farming can bring the total value with them so far as they can count it, all of the benefits of institutions and improvement of the environment of farming may flow into urban cities. Agriculture may remain the cluster of poverty forever. From the wording itself, the farming right should be the right for farming that lapses when its holders quit farming.
>
> *(YKCW 16: 342)*

To Yanagita, who regarded the cultivated land of the nation as the product of the everlasting continuity of collaboration, reviving the old idea of 'village uses the land of the village' was more suitable to promote the effective use of land than the transaction of land and its use on commercial base. His conviction was that self-sustained agriculture would develop under the collaborative relations of the rural community. Production unions that Yanagita advocated in his guidebook should renew the collaboration of direct producers living in the rural community.

As we read the paragraph in the preface to his guidebook on production unions, Yanagita's concern about rural poverty manifested twofold. The first was the general pauperization of the small producers in the rural area. Yanagita's recommendation was the modernization of their production (farming) with the help of the services of production unions. However, this recommendation presupposes the maintenance or revival of initiative and collaboration of the individual producers and their community. Thus, his second concern was that the massive urban exodus and the depth of the poverty of the remaining rural population might degenerate the nation's morality. He admitted that the change or modernization itself was inevitable, and the lifestyle of the people was changing with high speed. Then, Yanagita concluded that the immediate task of the present generation was to conduct systematic research on the ways of living ordinary people in the rural area (Jōmin: common man) to find a way of preserving their merits and reviving them in modern ways. This concern drove Yanagita after his leave from public service to folklore studies.

6.3 Discovery of Ie and *Mura*

Yanagita was fond of traveling. It gave his mind a spatial perspective of the nation. Its first axis was the division of urban area and rural area. Including the commentaries on the people's daily life, most of his writings had this contrast. This axis placed the massive existence of the rural population living in traditional style on one side and the urban residents in a modern living style on the other. This axis could also contain urban residents who could not quickly adapt to urban life and thought of their native country as their true home.

Further, he extended this horizontal axis to the mountainous area behind the rural areas. Those who lived in mountainous areas could not live in a similar style to farmers in the plains and kept a different lifestyle that appeared strange in the eyes of the people in planes.

The discovery of the secluded life in the mountains not only gave Yanagita's spatial vision of Japan a horizontal depth but also animated his literary imagination. *The Legends of Tōno* (1910)[8] that Yanagita published as the collected old stories and memoirs of the province Tōno (in Iwate Pref.) related to another life in the mountains and the world of the dead is now regarded as the founding work of Japanese folklore studies. Local communities were not only confronted with the commercialized market towns but also kept subtle relations with the mountainous area behind them and the realm of the dead. Figure 6.1 illustrates the space structure we guess Yanagita had in mind.[9]

Yanagita found that he could read the time axis in the spatial constellation of Japanese society. He visited a mountainous village in South Kyūshu (Shiibamura) and observed the lifestyle there. He wrote, "How far is the life in the mountain from the present! In my view, the past and the present don't make a vertical axis, but they lie sideways in the direction of the mountains. Such is the state of our nation" (YKCW 27: 8). Time axes are spatially structuralized as the cultures that originated in the capital city draw diffusion frontier lines from the urban area to the rural area and finally to mountains on the map of Japan. The past or history remains alive in the spatial constellation of Japan! In reality, such structuralized history exists in the mind of the living people. Tsurumi Kazuko named it as 'icicle model' of time (Tsurumi 1975: 227–229). The investigation of the surviving customs of the local life and that of the inherited oral tales would create the learning of the history of the 'common man.'[10]

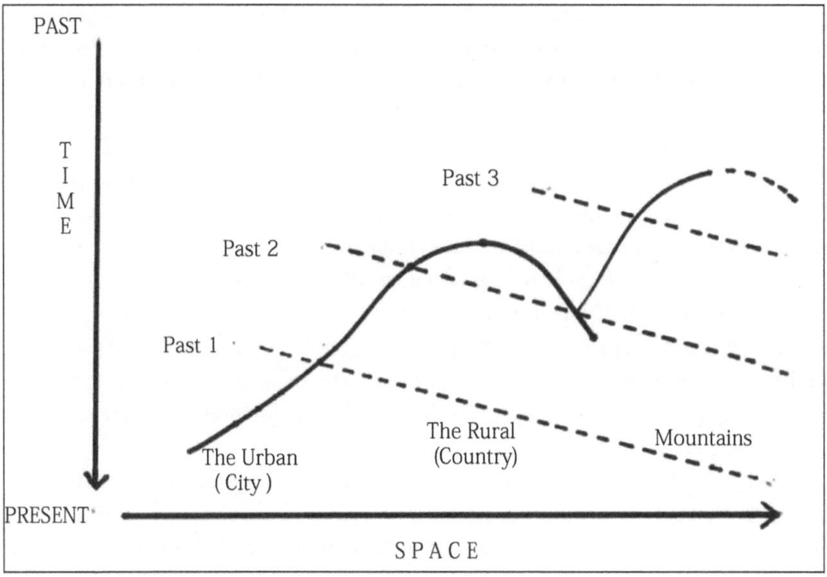

FIGURE 6.1 Yanagita's spatio-temporal view of Japan
Source: Yagi (1999), p.59 modified

> As modernization occurred in Japan quite recently, the past cohabits with the present in the same village and the same house. The things of the past are diluting away at an incredible speed. Still, the flowers of the folklore art haven't faded away totally. Japan is a rare country where those born there can learn them with their familiar sense of the mother tongue.
>
> *(YKCW 25: 103)*

Fukuzawa once talked about the privilege of his generation that lived the old and the new age. In Yanagita's case, it was the advantage of Japanese scholars to know the past and the present by studying the life of their nation.

Yanagita's folklore study had double aspects of the study of the external life of the people in work, consumption, and living, and that of the inner life of the people and its cultural manifestation. If we integrate both into one, it is worth the name of 'social economy.' In this sense, Hashikawa Bunzō compared Yanagita's work with Max Weber, who departed from agrarian studies and attained a grand view of world history based on religion's sociology (Hashikawa 1977). Modern readers would mention *the Annales* School, which emphasizes the relation between material life and the people's mentality. Weber took an intellectualistic approach of focusing on the ethical teachings of the world religions and understanding the Western civilization stressed the impact of the transcendental idea derived from Judaism to Christianity. Contrastingly, Yanagita focused on the innate senses and sentiments of the 'common man' combined with their everyday life. It is the inner world that welcomes the various spirits that visit the community regularly in each season and cohabits with the spirit of ancestors that would not leave their native home. Yanagita, who stayed within the range of national folklore studies, would not maintain the universality of such a mental world. However, even in the Western nations where the monistic religion dominated, the gods and heroes of the old domestic religions survived in the mean figures of the tales and legends (Heine 1853). Yanagita knew it from the writings of Heinrich Heine, whose ardent reader Yanagita once had been. In the rural life of the non-Western world, in particular, the effect of folklore would counter or even surpass the doctrines of the established religions. As Weber's methods and aspects are recognized as the model of social scientists, Yanagita's contrasting approach, too, may have the equal right for present social scientists to be utilized.[11]

The basic units of the rural society are *Mura* 村 (village or local community) and *Ie* 家 (household or family), which collectively form the former. Both have the dual aspects of the organization for the distribution of labor and collaboration on one side and of the entity to maintain the mores and rituals of the community life. *Ie* is the elementary unit of the life and production whose ritual for ancestors is succeeded by the generations of the family head. Since the mid of the Tokugawa period, the core of *Ie* consisted of a small family with the pair of the family head and their children and its supplementary constituents (retired parents, unmarried brothers, sisters, and servants). Though the lineage system generally stands on the male line principle with the priority of the first son, the necessity of continuity of *Ie* household allows considerable flexibility as the adoption of stepchildren, allowance of a female head, and creation of a branch family (Bunke). There are many rural villages (*Mura*) in Japan, where those *Ie*s that belong to several or a few lineages occupy the majority of their *Ie*s. Still, lineages are no more the basic unit of production and life in the local community. It is *Mura* that supplements Ie by various productive collaboration (irrigation, road repairment, collective prevention of harmful insects, administration of commons, etc.), neighborhood services (funerals and marriages), and seasonal festivals. Various groups of *Mura*, such as the youth group and maiden group, performed further education and training functions.

In English, *Mura* is usually translated into 'village.' However, the 'village' in the official local administration since the Meiji era (*Mura* or Son) is a larger legislative entity that consists of several clusters of settlements. Thus, the '*Mura*' or 'Son' (Village) range in the administrative term is more extensive than the '*Mura*' as the living rural community. Japanese sociologists invented the term 'natural village' to signify the latter. '*Mura*' in this sense usually consists of ca. 30~200 *Ies* and has its local shrine, fests, and commons.

Mura was once the local unit that represented the interest of its members (*Ies*) and prepared to contest with other entities. In the Tokugawa era, *Mura* was collectively responsible for tribute of the chartered amount of the product.

The head of *Mura* and his supporters (*Mura* officials) fixed the quota of tribute to each farmer and made a bargain with the officials of the clan lords. On the other hand, *Mura* was the unit of struggle with other *Muras*. Further, as *Mura* was a collective unit that received the visit of various spirits and sent them back, it kept hidden relations with mountains behind it and with the realm of the dead, including the ancestors of the present residents. While *Ie* keeps the ritual service for its ancestors, the fests of Mura are dedicated to the spirit of ancestors that is conceived to be united with the local indigenous spirit or the protector gods that the residents invited.[12] Compared with *Ie*, whose core consists in the time axis from the ancestors to the descendants, *Mura* is the entity that is more oriented to the spatial dimension that can contain the group of *Ie* collectively.

Yanagita made much of the peculiar Japanese idea that the spirit of the dead would stay in this land eternally and not leave it far away. In a usual pattern, it is conceived that the spirit of the deceased would observe the daily life of descendants from the top of the hills behind the *Mura*. The typical picturesque image of *Mura* is such one: A cluster of farmers' houses is settled with the mountains behind, a tutelary shrine is in its center, and the graveyards are on the mountainside.

6.4 Synchronization of *Ie, Mura,* and *Kuni*

Why *does Ie* occupy the center of Yanagita's thought? Taking each Japanese, Yanagita thought, an inner drive comparable with the quest for the soul's salvation in the Christianity exists in Japanese that wishes a peaceful rest after death, receiving ritual services of the offspring as they performed for their ancestors. Thanks to this inner drive, *Ie* becomes the entity that transcends the present generation of individuals and connects the future. However, with no communal or spatial dimension with others, *Ie* itself does not guarantee morality. It may intensify the selfishness of the people and bring them into fierce competition. As Yanagita's concern in the Preface of his *New Guide of Production Unions*, the urban exodus might cause the decline of the morality of *Ie* since the joint spatial collaboration is missing in urban life. In the cities, *Ie* would lose its productive nature and the socio-cultural common space that the alive could live with the spirit of ancestors. The *Ie* that just rode on the back of the individual who deserted the home would become a vanity if he succeeded in the urban life. If he failed, his *Ie* would disappear.[13]

In his *Meiji Taishō-shi, Sesō hen* (History of Meiji and Taisho Era, The Part of Social Affair: Yanagita 1931), Yanagita referred to a piece of news reporting. A 95-year-old man was protected by the police of Moji City (at present Kitakyūshū City) while walking alone with no destination. His whole belonging was a cloth wrapping of 45 mortuary tablets of his relatives (YKCW 24: 307). Yanagita saw in this trifle news the destination of the uprooted *Ie*.

The second reason for his attention on *Ie* is its relation to *Kuni* 国 (Nation or State). *Ie*, which contains the continuity due to the succession and ancestor worship, can support the nation's perpetuity. "The recognition of the relation between individuals and their ancestors, i.e. the recognition of the existence of *Ie* means in such feature of a nation like Japan, at the same time the recognition of the connection between individuals and the state." (YKCW 16: 39) The 'feature of a nation' here suggested the sacred continuity of the emperor's lineage.

Since the years when he lectured on agricultural policy, Yanagita conceived of the nation with a temporal axis.

> Even if all members approve a nation's policy at a time, we cannot adopt it directly as the state's policy. The people the state represents by its existence are not limited to the present nation living now. Those people in succeeding later years, too, consist of the state together with the present.
>
> *(YKCW 28: 196)*

In a similar way to the continuity of *Ie*, if the present nation behaves for the sake of the future nation and the principle of reciprocity should work there. The present nation would be respected by the future, as the former respect the past nation. This reciprocity forms the continuity of the nation.

However, the hasty combination of *Ie* and *Kuni* (Nation or State) may miss the spatial vision of Yanagita's folklore studies. We must locate Mura, that has a spatial dimension in his view of the nation. In the urban area, where direct relations of individuals or their *Ie*s prevailed, their links to the state (nation) were more direct. Those individuals or their *Ie*s that could accompany the growth of *Kuni* would thrive, and those that couldn't have to decline. However, in the countryside, *Mura* existed as the unit of the collective destiny of its residents. Thus, it assumed an intervening position between *Ie* and *Kuni*. It is symbolic that a high wave of peasant rebellion emerged in 1873 when the Meiji government fixed the order of general conscription. This wave was called Ketsuzei Ikki (revolt against blood taxation). 'Ikki' was the violent form of the unified protest of the people, particularly that of peasants. As *Mura* was an intervening unit of taxation (tribute of the product) of clans under the Tokugawa period, the introduction of the direct land taxation of the Meiji government did not fit the autonomy of Mura, not to say the general confiscation.

We saw before that *Mura* was the unit by which its members and their interest were represented in their relations to other *Mura* units, the rulers, the mountains behind, and the world of the dead. As such units, *Mura* retained its norms that were effective to its members only. Though the activities of the members of *Mura* were not confined to the range of *Mura*, the affairs outside of the Mura were called '*Seken*' 世間 (social world). *Seken*, constituted by the interactions and contracts, was the realm in which individuals had to manage their success on their sense and talent. It was not the place where they could settle their *Ie* without worry. However, in such closed communities of *Mura* (and *Ie*), even those who lost the fame to interact with others in the outer world (*Seken*) could have a living place. The logic of the local community was not the competition that would ruin others but that of long-term symbiotic life that should moderate the competition in the level of difference.

Kuni was supposed to be higher than *Mura*, which had definite membership and borders. However, *Kuni* was not always a foreign element in *Mura* because there were always some mental moves to assimilate the demand and norms of the higher entity and adapt themselves to it. Without such activities inside, *Mura* as an autonomous community might fall into chaos inside or run into blind alleys.

In the last years of the Tokugawa period, the concept of *Kuni* (national unity) emerged in Japan when the Shogunate was forced to open the port under the military threat of Western powers. The immobility of the clan rules failed to keep the sense of a higher entity to themselves. After some tumults and confusion, the new government finally succeeded in assimilating this concept of the higher entity, *Kuni*, as the credo of its rule. The government, which now appeared as the state, would lead the whole nation toward the Fukoku Kyōhei (Enrich the Nation and Strengthen the Military), following the mighty Western countries. Yanagita affirmed all of these, but he would be attentive to the reality of the 'agonizing nation.' The nation's agony was that with the rapid change of life under marketization and Westernization, the poverty and immaturity of the people emerged into the front. *Kuni*'s choice of this course was the unquestionable premise to Yanagita. He described the process in which the traditional view of the soul was assimilated by the state as follows:

> We cannot imagine to what a height did the heroic will to become the protecting god of the state after the death purified the mind of the brave youth that stood on the war front.
>
> Raising up for twenty-one years in my hands,
> Now a god of the state, after three months that I couldn't see him
>
> Such phrases were sung variously in the years of the Russo-Japanese War. This was the old idea of the soul that slept long in the depth of the mind of the archaic majority of the nation. Together with the enhancing new nationalism, this old idea got away from the home's borders and promptly created great solidarity.
>
> *(YKCW 24: 314)*

Fukuzawa translated the English term 'society' first as 'Seken' or 'Kōsai' (interactions). A local community such as *Mura* didn't exist for him. The people who established their independence in urban life could directly identify their fortune and their *Ie* with that of *Kuni*. However, the common people in the rural area would associate themselves with the state and the intermediary unit of *Mura* that performed the distribution of the common burden and benefits of *Kuni*. Those *Mura*s that had resisted the introduction of compulsory education and conscription in the early years of Meiji changed rapidly to support the state's policy. Yanagita did not oppose the Meiji state as the modernization power in principle.

Instead, he believed that to attain this national goal, not the authoritarian and bureaucratic control but voluntary collaborations that had been once alive in *Mura* should support the state's mission.[14]

Interpreting Yanagita's works in such a way, we face whether such a voluntary collaboration of common people was possible in Japan's real, local society in the years from the Meiji to the Taisho era. As we mentioned in the previous section of this chapter, the main advocators of promoting agriculture and production unions were absolutistic bureaucrat-politicians, and the systematically organized agricultural societies were just the assembly of renowned landowners. Even the adoption of the 'Sonze' (Program of Village) and 'Gunze' (Program of County) that had been originally intended to encourage the initiative and industrial mind of the rural producers, the actual process of its making was too uniformly patterned that disillusioned Yanagita.

In the twenties of the 20th century, from the late Taishō era to the early Shōwa era, the peace in the agricultural area was periled by the outbreak of tenant disputes. Under such a situation, Yanagita talked about the distinction between two forms of united action.[15] The one was the 'old style unity' of the unanimous concord of total members of the *Mura*. The other was the united action grounded on voluntary and egalitarian principles. The former, which once had been so mighty, was supported by their members' acknowledged order and mutual consideration. It failed to function at present due to the emergence of actual conflicts and struggles of interest. On the other hand, the latter form of the united action is currently realized in various forms of production unions. Yanagita argued that the latter also had its origins in various sorts of local united action. It was once called 'Ikki' (united action), whether peaceful or not. Yanagita named its motive 'Kunmiai-shin' (mind of collaboration and solidarity).

Could this type of combination based on 'Kumiai-shin' go beyond the level of the persistence of the immediate interest or the politicized struggle? Could it succeed in producing 'moderate men of collaborative solidarity'? Yanagita thought that the success or failure of the new self-governance of rural society depended on the above two questions. Production unions were initially conceived to cover the wide-ranging interests of the whole rural village. They have now degenerated into the organization to defend the current interests of mighty persons. On the other hand, the farmers' unions that were organized as the fighting tenants' union lacked the perspective for developing agriculture in the cooperation with the landed farmers.

Thus, what Yanagita recommended was to reconstruct the self-governance of *Mura* by integrating newly emerging unions on the recognition of the basic fact that the common people in Japan had lived long on the reciprocal collaboration in *Mura*.

However, if the 'moderate man of collaboration' had not emerged, the autonomy of rural entities would degenerate to superficial independence with the reality of the rule of the administrators. In the years when the traditional ties of the old rural community (*Mura*) weakened, how persuasive was Yanagita's hopeful view?

> Indeed, the bright future perspective is enhanced with no limits by the extension of the non-selfish activities of the production unions, reconstruction of the tenants federation with a clear conscience, and other improving efforts of the existing unions. However, if we would examine the interests of various classes and endeavor to harmonize the conflicts and avoid the confusion with the least pain as far as possible, it would be most convenient to rely on the working of the old public community that is equipped with rich experiences on a broad perspective.
>
> *(YKCW 16: 360)*

Notes

1 In this respect, Satsuma Clan (Kagoshima Prefecture) was different because most of its warriors lived in the country.
2 Mayet stayed in Japan from 1876 to 1893. His recommendation for agricultural insurance and other remedies for the pauperization of Japanese farmers were published in Japanese in 1890 and 1893. Eggert, whose recommendation was published in Japanese in 1891, came to Japan in 1887 and died there in 1893, just before his return. See Mayet (1888), Eggert (1890), and Kondō ed. (1975).
3 Thanks to their contribution to its legislation, Shinagawa and Hirata were usually regarded as the founders of industrial cooperatives in Japan. However, their control-oriented policy was what Yanagita would oppose from the beginning. Saga (1987) offers a critical view of Hirata's position in this area.
4 Compared with a heap of Yanagita literature in Japan, English literature on him is rather scarce. Starting from his dissertation in 1974 (Morse 1977 and 1990), Ronald A. Morse has contributed much to introducing Yanagita to the international public. Kawada (1993) followed him, and Ortabasi (2014) appeared recently.
5 Kawakami Hajime, whom we discuss in the next chapter, studied under the same mentor a few years after Yanagita. He took a strong position on agricultural protectionism in his early years.
6 On Yanagita's agricultural economy and policy, see Iwamoto (1976), Fukutomi (1978), Fujii (1995), and Kikuchi (2021).
7 On this latent conflict, see Iwamoto (1982: 167–170).
8 R. A. Morse provides its English translation (Yanagita 2008).
9 Yanagita himself provided an illustration in which horizontal timelines crossed the vertical line of the town and the country, and diffusion lines of illumination methods ran a slant. (YKCW 25: 512) If we take the profile of life at a given time and place, we can acquire Tsurumi's 'icicle model' (Tsurumi 1975).
10 In Yanagita's term 'Jōmin.' Tsurumi Kazuko defined it in her words: "He is a ruled rather than a ruler, one of the majority of a people, whose life and work depend on a spoken rather than written language, and who has a settled domicile in a specific area. He inherits the patterns of doing, thinking, and feeling from the previous generation who have dwelled in that area and takes time to transform those inherited patterns with his own wisdom to make them fit the changing conditions of his life. He does not succumb to what he considers contrary to his standard of reasonableness, whoever the opponent may be" (Tsurumi 1975: 227). This concept fixes the criterion on the settled farmers that live in the community life of *Mura*. The challenge against this view was made by Amino Yoshihiko, that refocused the research attention on

non-cultivating people such as craftsmen, fishermen, hunters, traveling entertainers, discriminated peoples, and so on.

11 *Ie* and *Mura* have been the basic concepts of rural sociology in Japan since Aruga Kizaemon. The model of *Ie, Mura, Seken*, and *Kuni* may have resemblance with several attempts of theorizing the model of Japanese society; Murakami, Kumon, and Sato (1979) on *Ie* society, Hamaguchi (1985) on 'contextual mode,' Abe (1992) on 'Seken,' and so on.

12 Here, we follow the interpretation of Fukuda (1992). However, this is not a fixed view of researchers.

13 Kamishima (1961) viewed the urban society in Japan as a mass society with no autonomous principle of social formation. In his view, Japanese urban society is the sphere where various fictitious *mura* orders form competitively and decay.

14 Tsurumi (1975) discovered 'a model of endogenous development' in Yanagita's work.

15 Yanagita (1929: chap.8).

References

Western Languages

Eggert, Udo (1890) *Land Reform in Japan: Specially Based on the Development of Credit Associations*. Tokyo: Kokka Gakkai. [Japanese translation by Oda Hajime: Eggert (1891) *Nihon Shinkō-saku*. Tokyo: Hakubunkan. Included in Kondō ed. (1975)].

Hamaguchi, Eshun (1985) "A contextual model of the Japanese: Toward a methodological innovation in Japan Studies." *Journal of Japan Studies*, 11(2), pp. 298–322.

Heine, Heinrich (1853) "Götter in Exil [Elend]." *Blätter für literarische Unterhaltung*, 18 (April 30).

Kawada, Minoru (1993) *The Origin of Ethnography in Japan: Yanagita Kunio and His Times*. London: Routledge.

Mayet, Paul (1888) *Landwirtschaftliche Versicherung in organischen Verbindung mit Sparanstalten, Bodencredit und Schuldenablösung. Vorschläge zur Besserung der Lage des japanischen Landmanns*, im Auftrag des Kais. Jap. Ministeriums des Innen. Tokyo: Kokubunsha. [Japanese translation by Saito Tetsutarō and Watanabe Junnnosuke: Mayet (1890) *Nōgyō Hoken-ron, Ichimei Nihon Nōmin Ichi Kairyō-saku*. Tokyo: Nihon Shoseki].

Morse, Ronald. A. (1990) *Yanagita Kunio and the Folklore Movement: The search for Japan's national character and distinctiveness*. (Ph.D. Dissertation, Princeton University, 1974). New York and London: Garland Publishing. [Japanese translation: Morse (1977)].

Ortabasi, Melek (2014) *The Undiscovered Country: Text, Translation, and Modernity in the Work of Yanagita Kunio*. Cambridge MA: Harvard University Asia Center.

Tsurumi, Kazuko (1975) "Yanagita Kunio's work as a model of endogenous development." *Japan Quarterly*, 22(3), pp. 223–238.

Yanagita, Kunio (2008) *The Legends of Tōno: 100th Anniversary edition*, tr. by Ronald Morse. New York: Rowman & Littlefield.

Japanese

Abe Kin'ya (1992) *Seiyō Chūsei no Ai to Jinkaku – Seken-ron Josetsu* (Love and Person in Medieval West: Introduction to the Theory of Seken). Tokyo: Asahi Shimbun-sha.

Fujii Takashi (1995) *Yanagita Kunio, Keisei Saimin no Gaku* (Yanagita Kunio, Study of Kesei Saimin). Nagoya: Nagoya Daigaku Shuppankai.

Fukuda Ajio (1992) *Yanagita Kunio no Minzoku-gaku* (Folklore Studies of Yanagita Kunio). Tokyo: Yoshikawa Kōbunkan.

Fukutomi Masami (1978) *Nihon Marukusu-shugi to Yanagita Nōsei-gaku* (Japanese Marxism and Yanagita's Agricultural Policy). Tokyo: Mirai-sha.

Fukuzawa Yukichi (1892) "Chiso-ron" (On Land Tax). *Jiji Shimpō*, Editorials, April 29–May 8.

Hashikawa Bunzō (1977) *Yanagita Kunio: Sono Ningen to Shisō* (Yanagita Kunio: Person and Thought). Tokyo: Kōdansha.

Iwamoto Yoshiteru (1976) *Yanagita Kunio no Nōseigaku* (Yanagita Kunio's Agricultural Policy). Tokyo: Ochanomizu Shobō.

———. (1982) *Yanagita Kunio: Minzoku-gaku he no Mosaku* (Yanagita Kunio: Road to Folklore Study). Tokyo: Kashiwa Shobō.

Kamishima Jirō (1961) *Kindai Nihon no Seishin Kōzō* (Mental Structure of Modern Japan). Tokyo: Iwanami Shoten.

Kikuchi Kiyomaro (2021) *Meiji Kokka to Yanagita Kunio* (Meiji State and Yanagita Kunio). Fukuoka: Gen Shobō.

Kondō Yasuo ed. (1975) *Meiji Taishō Nōsei-Keizai Meicho-shū* (Major Works on Agricultural Policy in Meiji and Taisho Era). *Eggert and Mayet*, Vol. 3. Tokyo: Nōsangyoson Bunka Kyōkai.

Morse, Ronald A. (1977) *Kindaika he no Chōsen – Yanagita Kunio no Isan* (Translation of Morse (1990) from his dissertation by Okada Yōichi and Yamano Hiroshi). Tokyo: Nihon Hōsō Shuppan Kyōkai.

Murakami Yasusuke, Kumon Shunpei and Satō Seizaburō (1979) *Bunmei to shiteno Ie Shakai* (Ie Society as a Civilization). Tokyo: Chuō Kōron-sha.

Saga Ikurō (1987) *Kunshin Hirata Tōsuke-den* (Biography of the Loyalist Hirata Tosuke). Tokyo: Nihon Keizai Hyōron-sha.

Yagi Kiichiro (1999) *Kindai Nihon no Shakai Keizai-gaku* (Social Economics of Modern Japan). Tokyo: Chikuma Shobō.

Yanagita Kunio (1902) *Saishin Sangyō Kumiai Tsūkai* (Newest Guide of Production Unions). Tokyo: Dai Nihon Jitsugyō Gakkai. [YKCW 28].

———. (1929) *Toshi to Nōson* (Towns and Rural Villages). Tokyo: Asahi Shimbun-sha. [YKCW 16].

———. (1931) *Meiji Taishō-shi, Sesō-hen* (History of Meiji and Taisho Era, the Part of Social Affairs). Tokyo: Asahi Shimbun-sha. [YKCW 24].

———. [YKCW] (1962–1971) *Teihon Yanagita Kunio-shū* (Authorized Works of Yanagita Kunio). 31+5 vols. Tokyo: Chikuma Shobō.

7

EGOISM AND ALTRUISM IN THE SENTIMENT OF AN ECONOMIST

Kawakami Hajime's Difficult Path to Marxism

7.1 Economics of *Bimbō Monogatari*

Apart from Fukuzawa Yukichi and Yanagita Kunio, who are generally not considered economists, Kawakami Hajime (1879–1946) was outstanding among Japanese economists in pre-1945 Japan in catching the mind of people with his contributions to the newspapers.

First, his series article *Shakaishugi Hyōron* (Critique of Socialism) that young Kawakami contributed to the *Yomiuri Shimbun* in 1905 brought new knowledge on socialism to the public out of the closed circle of academicians and journalists. This article told the people about the coming intellectual anguish of the new age, amplified by its abrupt closing. Apologizing for his writing so far under a pseud name, the author confessed the conversion that guided him to join a religious circle that advocated the agape of altruism.

Next, after a decade, in 1916, Kawakami, then a professor at Kyoto Imperial University, contributed to the *Osaka Asahi Shimbun* series *Bimbō Monogatari* (Tale of Poverty), which became a book in the next year. Kawakami warned the readers that mass poverty had emerged in the developed nations under the surface of prosperity. It changed the people's minds in the euphoria of the war boom. When Kawakami began this series, saying, "what astonishes us is the poverty of the mass in the present civilized countries" (KHCW 9: 9), the dominant obsession of catching up with Western nations through industrialization received a fatal blow. When *Bimbō Monogatari* reappeared as a paperback edition in 1947, Ōuchi Hyōe recollected its appearance:

> Every intellectual in Japan over a middle age has a memory of this book. Of them, all who are proud of having basic knowledge of social problems will confess without exception that they were enlightened by this book.
>
> *(Ōuchi 1947: 182)*

DOI: 10.4324/9781003081319-7

However, it is not the same to say that they were awakened to social problems by this book and that they agreed with its conclusion. Kawakami listed three solutions to poverty, the voluntary abolition of the luxury of the rich, the remedy of the disparity in income distribution, and the transition from private production to public production. Then he recommended the first, saying, "the renovation of the people's mind is a more fundamental task than the renovation of social organization." (KHCW 9: 96)[1] However, it is doubtful that this ending thoroughly convinced all readers. Sakai Toshihiko (1870–1933), a senior pioneer of Japanese socialism, commented on Kawakami's moralism in the concluding part of the *Bimbō Monogatari*, as he had felt "as if being guided from a labyrinth to another."

> The mixing of moralism and economics! If we can be satisfied by such moralistic preaching, we need neither the lecture on economics nor the explanation of the social reorganization.
>
> *(Sakai 1919 [initially in 1917] in Suekawa ed. 1965: 201)*

In part on the causes of poverty, Kawakami argued that the progress in the productive powers by introducing machinery had made the Malthusian population law invalid as the explanation for the existing poverty. In his view, the main reason for poverty was the relative limitation of the production of necessary goods due to the excessive absorption of resources by producing luxury goods for the rich. Thus, the total abolition of luxurious consumption of the rich would surely increase the product for the mass and raise their standard of life. But Sakai's criticism was sharp.

> Didn't Dr. Kawakami mention before that production would not occur without purchasable demand under the present economic organization? If so, how can the supply of the necessaries demanded by the poor majority increase while the purchasing power is missing them? Further, Kawakami argues that if men of business should decide not to produce goods 'which do not benefit people, ' 'the shortcomings of the present economic organization are rectified.' How can businesspeople choose the production based on the criterium of being beneficial or harmful under the present economic organization in which production follows the demand with purchasing power? If it should be possible, it presupposes the destruction of the current economic organization!
>
> *(ibid.: 202)*

To Sakai, who had reached Marxism so early at the beginning of the 20th century and endured the suppression in the 'winter years' after the High Treason Incident, it was easy to discover the flaws of Kawakami's argument. Sakai refrained from continuing his criticism saying, "it becomes boorish to continue the criticism if we think over the limit of freedom of a university professor, who is an official of the government." His final sentence was: "This book will bring no effect in the recommendation of the voluntary restriction of luxurious consumption. I believe rather it will help other readers conclude the necessity of improving society" (ibid.: 202). This prediction was realized more in the very case of the author than in most other readers of the book.

Since acquiring the Kyoto Imperial University position in 1908, Kawakami devoted himself to academic investigation. At the early stage, he got influenced by the German historical school that he studied at the (Tokyo) Imperial University. In this stage, he was an economist with nationalistic traits and advocated the agriculture-centered economic policy. However, during his years in Kyoto, holding an ambition to establish his theoretical system, Kawakami widely studied the literature on economic theory. It covered the works of Austrian School Economists (C. Menger and E. Böhm-Bawerk) to such early neo-classicists in Britain and the United States as F. A. Fetter, K. Pearson, I. Fisher, and J. B. Clark. His understanding of the history of economics, too, was considerably influenced by the view of then-leading scholars such as F. W. Taussig and E. Cannan. Kawakami's motif of the integration of economics and ethic, too, reminds us of the echo of ethical economics of the historical school and Alfred Marshall's view of 'economic chivalry.' *Bimbō Monogatari*'s theoretical background was far from Marxian economics. Instead, this book had its background in Kawakami's wide-ranged study of the economic orthodoxy in the transition years from the classical school to the neo-classical school.[2]

Kawakami's argument that the cause of the poverty lay in the luxurious demand of the rich and thus its abolition could be the solution to the poverty problem might have its origin in Hartley Withers's *Poverty and Waste* (1914), from which Kawakami cited in the closing part of *Bimbō Monogatari*. Fukuda Tokuzō (1874–1930), a senior to Kawakami both in age and in the membership of the Shakai Seisakugakkai (Association for the Study of Social Policy), tied up Kawakami and Whithers and named the 'theory of liberation of productive power.' As we saw before, Sakai had raised the question of how the abolition of the rich's luxurious consumption could increase the poor's production. In this respect, if we assume that Kawakami, together with Whithers, followed the classical compensation view that argued no unemployed capital exists so far as the market works, we can understand Kawakami's point at least. We'll cite his reasoning from his theoretical article "*Shashi to Hinkon*" (Luxury and Poverty), written in the same period *as Bimbō Monogatari*.

> What would happen if the people of the prosperous class should abolish all of their luxurious consumption? On the one hand, capital would increase due to a reduction in unproductive consumption. On the other hand, capital and labor which were so far employed in luxury production would be liberated. The increased and saved productive powers of the society would be used entirely to produce necessary goods. Thus, despite the nonproduction of luxuries, useful daily necessities would be supplied

> abundantly and cheaply. With the rise in wages due to the increase in labor demand, the poor's life would change drastically. At last, we can see all the people enjoying their life.
>
> *(KHCW 9: 204)*

Kawakami would never write such a paragraph if he were already a genuine Marxian economist. Even if we put the central problem of the class relations aside, this argument implied a group of dogmas of the orthodoxy such as Say's law, wages funds theory, and compensation theory that Marx had opposed. It is regrettable that since the dispute between Fukuda and Kawakami had not deepened theoretically, economics in Japan evaded the chance to proceed further in the theoretical analysis of poverty.

A fatal blow came from Kawakami's close disciple Kushida Tamizō (1885–1934), whose theoretical sense exceeded Kawakami's. Kushida criticized his mentor: "The luxury in the society is grounded on the poverty in the society. Not the poverty is grounded on luxury. My professor seems to have made an error in the understanding the causality adversely" (Kushida 1935, I: 273). In Kushida's view, poverty as a social problem was grounded because "capitalists as partners in the exchange relation acquire extra profit on the loss of the counterparts of workers" (ibid.). Thus, Kushida attributed the cause of poverty to the distribution of capital-labor relations. In Marxian terms, Kushida maintained that the cause of poverty was capitalists' exploitation of surplus-value. However, as Kushida then had not been thoroughly acquainted with Marxian terms, similarly to Kawakami, he expressed his view that poverty as a social problem was a 'distribution problem' and not a 'production problem' (ibid.).

The core of the Kawakami-Kushida controversy lay in understanding the class relations between workers and capitalists. However, Kawakami could not grasp it in his direct answer to Kushida. He only asked Kushida to appreciate his definition of poverty in the objective criterium, "the inability to perform necessary consumption," and commented that Kushida seemed to understand poverty "in its relative meaning that compares the rich and the poor," Kawakami interpreted Kushida's view as if he had maintained that poverty should occur from the unfair distribution. In Kawakami's view, the problem of poverty was not a 'distribution problem' but a 'production problem' in which the affluent production of necessaries for the poor was hindered by luxury production. However, Kushida's criticism echoed in his mind for a few years further.[3]

7.2 Production-Oriented Policy and Distribution-Oriented Policy

When Kawakami published *Bimbō Monogatari* as a book in early 1917, he wrote that he considered it the best work he had ever had. It sold well. But Kawakami stopped its printing in 1919 when he acquired his journal *Shakai Mondai Kenkyū* (Research on Social Problems) (Kawakami 1919–1930). Kawakami struggled to find a new direction in the intervening two years and finally became a Marxist economist.

The situation before the turn is that of being unsettled. In January 1918, Kawakami contributed an article titled "Miketsu-kan" (House of Detention) to the *Osaka Asahi Shimbun* with his poem that confessed his mental situation at the age of 40: "Being perplexed further and further, I reached the age to be free from vacillation" (KHCW 9: 219). This article compared the situation of contemporary economists that had no fixed criterion over the priority between production and distribution with that of the unsettled prisoner. With this article, Kawakami declared his will to escape the dilemma between production and distribution.

> Many scholars and politicians stressed the need for the protection of small entrepreneurs or the protection of workers under the name of social policy. They strived to prove its harmlessness for the increase in production or its contribution to the growth. I dare ask them: If the social policy should be harmful to the rise in production, would they retract their appeal? Then, their social policy, in reality, is nothing but a production-oriented policy. The production maximization is the end, and the remedy of distribution is the mean for this end. If they should admit some harmful effects of social policy over the production increase and still maintain the necessity to approach a fair distribution, I would ask them once more: To what degree the growth of production should be sacrificed for the fairness in distribution? When the discussion should reach this question, all scholars must remain silent. In this respect, all the modern economists are in the situation of unsettled prisoners. Only the person that is so brave as to break this barrier can gain the honor of the second Adam Smith. So far as such scholars would not emerge, all current economic policies remain without unity, principle, philosophy, and wisdom. Isn't this a sorrowful situation?
>
> *(KHCW 9: 218f.)*

Declaring his will to devote himself to a new investigation, he examined the view on production and distribution of eminent economists. First, regarding utilitarianism as the core of the economics orthodoxy, he studied Jeremy Bentham and James Mill. He was disappointed to find them giving priority to the safety of private property despite their reasoning that an egalitarian distribution might increase the total utility of the society. The principle of the maximum utility without egalitarian redistribution is, in its nutshell, the maximization of production. Thus, Kawakami constructed the series equation, selfish individualism = sacred private property = utilitarianism = production-oriented policy. So long as social policy should have its *raison d'etre*, it should not serve this serial equation of production-oriented policy.

> The policy for the production increase is legitimized only in the situation when the stock of the wealth is too scarce, and the need for its increase is

> apparent to everyone. Increasing production is the means, and the appropriate product is the end. The distribution-oriented policy is the master, and the production-oriented policy is the servant. I believe that we can approve the actual social policy, which differs from the social policy as a production-oriented policy, only in this viewpoint.
>
> *(KHCW 9: 234f.)*

In Shakai Seisaku Gakkai (Association for the Study of Social Policy), 'social policy as production-oriented policy' was the position that the group took near to industry and government, that would admit the social policy such as factory legislation so far as it didn't hinder the development of the industry. In opposition to them, such scholars who had learned German economics à la Adolf Wagner as Kanai Noburu and Matsuzaki Kuranosuke adhered to 'social policy as distribution-oriented policy.' As Kawakami deserted the viewpoint on production, which had been taken in *Bimbō Monogatari* and approved distribution-oriented policy as the *raison d'etre* of the social policy, he seemed to have returned to his old position as an ethical nationalist.

At this stage, he considered socialism as a radical extension of the distribution-oriented policy. However, his dualism between production and distribution-oriented policy failed when Kawakami began to study Marx as the representative socialist economist. Kawakami thought that a socialist scholar would take the side of distribution at the expense of production when two policies should collide. Marx contradicted this anticipation. Marx maintained that capitalism collapses when it becomes the obstacle to the development of the productive forces and anticipated the coming of socialism that would realize the total emancipation of productive forces that have been prepared under the epoch of capitalism. In Kawakami's dual classification, he surely would come under the camp of 'production-oriented policy.' Further, Marx denied the ethical criterium that Kawakami had endeavored to introduce as the ground of social policy.

> He [Marx] did not raise the ethical claim that the organization of capitalism should be abolished due to the inequality of the distribution under it. …. He told only that this organization, after the stage when the productive forces of the society should reach a stage and the restriction of the growth of production should emerge, […] this organization is destined to collapse soon. He did not demand socialism from the viewpoint of distribution but forecasted it from the viewpoint of production.
>
> *(KHCW 10: 215)*

In January 1919, Kawakami published 'Socialism as Production-oriented policy' (January 1919), whose half was occupied by three long citations from Marx. The first citation was the famous summary of the materialistic view of history in the preface to the *Contribution to the Critic of Political Economy* (1859). The second is also a famous passage in the chapter on capital accumulation in the first volume of *Capital*, in which Marx forecasted the end of capitalist ownership under the concentration of the means of production and socialization of labor. The third was the citation from the chapter 'Production relations and Distribution relations' of the third volume of *Capital*, in which Marx criticized the separation of distribution relations from production relations and regarded the former as the presentation of the latter. After this citation, Kawakami added: "In short, the dichotomy between production-oriented policy and distribution-oriented policy was foreign to Marx from the beginning" (KHCW 10: 217). Kawakami realized that the traditional viewpoint of social policy had no merit in learning from Marx.[4] Under the impact of reading Marx's original text directly, Kawakami decided to start again from the beginning under Marx's guidance.

7.3 Egoism and Altruism

Kawakami's relation to the *Osaka Asahi* was broken with the retreat of liberals in this newspaper due to the alleged lese-majesty incident that occurred in 1918. However, in January 1919, Kawakami acquired his journal *Shakai Mondai Kenkyū* (Research on Social Problems), thanks to the circle close to him and the publisher of *Bimbō Monogatari*. It was more convenient to him, as he "in these days decided to propagate Marxism with the guess of the direction of the truth despite the lack of exact understanding" (Kawakami 1947, KHCW Sequel 5: 227).

In the Preface to the foundation of the journal, Kawakami declared that "I criticize every social policy, setting the fundamental solution of social problems as my ultimate criterion" (KHCW 10: 227). Though this statement retained the continuity between social policy and socialism on the surface, adopting 'the fundamental solution of the social problem' as his criterion meant that Kawakami assumed the position of a revolutionary that quested for socialism or communism as the 'fundamental solution of social problems,' not that of a reformer.

However, as an ethical truth-seeker, Kawakami then was not a fully convinced Marxist. Kawakami added one more criterion that occupied a deeper position than the 'final criterion.' As he could not throw his ideal of the 'perfection in human morality,' he set it as "the ultimate and final criterion." "Not perish the spirit for the sake of flesh" was Kawakami's "ultimate and final criterion" in criticizing every policy to solve the social problem, including its final solution (ibid.: 228).

As this dual criterion shows, Kawakami's 'unsettled situation' had another dimension that lay deeper than the collision between 'production-oriented policy' and 'distribution-oriented policy.' It was the conflict between egoism and altruism in his mind. The former was the appearance of the deeper inner conflict in his mind on the surface of academic discussion. Even after his adhesion to the 'unity of economy and ethics' had been ridiculed and his attempt to prioritize the 'distribution-oriented policy' from an ethical viewpoint failed, the call for the second Adam Smith kept the echo in his mind.

Determining himself to follow Marx, Kawakami found that Marx provided him with no solution to the conflict of egoism and altruism that had anguished him for so long. After filling several issues of his journal with studies on Marx, in its sixth issue (June 1919) at last, Kawakami allowed himself to confess his mental suffering as a 'belief' that differed from his scientific research in an essay of the title Egoism and Altruism (Kawakami 1919).[5] In this essay, he recollected his mental journey in which he had continued to anguish over the conflict between egoism and altruism since he had received a profound impact from knowing Jesus's words in the Sermon on the Mount: "To him, that smiteth thee on the *one* cheek offer also the *other*; and from him, that taketh away thy cloak withhold not thy coat also." Even after entering the religious circle of altruists, abandoning everything, including jobs and home, his mind had not become composed. In the days when he had so tortured himself as to regard even sleeping as a selfish act, he had reached the awakening of the identity of egoism and altruism.

> Then, I felt myself sinking to the far depth below the ground and received the awakening that this body was not mine. Thus, no distinction exists between selfishness and unselfishness.
>
> *(KHCW 10: 386)*

The 'belief' that Kawakami acquired from his mental agony was that "a thoroughgoing altruism coincides with thoroughgoing egoism." If a person decided to live an utterly altruistic life, he would not be able to live. However, "under the belief of absolute altruism," the whole of my soul and body is the dedication to God. Thus, "we should keep this dedication to God carefully. This is the true sense of egoism" (KHCW 10: 86). From the viewpoint of absolute altruism, the act which appears to be selfish is no other than a service to God. Developing one's capability is also justified selfishness. After attaining this recognition, he left the community of altruists and returned to the career of an economist.

In his *Autobiography* (Kawakami 1947b), Kawakami described this awakening as 'a religious experience' and defined himself as an unordinary Marxist that admitted 'religious truth.' Indeed, the paradoxical logic that the return to the secular world as a tool of the service under the thoroughgoing altruism sounds religious like that of Christianity. Kawakami, in 1919 when he started the propagation project of Marxism with the preparedness to lose the established position and to receive persecution, thought it necessary to confirm his old starting point of the 'justified selfishness' under 'throughgoing altruism.'

However, from the viewpoint of economics, Kawakami then was far from his destination Marx. What Kawakami studied for an antecedent decade was the orthodox economics that approved self-interest since Adam Smith. From the viewpoint of Kawakami's 'belief,' the economics that would vindicate self-interest and the interest of the own nation was what Kawakami quested for. He thought that the element of 'mental revolution' should work in economics and started to review the history of economics from this viewpoint.

Kawakami would discover "his own mental history in the history of economics." He realized that John St. Mill's conversion from the strict utilitarianism and the criticism of capitalism by T. Carlyle and J. Luskin's mental history as the steps toward the self-negation of the bourgeois economics, he could regard the history of orthodox economics in total as the prehistory of altruistic economics, i.e. economics of socialism. So, he conceived his history of economics, *Shihonshugi-Keizaigaku no Shiteki Hatten* (Historical Development of the Capitalist Economics) (Kawakami 1923), under the following construction: "Description of the historical metamorphosis of the idea that legitimate the selfish economic activity – Its emergence, development, death, and the replacement by the opposite idea" (KHCW 15:142).

Kawakami's voluminous *Keizaigaku Taikō* (Fundamental Principles of Economics), which appeared in 1928, the year when Kawakami was expelled from the Kyoto Imperial University, was the certificate that Kawakami's approach to Marxism was completed. In the preface of this book, Kawakami contrasted 'capitalist economics' and 'proletarian economics.' He maintained that as the former had begun with Mandeville's slogan 'private evil public virtue' that had legitimated the egoistic profit-seeking of capitalists, the latter would start with legitimating the selfish acts of the working class. As the proletarian class replaced the bourgeois class in the representation of the developed productive powers, the egoistic pursuit of the interest of the proletarian class would lead to the realization of the benefit of the whole human race. Here, by replacing individuals with class, Kawakami adjusted his duality of egoism/altruism to the Marxian thesis. From then on, Kawakami should only devote himself to selfish activity as the being dedicated to God (proletarian class).

> Strikes, sabotage, and so on. Every class struggles proletarians engaged are always morally reproached. However, as the idea of 'private evil, public benefit' emerged in the early eighteenth century, in the present society we live, the idea of 'the struggle of the working class for the interest of their own class is the struggle for the interest of human race as a whole' should emerge and is really emerging. Under the class society, the realization of public benefit needs necessarily the intervening struggle for the realization of the private interest.
>
> *(KHCW 15: 143)*

7.4 Sentiment under the Developmentalist State

We followed Kawakami's swaying approach to Marxism from the viewpoint of his dualism between egoism and altruism. In this closing section, we will place him in a large constellation of the society in Japan, whose industrialization was led by a government that resolutely sought prosperity and power.

First comes the characterization of *Bimbō Monogatari*. Kawakami was in accord with Yanagita in considering the present poverty with the civilization or industrialization that Meiji Japan had pushed forward.[6] However, while Yanagita took the position of small farmers and asked why we were so poor, Kawakami began his *Bimbō Monogatari* with the observation of the poverty in Western industrialized nations, in other words, from the viewpoint of an observer. As for the solution to poverty, while Yanagita expected much for the own initiative of small producers, Kawakami advocated the voluntary abolishment of the luxury consumption of the rich. It was a call for the rich, not for the poor. The other two solutions, i.e., redistribution and social reorganization, were the measures taken from above. They, too, were not the own acts of the poor. In other words, the author of *Bimbō Monogatari* talked to the public from the position outside of the poor people concerned. As Kawakami expected much from Lloyd George, Kawakami then was sympathetic to the direction of 'new liberal reform.' However, the core idea of new liberalism, which aimed at the reconstruction of the liberty of citizens on the social service such as labor exchange and social insurance, was missing in Kawakami. His primary interest lay in the vindication of self-interest by B. Mandeville and Adam Smith on the one hand and the teaching of morality in Chinese and Japanese classics on the other. As Sakai noticed, the contrast between the novelty of the theme and the moralistic attitude in dealing with it was striking, at least for modern readers.

Fukuda, the rival of Kawakami both in academism and journalism, advocated, as we saw in the preceding chapter, the 'right to live' of all individuals, including the poor. Applying this idea to the reality of the ongoing class struggle, he would liberate social policy from the hand of the state to society. Along with Ishibashi Tanzan (see the next chapter), we can regard him as the leading figure of the new liberalism in Japan. In the 1910s, Fukuda and Kawakami shared the same objectives in the foundation of original economics in Japan and renovating social policy. Even after Kawakami's turn to Marxism, they continued their debates openly in publication.[7]

From a retrospective view, the chance of fruitful discussion between the two had existed still at the stage of *Bimbō Monogatari* if Kawakami had grasped the core of new liberal reform in the early 20th century. However, under the impact of the Russian Revolution, Kawakami shifted his position from a reformer to a revolutionary, keeping his moralistic thinking intact. Fukuda, a well-read senior to Kawakami, had often shown his advantage by finding faults in Kawakami. Kawakami came to regard Fukuda as belonging to his enemy's camp of 'bourgeois economics.' Their debates proved fruitless after all.

On the topic of the conflict of egoism/altruism in Kawakami, we need to answer a few further questions. The first question is, while what was contrasted to the self-interest was 'the general interest of the society' in the case of Adam Smith and 'common public interest' in the case of historical school economists in Germany, why 'altruism' was contrasted in Kawakami's case? The second question is why Kawakami adopted the paradoxical logic of vindicating 'legitimated self-interest under the absolute altruism' to reconcile the contradiction between egoism and altruism, not to proceed on the path of refinement or extension of self-interest to subsume altruism or public interest. The third is on the relation between this inner conflict of egoism/altruism and Kawakami's entry into the underground activity of the illegal communist party in 1932 after his leave from the Kyoto University in 1928.

As for the first question, we should note while 'social interest' is the term related to politics, the egoism/altruism conflict is the mental problem of the individual concerned. 'Public interest' presupposes some calculation even at the level of subjective guess. Contrastingly enough, a genuine act of altruism rejects such calculation. What Jesus's Sermon on the Mount appeals to is the soul of individuals that is foreign to the reason of calculation.

Kawakami found the path that proceeds to subsume altruistic elements by refining or modifying selfishness in the historical development of British economic thought from B. Mandeville, D. Hume, A. Smith to J. St. Mill and A. Marshall. Cooperation can emerge among egoists if we assume a long-range perspective and mutual trust. The state that had its ground in the ensemble of families, local and working communities, unions and associations, and political parties is not the Leviathan that absorbs the whole elements of an individual. However, according to Kawakami, while 'individualism' is dominant in the West, the state is dominant in Japan. "In Japan, we cannot consider an individual as an independent being that has its own value and purpose. Only the state has its own value and purpose" (KHCW 6: 119). The path that Westerners trod was closed to the Japanese. So felt Kawakami.

'Self-interest' did not countervail the state, but it could collaborate with the state. Receiving higher education and climbing the ladder of bureaucracy or collaborating with the government in the business was the path to wealth and success. Where wealth and success depended on the state, the direction of 'self-interest' was far from the 'independence and self-reliance' that Fukuzawa had praised. What appears as the opposite of egoism was not the fair public mind but a total 'self-denial.' The others to whom the altruism of young Kawakami directed were such people as the victims of the Ashio ore poison case, that the state and the industrialization had deserted.

If we apply the term 'development state' to the matured Meiji state, egoism and altruism had a correspondence with insiders and outsiders under the development state of Meiji. Individuals could not become free so far as they would seek wealth and success in the state with traits of 'developmentalism.'[8]

Then, how to think about the last question, the moral dimension in Kawakami's political engagement? At the age of 50, in our interpretation, Kawakami placed the proletarian class or its party – the illegal Japanese Communist Party (JCP) – as the target of his altruism and wished to be selfish in his dedication. Many of his inscrutable behaviors that hurt his supporters and friends might result from his political engagement with his religious altruism.

In Kawakami's case, the problem consists of the retardation of this outcome from his mental journey holding the egoism/altruism problem under the development state. Kawakami kept questing for the solution to his inner problem for three decades from his youth and two decades from his religious experience in the altruist collective. Why did he adhere to his 'ultimate and final criterion' of moral perfection even after turning to Marxism?

Its main reason lay in the historical development of the Japanese society, in which the formation of the working class and the political organizations that would represent its interest were too unmatured. While the appeal of the public interest by the German Society of the Social Policy had been addressed to both sides of the struggling classes, the founders of the Japanese Association for the Study of Social Policy had wished to study social policies as preventive measures taken by the government for the possible class conflicts in the future. Before Fukuda's innovation to admit class struggles as the formative elements of social policies, the working class was not conceived as the actor in forming social policies. In Kawakami's case, his first understanding of Marxism was economic determinism, inevitably directed toward socialism. During his academic years, his view of history had been parallel with his idea of economic theory in the point both were driven by self-interest or class interest. Beyond this scientific view, Kawakami drew his moralistic vision by parallelly citing Mencius and the Bible. According to him, the purpose of life was to accomplish moral perfection beyond the horizon where the economic and historical laws were valid.

We characterized Kawakami's initial view as the preacher standing in a detached position from both the state and the people. The tentative solution to the egoism/altruism conflict made him acquire the chair at the university and go abroad as he had wished. However, when social problems began to menace the social order, the Russian Revolution occurred, and proletarian parties emerged, the tentative solution became the solution no more. Even in such a situation, Kawakami preferred individuals' mental conversion and moral commitment to the voluntary collaboration and collective learning process in the social movements. As a whole, Kawakami as a scholar always regarded himself as a concerned critic of the developmentalist state. Most of his writings' ardent readers recognized this nation's intellectual structure through Kawakami's overdoing words and behaviors.[9]

His missionary quest, at last, made him leave the academism in 1928 and enter the world of real politics. After a brief period of serving the illegal communist party as its lay member, he was arrested in January 1933. Enduring the troublesome agony of choice between conversion and non-conversion, Kawakami completed the term of imprisonment. On his leave from the prison, he declared the closing of his life as a Marxian scholar. Since then, Kawakami has lived the life of a hermitage under the monitorship of the police. He could see the collapse of the Japanese Empire and died on January 30, 1946, in Kyoto. The manuscript of his *Autobiography* (Kawakami 1947a), which Kawakami wrote during his years under probation, was published after his death. It revived him in the intellectual life of the Japanese. Though he confessed his troublesome path openly, the figure of a man who sacrificed everything for his conviction emerged as a purified investigator. Of the many scholars in pre-1945 Japan, Kawakami is probably one of the most beloved figures that attracted Japanese readers by his sentiment.

Notes

1 So far as we read the text of *Bimbō Monogatari* on the surface and took the choice of the voluntary abolishment of the luxury granted, it is natural to regard this as moralistic preaching to the rich. However, Sugihara (1996) raised a question about this prevailing view on the ground of Kawakami's lecture after his study abroad on the transition from a war economy to socialism. According to Sugihara, Kawakami could not reveal his true vision openly to the mass media. This topic we once discussed in Yagi (2013). Another critical view on the prevalent reading of the *Bimbō Monogatari* was offered by Makino (2008) from the viewpoint of reading it as a starting point for the development program of the Japanese economy.

2 Ōuchi (1965) regarded the economics in *Bimbō Monogatari* as 'simple bourgeois economics.' Similarly, Kobayashi (1994), that followed Kawakami's writings in this period in detail called it the 'equilibrium theory of the poverty.'

3 So far was the first round of the discussion between Kawakami and Kushida. The two made the second-round discussion in 1924–1925 on understanding the Marxian notion of the materialistic view of history. Kushida criticized Kawakami's *Shihonshugi Keizaigaku no Shiteki Hatten* (Historical Development of Capitalist Economics) (Kawakami 1923; Kushida 1924), and Kawakami approved Kushida's criticism. Cf. Ōuchi and Ōshima eds. 1947. See also Yagi (2007) on this topic.

4 As we saw before, Kawakami ordered the publisher of *Bimbō Monogatari* to stop its printing in mid-1919. Omitting the much-discussed concluding part, he included the first and the second part of its text as Fragments from *Bimbō Monogatari* in the *Kaiban Shakai Mondai Kanken* (Revised Version, Current Views on Social Problem) that appeared in April 1920. However, in the rescued part, redistribution was erased out of the three conceivable remedies to the social problem. From such treatment of the text of *Bimbō Monogatari*, we can assume that Kawakami rejected the leading idea of social policy and moved to that of a revolutionary who quested for both moral revolution and social revolution.

5 In his *Jijoden* (Autobiography), Kawakami defined himself as the unique Marxist that approved 'religious truth' beside the 'scientific truth.' On this topic, confer Sumiya Etsuji (1962) and Deguchi (1962).

6 Cf. Sumiya Kazuhiko (1965) on the comparison between Kawakami and Yanagita.

7 Inoue and Yagi (1998) discussed the life and work of Fukuda and Kawakami in parallel. Sugihara (1979) mentioned Fukuda's guess on the origin of Kawakami's *Bimbō Monogatari* in Withers (1914).

8 We use the term 'developmentalism' to suggest the traits of the state and society that prioritize economic development before liberal and democratic elements. See Woo-Cummings ed. (1999). See also Yagi (2000) that applied this concept to modern Japanese economic history.

9 In her attractive Kawakami's biography, Bernstein (1976) regarded Kawakami's Autobiography as "the story of a member of the traditional Japanese elite who, caught in the unsettling changes of the past 100 years, persistently tried to adapt old values to the new circumstances of his existence" (p. 172). She would directly find the inner conflict between Japan and the West in Kawakami's quest. At the same time, we would place this moralist scholar in the intellectual constellation under the developmentalist state of Japan.

References

English

Bernstein, Gail Lee (1976) *Japanese Marxist: A Portrait of Kawakami Hajime*. Cambridge, MA and London: Harvard University Press.

Inoue, Takutoshi and Yagi, Kiichirō (1998) "Two inquirers on the divide." In Sugihara, Shirō and Tanaka, Toshihiro eds. *Economic Thought and Modernization in Japan*. Cheltenham and Northampton: Edward Elgar, pp. 60–77.

Withers, Hartley (1914) *Poverty and Waste*. London: Smith, Elder.

Woo-Cummings, Meredith ed. (1999) *The Development State*. Ithaca, NY: Cornell University Press.

Yagi, Kiichiro (2000) "Intensive and extensive mobilization in the Japanese economy: An Interpretation of Japanese capitalism in historical perspective." In Koslovsky, Peter. ed. *The Theory of Capitalism in the German Economic Tradition*. Heidelberg: Springer, pp. 419–448.

———. (2007) "Emergence of Marxian scholarship in Japan: Kawakami Hajime and his two critics." *Rekishi to Keizai* (The Journal of Political Economy and Economic History), whole no. 194 (Vol. XLIX, No. 2), pp. 34–45.

———. (2013) "Sugihara Shirō on Kawakami Hajime." *Keizaigakushi Kenkyū* (The History of Economic Thought), 54(2), pp. 1–10.

Japanese

Deguchi Yuzō (1962) "Kawakami Hajime ni okeru ni-shurui no shinri" (Two sorts of truth in Kawakami Hajime). *Keizai Ronsō* (Kyoto University) 90(3). Included in Suekawa ed. (1965), pp. 180–197.

Kawakami Hajime (1905) *Shakaishugi Hyōron* (Critique of Socialism). Tokyo: Yomiuri Shimbun.

———. (1916) "Shashi to hinkon" (Luxury and poverty). *Keizai Ronsō* (Kyoto University), 2(4), pp. 510–524.

———. (1917) *Bimbō Monogatari* (Tale of Poverty). Kyoto: Kōbundō.

———. (1918) "Miketsu-kan" (House of detention). *Osaka Asahi Shimbun* (January 16, 17, 18, 19, each p.1).

———. (1919) "Rikoshugi to ritashugi" (Egoism and altruism). *Shakai Mondai Kenkyū*, 6, pp. 9-25.

———. (1920) *Kaihan Shakai Mondai Kanken* (Revised Version, Current Views on Social Problems). Kyoto: Kōbundō.

———. (1923) *Shihonshugi Keizaigaku no Shiteki Hatten* (Historical Development of the Capitalist Economics). Kyoto: Kōbundō.

———. (1928) *Keizaigaku Taikō* (Fundamental Principles of Economics). 2 vols. Tokyo: Kaizō-sha.

———. (1947a) *Jijoden* (Autobiography). 5 vols. Tokyo: Sekai Hyōron-sha.

———. (1947b) *Bimbō Monogatari* (Tale of Poverty). Tokyo: Iwanami Shoten.

———. ed. (1919–1930) *Shakai Mondai Kenkyū* (Research in Social Problems). Total 106 ns. Kyoto: Kōbundō.

———. [KHCW] (1982–1986) *Kawakami Hajime Zenshū* (Complete Works of Kawakami Hajime). 28+ sequels 7+ separate 1, in total 36 vols. Tokyo: Iwanami Shoten.

Kobayashi Kanji (1994) *Kawakami Hajime: Marx Keizaigaku ni itaru Kiseki* (Kawakami Hajime: Trajectory to Marxian Economics). Kyoto: Hōritsu-Bunka-sha.

Kushida Tamizō (1924) "Shakaishugi wa yami ni mensuru-ka hikari ni mensuru-ka" (Does socialism face toward darkness or light?). *Kaizō* (July), pp. 2-38. (Included in Suekawa ed., 1965).

———. (1935) *Kushida Tamizō Zenshū* (Complete Works of Kushida Tamizō). 5 vols. Tokyo: Kaizō-sha.

Makino Kuniaki (2008) "*Bimbō Monogatari* Saikō: Nationalist Kawakami Hajime karano Kaishaku" (Reconsidering Tale of Poverty: Interpretation from Kawakami Hajime as Nationalist). *Shisō*, (1013), pp. 128–147.

Ōuchi Hyōe (1947) "Kaidai" (Bibliographical introduction) to Kawakami Hajime (1947b) *Bimbō Monogatari* (Tale of Poverty). Tokyo: Iwanami Shoten.

———. (1965) "Keizai Gakusha to shiteno Kawakami Hajime" (Kawakami Hajime as an Economist). In Suekawa ed. pp. 135–156.

Ōuchi Hyōe and Ōshima Kiyoshi eds. (1974) *Kawakami Hajime yori Kushida Tamizō he no Tegami*. Tokyo: Hosei Daigaku Shuppannkyou.

Sakai Toshihiko (1919) "Kawakami Hajime kun wo hyōsu" (Reviewing Mr. Kawakami Hajime). *Shin-Shakai*, 5(7). [Included in Suekawa ed. (1965)], pp. 198–209.

Suekawa Hiroshi ed. (1965) *Kawakami Hajime Kenkyū* (Studies on Kawakami Hajime). Tokyo: Chikuma Shoten.

Sugihara Shirō (1979) "Kawakami Hajime to Fukuda Tokuzō" (Kawakami Hajime and Fukuda Tokuzō). *Keizai Ronsō* (Kyoto University), 124(5/6), pp. 223–242.

———. (1996) *Tabibito Kawakami Hajime* (Kawakami Hajime as a Traveller). Tokyo: Iwanami Shoten.

Sumiya Etsuji (1962) "Shakaikagaku-teki shinri to shyūkyō-teki shinri no tōitsu" (The unity of scientific truth and religious truth). *Dōshisha Daigaku Jinbun-Kagaku Kenkyū-sho Kiyō*, no. 5. [Included in Suekawa ed. 1965], pp. 3–37.

Sumiya Kazuhiko (1965) "Kawakami Hajime to Yanagita Kunio" (Kawakami Hajime and Yanagita Kunio). In Suekawa ed., pp. 157–179.

8

NEW LIBERALISM IN THE FAR EAST

Ishibashi Tanzan and J. M. Keynes

8.1 Consequences of the Peace in the Far East

When we think over Japan's modern history, we always face whether the long war and the last disaster of 1945 were an inevitable outcome of the modernization/ industrialization of Japan. Since the Meiji Restoration, state-led industrialization went hand in hand with aggressive nationalism. Through repeated victories in war (Sino-Japanese War and Russo-Japanese War), most Japanese began to regard Japan as the leading nation of the Far East. The dual spatial structure of a developing nation (Figure 3.1) – the center and the periphery – was extended beyond the border. After a period of Japanese patronage, Japan annexed Korea (1910). The north-eastern part of China (Manchuria) was considered a special zone where Japan kept its privileged interest. The central part of China was viewed as a golden market for Japanese industrial products. In this development course, it was clear that Japan's collision with Asian nations (particularly China) was unavoidable.

In the author's view, Japan failed to switch its course while several chances existed. After World War I (WWI), all the participating nations gathered to establish a new international order in Versailles. Japan, as well as China, sent delegates to this Conference. However, as Japan forced through its claim to succeed Germany's privilege in Shandong Province, China called back its delegation under the rising protest of the Chinese youth. As the Peace Treaty of 1919 did not enter the international relations in East Asia, a vacuum of order remained there.

It is well known that John Maynard Keynes, soon after the conclusion of the Treaty, warned against the unpleasant outcome of the unfair treatment of losers of war with his *Economic Consequences of the Peace* (Keynes 1919). In the Far East, it was Ishibashi Tanzan (1884-1973)[1] that criticized the Treaty and advocated a drastic change in Japan's foreign policy.

DOI: 10.4324/9781003081319-8

Probably it was Ishibashi Tanzan's sympathetic introduction of Keynes's *Economic Consequences* in his serial editorials of the *Tōyō Keizai Shimpō* (*Weekly Toyo Keizai:* lit. Newsjournal of Eastern Economy) in 1920 that made Keynes's name widely known to the Japanese.[2] In the first editorial of March 27 with the title "Victors of the War," Ishibashi introduced the book's author in his full name as the attendant of the Paris Peace Conference sent from the British Treasury. Considering the days of book trafficking from London to Tokyo, we notice Ishibashi's acute sensitivity to catching the world economy and political discussion.

In the next issue, Ishibashi explained Keynes's view under the title "Consequences of the Peace: Mr. Keynes' s Investigations" in five sequels (April 3, 10, 17, 24, May 1). First, he introduced several estimations of the possible amount of the reparation grounded on the damage to the allied nations and Germany's capability of paying reparation. Ishibashi surmised that its upper limit could not exceed 10 billion US dollars. Next, he described the state of the post-war European economy facing three significant obstacles of decline in production, paralysis of railroad traffic, and the overissue of paper currencies. Last, Ishibashi presented Keynes's remedy program for Europe in four points: (1) revision of the peace treaties, (2) cancellation of the credits and debts among the allied nations, (3) international public bonds, and (4) on Russia and middle Europe.

Viewing Ishibashi's journalism before and after this serial introduction and his activities in the 1920s and early 1930s, Ishibashi seems to have shared similar concerns and aims after the WWI in the Far East and Pacific Area with Keynes, that lived in the Atlantic world. Keynes's stance of demanding the retreat of the governments responsible for the 1919 Treaty and expecting its revisions through international conferences and the League of Nations coincided with Ishibashi's attitude that emerged as a young journalist in the age of the so-called Taishō Democracy. He demanded the retreat of the governments of absolutistic bureaucrat-politicians and supported the solution of international tensions and restriction of armament through international conferences. Keynes's second and third points, which were the consequences of recognizing that the reconstruction of the order of international finance would be impossible without the collaboration of leading nations, including the United States, would have been the guideline for Ishibashi's thought on the global economic order in this age. Even Keynes's fourth point of the necessity of the turn from the intervention and containment policy against Soviet-Russia and his proposal to let Germany release Russia might resonate with Ishibashi. So early in the summer of 1918 (July 25 issue), Ishibashi criticized the Siberian Expedition and demanded the recognition of the 'Radicals' government' in Russia.

Since the outline of the Peace Treaty got known to the public, thus before he introduced Keynes's *Economic Consequences*, Ishibashi continued to criticize the Versailles Treaty. At the outbreak of the war, Ishibashi opposed Japan's participation in the war. During the war, he continued to talk about the lack of its benefit even to its victors. He argued for 'no annexation,' 'no repartition,' and 'guarantee for future peace' as the fundamental premises of the peace. (1917, June 25 issue) The draft of the Treaty of the allied nations, though in accord with Ishibashi's hope of establishing the League of Nations, betrayed Ishibashi's hope by demanding strict obligations against Germany in cessions of the territory, a tremendous amount of repartition, restriction of forces, and limitations on the sovereignty in transport and traffics. Knowing it, Ishibashi promptly published the alarm in the editorial: "Peace Treaty involving roots of evils" (May 25, June 5, and 15 issues of 1919).

> The peace treaty that allied nations submitted aims to push forward the lofty ideals represented by the Covenant of the League of Nations and the foundation of the International Labor Organization on the one hand. Except for the repartition and some other obligations, the various demands on Germany could be generally imposed on every other nation. They are conditions for establishing freedom, fairness, and fraternity in the world. However, their application to every nation is, in fact, impossible at present. Thus, allied nations inserted all of them in the Covenant of the League of Nations and hoped for their solutions in the future. I agree with it. However, the allied nations coerced Germany into those conditions that they regarded the implementation as impossible for themselves. They postponed the future from the concern of the delusion of world peace. The clean idealistic stream of the League of Nations could not prevent now the pollution from the dirty stream. Such dirty ideas emerged in the repartition problem as aiming at despairing Germany as deeply as possible, as acquiring own advantage as large as possible merged with the lofty ideal of the League of the Nation. Thus, allied nations forced Germany mercilessly to the conditions they themselves couldn't implement. Think of the fact that those they themselves thought it hard to implement are equally hard to Germany. Their merciless enforcement over Germany would endanger the world's peace, as it would occur when the allied nations reciprocally forced them.
>
> *(ITCW 3: 141)*

While Keynes's thought stood on the traditional thinking of British politicians that aimed to maintain the peace by sustaining the balance of powers in the European Continent, including Germany, a fresh idealism longing for the world peace by way of international collaboration colored Ishibashi's article. The conditions that allied nations forced Germany but suspended their application on themselves were the cession of the territory on the principle of the self-determination, the limitation of the armed forces as the first step of the general restriction of the armament, and international openness of airspace, rivers, canals, ports, and so forth. As the principles or ideals, they, the self-determination, the pacifism that does not rely on armaments, and the economic internationalism, are the ideals that Ishibashi supported lifelong. Though Ishibashi did not believe in their immediate realization, he hoped that the establishment of international organizations could open the way for their implementation through international accords.

The Japanese government's basic stance was the allied nations' conformism. Indeed, the Japanese delegation proposed to insert the principle of ethnic equality in the Covenant of the League of Nations; it withdrew this proposal facing a stern reaction from other delegations. On the other hand, what the delegation of Japan stuck to and finally acquired the approval even from the idealist US President Woodrow Wilson, was the approval of Japan's succession of the privileged German interest in Shandong Province. When the news reached China, a passionate anti-Japan movement (Wusu Movement) broke out in Beijing and other major cities of China, making the Chinese government call its delegation back without signing the Treaty.

Japan joined the rank of the five major victorious nations (Britain, the United States, France, Italy, and Japan) and assumed important positions in the League of Nations. The general diplomatic stance of its diplomacy in the nineteen-twenties was that of the cooperation with the hegemony of Britain and the United States, which was often called by the name of the Foreign Minister Shidehara Kijūrō (1872–1951). However, the stance of Japan to consolidate its interest in the Far East did not change and caused successive conflicts with the nationalism of the neighboring nations. WWI made the collapse of not only the German Empire but also that of the multi-national Empire of Austro-Hungary. With the decay of the Tzarist Russian and Othman-Turkish Empires that had suppressed indigenous ethnic groups, many nation-states emerged after WWI. The winners continued their imperialistic rule (the rule over other nations and ethnic groups) by limiting the application of the self-determination to losers. Japan acquired international recognition of its position as an imperialistic power by joining the group of winners of this World War.

Wilson's Fourteen Points (1918) had echoes also in Korea. The signers of the March 1 Declaration of Korean Independence (1919) and the people who joined in the demonstration expected that their wish for independence would attract the delegates of the nations at the Versailles Conference. However, as Ishibashi wrote in his editorial, a prominent high official of Japan declared openly: "Koreans misunderstand the meaning of self-determination in the agenda of Paris Peace Conference. It is not the principle that applies to the winning allied nations. It is the principle applied to Germany and its allies only" (ITCW 3: 132). Citing this bold saying, Ishibashi revealed the genuine attitude of the Japanese government that stood on the side of self-righteous winners.

The Peace Treaty approved Japan's succession of the privileged interest of Germany in China. However, as its contradiction to the ideals of international relations was known to almost all countries other than Japan, Japan's diplomatic position deteriorated even compared to China, which refuted signing the Treaty. The United States, whose Congress denied the ratification of the Treaty, had a free hand, particularly in the Pacific region and the Far East, where it had considerable interest and influence. In contrast with Europe, the post-war order did not exist in this area.

Japanese interest and influence in China, which extended in the years of WWI, were not stable and faced the hostility of the native people. Such prominent demands against China as the Twenty-One Demands (1918) might conflict with the interests of other Western powers. The prolonged military expedition in Siberia that continued after accomplishing the original goal (protection of the Japanese and other allied nations' citizens in Russia in the war and revolution and the rescue of the Czechoslovak Legion) heightened the suspicion of the United States. In such a situation, the new US President, Warren Harding, proposed the Washington Conference that dealt with reducing naval forces and the international order in the Pacific and the Far East. Both the government and the military of Japan were at first suspicious that this conference might work to contain Japanese influence in this area. In vain, they endeavored to exclude the regional order in the Pacific and Far East areas from the agenda.

Ishibashi, who had confessed his concern about the deepening conflict between Japan and the United States, welcomed Harding's initiative positively. However, he was not a simple follower of the international order under the hegemony of Britain and the United States. Ishibashi aimed to demise the order of vested interests in Asia of the leading imperialistic powers by activating the new principles of self-determination, pacifism, and internationalism. New principles should be implemented openly and fairly, not in such an unfair and partial way as in the Versailles Treaty. To realize it, Japan should take the lead. Ishibashi wrote the editorial titled "Issai wo sutsuru no kakugo – Taiheiyō kaigi ni taisuru waga taido" (Preparedness to abandon all: Japan's attitude at the Pacific Conference) for the July 23, 1921 issue of *Tōyō Keizai*. This now famous editorial urged the Japanese government to attend the Conference, showing the preparedness to renounce all privileged interests and pressures in the China Continent and give freedom to Korea and Taiwan. It would give Japan a moral advantage against Britain and the United States, and other countries and enable Japan to take the initiative in establishing non-imperialistic order in the Pacific and Far East region. In the following editorials (1921, July 30, August 6, 13), Ishibashi named the course that Japan had taken 'Dai Nihon-shugi' (Big Japanism) and argued for an alternative course, 'Shō Nihon-shugi' (Small Japanism). It was one of the most remarkable proposals Japan ever had before its fall into the successive war years.

Ishibashi was not a utopian that ignored the genuine economic interest of Japan. As Keynes did in his estimation of the outcomes of the 1919 Treaty, Ishibashi compared in the continuing editorial, "Dai Nihon-shugi no Gensō" (Illusion of the Big Japanism) (1921, July 30, August 6, 13) the benefit of Japan's imperialistic efforts so far and that of the peaceful trade by showing both in trade statistics. Taking the trade in 1920, the total trade (import and export) between Japan's homeland and its imperial territories (Korea, Taiwan, and Kwantung

Leased Territory) amounted to 916 million Yen, the trade with the US 1,438 million Yen, that with British India 587 million Yen, and that with Britain 330 million Yen. The main suppliers of strategically important import goods such as cotton, iron, and rice were out of Japan's imperial territories. The significance of the trade with the US and British Empire exceeded well over that of the trade with all of Japan's overseas territories. Further, the trade with China was 628 million Yen. Its growth from 1910 was 470 million Yen. However, this was far less than the trade growth with the United States in the same period, 1,240 million Yen. The effort to promote trade with China with all sorts of interventions might have hindered its growth.

As for another issue of the need for colonization that legitimated overseas expansion, Ishibashi rejected it. The number of the Japanese living in its overseas territories and other areas where Japan could exert some influence counted only 0.8 million in total. It was not possible to mitigate overpopulation by way of colonization. Both colonization and emigration needed considerable financial expenditure. The labor emigration without the means to establish the economic base in the destination could not ensure emigrants the advantage in the income. Ishibashi's negative view of emigration as the solution to the overpopulation problem of Japan was the same since he had discussed the US's restriction of Japanese emigration before WWI. He had warned against the rising irritation among the Japanese, arguing that the solution to the overpopulation problem consisted not of the emigration but the industrialization of Japan (1913, May 15).

What supported Ishibashi's criticism against Big-Japanism was the classical economic liberalism that taught the availability of foreign resources through ordinary trade and investment. Probably he acquired this conviction from his reading of the texts of classical economics in his daily commuting. His support for 'equality of the opportunity in the economy' or 'open-door policy,' too, came from his conviction in economic liberalism. These principles were the best policies that combined resources and capital. Foreign overseas investment might be helpful if Japan had plenty of capital. As capital accumulation remained an urgent task for Japan, spending precious public money to expand overseas territories and acquire a privileged interest in foreign countries was not recommendable.

> Capitals are rice cakes, and land is their case. Assembling cases without rice cakes is stupid. So long as you can make plenty of rice cakes, neighbors may lend you the cases promptly. The way to increase capital is to devote all the efforts of the people to the inquiry of science and technology and the progress of industry, standing on pacifism. Found schools instead of barracks, found factories instead of warships. If we invested half of the military spending, ca. 800 million Yen annually, in peaceful enterprises, the Japanese industry would renovate itself drastically in several years.
>
> *(ITCW 4: 29)*

Washington Conference held from November 1921 to February of the following year fixed the ratio of weight tons of battleships of the United States, Britain, and Japan 5: 5: 3. Japan had to renounce the interest in Shantung Province and give up the reserved points in its Twenty-One Demands against China. However, this Conference did not touch on the core part of Japan's interest in Manchuria and Mongolia on which the military of Japan extended its sphere of influence in China. The so-called Washington Treaty System grounded on the Nine-Powers Treaty of 1922 had the characteristics of the common control of their interest in China by Britain, the United States, and Japan under the phrase 'Open-Door.' It was not the order that stood on the denial of the imperialistic desires of the powers as Ishibashi wished. However, it provided the ground on which trades and investments in this region in the 1920s and early 1930s were maintained. The Japanese economy, whose trade balance recorded rapid deterioration after WWI, was hit further by the Great Kantō Earthquake (1923). It could get through the successive calamities by receiving foreign capital on the one hand and by the restraint of the military spending thanks to this reconstructed international order on the other hand.

8.2 Managed Currency and Economic Policies

The next time that Ishibashi introduced Keynes's work was in the fall of 1933, the following year of Japan's repeated gold embargo. At a meeting of the club that *Tōyō Keizai* organized for its readers, he gave a lecture on the part of currency administration of Keynes's *Treatise on Money* (1929) together with the preceding *Monetary Reform* (1923). He published it as the editorial titled "Proposal for currency control of Mr. Keynes" (October 1 issue). His motivation was to acquire the suggestions for future currency systems of Japan in the situation under the gold embargo. Thus, this editorial did not discuss the theoretical part of the *Treatise.*

For the maintenance of the system of international currencies, the financial policy of each country needs to be harmonized following the average action of other countries. However, every country seeks 'the autonomy in the short run' to enforce its own financial policy that fits the varied economic situation of the own country. Here is the imamate contradiction that every system of international currencies has in itself. Ishibashi first introduced Keynes' view on the ground of the working of the international gold standard that attributed its success to Britain's capability to control the world's financial transactions. Then, he asked himself whether the currency system must remain international. He answered that apart from short-term financial transactions, a reasonable degree of flexibility in the exchange rate is not bad for international trade.

> The question is whether it is a good institution that is very sensitive to international influence. Taking examples of wages, tariffs, domestic financial transactions, trades, etc., any of them does not receive the global power

> not so directly. Even if wages or prices in foreign countries should decline, we cannot conclude that wages in Japan should decrease or that the amount of debt and obligation should be reduced.
>
> *(ITCW 9: 242)*

Ishibashi considered that Keynes's conviction on the necessity of the managed currency was the same as both *Monetary Reform* (1923) and *Treatise on Money* (1930). Thus, he borrowed the former idea of prioritizing the stability of the domestic prices over that of the exchange rate. Further, Ishibashi added that the idea of the managed currencies was not an imaginary construction but a realistic concept that consciously developed those practical actions of the currency administrators. Even under the gold standard system, currencies were domestically controlled by the adjustment of discount rates and market operation of the central bank. In the international scene, the controllability existed to some degree by adjusting the discount rate or the change in the purchasing price of gold. The leave from the gold standard system did not mean the extinction of the role of gold holding as a last resort for international security or as the reserve for an emergent need. Last, Ishibashi concluded that Japan, which relied much on the gold exchange (foreign specie), had substantially practiced the control of currencies. In Japan, the circulation of the gold currency was missing, and paper money (Yen banknote) had been issued without limitation.

> Summing up, Japan unconsciously practiced currency control at the domestic level. At the international level, its promise of gold-convertibility had been practiced not often. Japan practiced its control by letting the Specie Bank trade the gold exchange. Further, to promote export, Japan endeavored to keep the rate of export-bill low. Thus, we have practiced currency control already. Therefore, we Japanese need not be surprised by hearing Mr. Keynes's idea. However, most of our controls had been practiced contingently and not consciously. Getting caught by the name of the gold specie standard, we could not consciously exert control. Thus, it is also a mistake to regard Mr. Keynes's view as saying it contains nothing new. The merits of his view consist in that he suggests we reflect consciously on what has been not new to us and practice it scientifically. At this point, we owe much to him.
>
> *(ITCW 9: 250)*

For several years before this lecture, Ishibashi had been in dispute over the lift of the gold embargo.[3] After the war, when the United States resumed the gold exchange suspended in war years, many countries followed the United States one by one in returning to the gold standard system. Also, in Japan, a return to the gold standard became the policy agenda associated with the nation's prestige. Prominent business leaders thought that the return to the international currency system would be beneficial to the Japanese economy to expand the global business and consolidate Japanese industry by eliminating inferior firms. Despite Keynes's alarm against Britain's return to the gold standard system in his *Monetary Reform* (Keynes 1923), the Conservative government of Britain returned to the gold standard system in 1925 at the same rate before the War. As Keynes had alarmed before, its impact on the British economy caused a large-scale labor dispute in the coal mine area.

In 1924, Ishibashi recommended a new realistic exchange rate for Japan's return to the gold standard. In collaboration with another economic journalist Takahashi Kamekichi, who was then in the same office of the *Tōyō Keizai Shimpō*, Ishibashi estimated an appropriate rate using Gustav Cassel's theory of purchasing power parity. It was considerably lower than the old official rate. However, in 1929 the new Minsei-tō cabinet under Prime Minister Hamaguchi Osachi nominated Inoue Junnosuke as its Minister of Finance. It adopted the lift of the gold embargo with the old official rate as its main policy agenda. With the backing of most business and financial leaders, Inoue rushed to resumption the gold exchange at the old official rate (1 USD=2.005JPY, 100JPY=49.875USD). Against the group's criticism that recommended the new rate, Inoue argued that the official rate could be practicable with some necessary measures to recover and sustain the rate in the exchange market.

The result of the resumption of gold exchange on January 11, 1930, was disastrous. The contraction of currencies and the decline in prices occurred with the massive outflow of gold. With the effect of the 1929 market crisis in the United States, the trade balance deteriorated rapidly by the sharp decline in export. Closures of firms and an increase of the unemployed nourished the social unrest and the bad harvest in the North-Eastern area of Japan. The resumption of gold exchange in 1930 triggered the so-called Shōwa Kyōkō (Economic Crisis of Shōwa).

> The cause of the present depression in Japan consists in Japan. The resumption of the gold exchange with the old rate appreciated the international value of the Yen. This is the cause of the disease. [...] It needs the contraction of the currency and the decline of prices of goods and share prices from its own logic. It requires, of course, the depreciation of every tangible and intangible asset. It needs the decline in wages. These evils are inevitable. If they are stopped, the disease will become chronic, and the outflow of gold will continue endlessly. The introduction of foreign capital may mitigate the outflow of gold for a while, but it would result in more significant damage. The reason for policymaking's difficulty coping with depression and unemployment lies here.
>
> *(ITCW 7: 224)*

When Britain left the gold standard again in September 1931, Ishibashi anticipated Japan's following and began to think that the maintenance of the gold standard system itself became impossible. Ishibashi's renewed attention to Keynes lay in his quest for a new currency system free from the gold standard's constraint. It must be such a system that could avoid domestic deflation and enable the government to execute the action to cope with depression. However, it would allow the fluctuation in the exchange rate to some extent.

Before, we saw a solid conviction of economic liberalism existed behind Ishibashi's criticism against 'big Japanism.' The reliance on Cassel's purchasing power parity assumption was also in accord with doctrines of liberalism. After the resumption of gold exchange, Ishibashi began to support the concept of managed currency under Keynes's influence. The dominant stance of Ishibashi's discourse in the early 1930s was to act to stimulate the economy and keep the stability in domestic prices while blocking the international influence by way of the managed currency.

In Japan, after the leave of the gold standard system, the group that oriented the collaboration with Britain and the United States to maintain the existing international order retreated, and a nationalistic view that advocated the block economy in the foreign policy and the controlled economy in the domestic policy gained the force. The concept of the managed currency itself may be considered one of the supporting blocks of such a trend of the view. Then, did this shift in the opinion of the currency system affect Ishibashi's liberal theory of international relations? Later in this chapter, we will discuss this question to investigate his 'new liberalism.'

From the classical viewpoint, *à la* J. St. Mill and G. Cassel, the effect of the leave of the gold standard is nothing other than replacing the decline of the domestic prices with the deterioration of the exchange rate. However, Keynes and Ishibashi thought that the leave from the gold standard would have no positive effect but that its merit lay in giving the government the allowance to use fiscal and financial policies to support the economy. In the editorial just after the repeated ban on gold exchange (December 17, 1931), Ishibashi questioned the new Minister of Finance, Takahashi Korekiyo,[4] as follows:

> I believe that the decline in the market rate of the exchange alone does not raise domestic prices much, thus cannot improve the present situation of agony. To stimulate the economy, the government must take measures to start new public works or increase the money supply to the business, raise the prices, and boost production. However, an irresponsible policy is hazardous. It touches on the management of public finance and the institution of public services. We want to ask Finance minister Takahashi what plans he had in mind for these problems.
>
> *(ITCW 8: 149)*

This passage suggests that Ishibashi's economic thought advanced over the classical type of liberalism and reached a kind of revolution in the ideas of economic policy. He sometimes went further to admit control over trade and investment. However, in Ishibashi's view, they were unavoidable interventions. His fundamental viewpoint was to avoid 'intricate controls' that might harm the economy. Ishibashi's aim consisted of the prospect that the success of the managed currency could enable the renewal of capitalism toward a more functional one, keeping the freedom of economic activities on the ground of successful currency control.

The concept of economic policy of Ishibashi (and Keynes) had a nationalistic character indeed in the point that it recommended an active policy stance on the unit level of the nation-state. However, it did not neglect the reciprocal dependence in international economic relations. If a country engaged so much in stimulating the economy (or on armament expansion) as to bring about inflation, its trade would shrink, and its economy had to move toward a closed economy. The concept of a block economy in Japan was a desperate idea that originated there. It was not sustainable in the economic sense. It served the interest of the military and politics-affiliated business groups at the cost of the nation's interest. What Keynes set as an ideal goal was the international organization that could control international currencies at the global level. In the 1930s, it was evident that the common agreement for such an international organization was too hard to attain. However, even after the repeated ban on gold exchange at the end of 1931, Ishibashi still kept the hope. A substantial consensus for the international administration of currencies could be reached either through some international conferences or through prudent currency control of each country grounded on the mutual consensus over the global economic relations.[5]

As mentioned, Ishibashi argued for the price hike and expansive fiscal policy. Then, what kind of macro-economic thought did Ishibashi have? From such a viewpoint, we can read Ishibashi's comments on the two talks that Finance Minister Takahashi Korekiyo made in May 1935.

In the first talk, which was recorded in the *Tōyō Keizai Shimpō* (May 4, 1935), Takahashi talked about the positive effect of military spending. "Though the defense of the nation itself is not productive, its expenditure has much to do with production. The defense needs materials and labor forces. This expenditure maintains the living of those producers and workers. Thus, the battleship itself is not for the production, but the expenditure itself is productive" (ITCW 9: 380). The famous unfettered parable that even the spree of the war riches at geisha houses had a productive effect appeared in this first talk. This anecdote often referred to certificate Takahashi's understanding of the multiplier effect of the original spending.

In the second talk, made after a few weeks, Takahashi talked more seriously about the limit of deficit spending. "Issuing the bond to cover the deficit means that the government absorbs the nation's savings. It would not be so harmful as it supports the yearly national economy and remains in its surplus. However, if it should exceed this limit, it would be nothing other than that the government wastes up the nation's savings, the value people diligently accumulated for many years" (ITCW 9: 379). Against those who might have read a signal of policy change in this second talk, Ishibashi interpreted that Takahashi had wished to revise his first talk to restrain the military from relying on it in its demand for armaments expansion.

Putting such delicate tactics inside the government aside, we would follow Ishibashi's macro-economic scheme to understand the problem of the limit of deficit spending. Signifying the amount of yearly national saving by S, the amount of annual investment that is needed to maintain the present level of the national economy by I, Ishibashi concluded that the limit of the amount of new deficit-covering public bond (D) must be S−I. If D exceeded this limit, I would decrease accordingly. At last, when D=S, the maintenance of the present production capacity itself would be perfectly impossible. Ishibashi argued further that to leave the growing capacity to the economy, not the limit S−I=D, but S−I>D would be necessary. Theoretically, it might be possible that thanks to some skillful operation in the currency or taxation, the government should acquire the resources it needs without affecting I and S. This is the case of 'forced saving.' However, a large scale of 'forced saving' would decline the people's living standards and accompany the deterioration of their health. The shift of taxation from the mass to higher income might contribute to the reduction of luxurious consumption. The amount of the decrease in consumption would be too small. It would turn out to be in decline in savings and investment.

Next, Ishibashi would explain the 'lower limit' of public finance by adding F (the expenditure of the government) and P (productive investment). Signifying the people's consumption by C, and the yearly income of the nation by E, then an equation C+P+F=E would be acquired. "The view that there is no lower limit of the public finance assumes that the contraction in F automatically increases P and or C, thus bringing about the future increase in production or the leveling-up of the living condition of the nation" (ITCW 9: 389). Ishibashi criticized such a view as it supposed exceptional situations such as the people's consumption were severely suppressed under the fiscal expansion under war or as the fund for investment was keenly demanded under the extremely high boom.

In ordinary conditions, "when the people's consumption is maintained following their habits and the shortage in the supply of the business fund is not felt, [...] we cannot anticipate the increase of C or P from the reduction of public finance directly. The contraction of F would first cause the decline of the demand of products and labor accompanying the decline of prices and then bring about the decline in production and depression" (ITCW 9: 389). When the public expenditure (F) should contain productive spending such as the construction of infrastructure, and industrial development, the adverse effect of fiscal contraction would be severer. After arguing so, Ishibashi concluded that "the lower limit of fiscal contraction should be in the point where C and P begin to increase instead" (ibid.: 190).

Ishibashi's argument above appeared before the emergence of Keynes's *General Theory* (Keunes 1936), and thus the terminology differs from the current usage in macroeconomics. In the first part that dealt with the upper limit of deficit covering public bonds, since Ishibashi did not mention the change of national income, we receive the impression that he made a model out of the classical or Marxian economic model that stipulated the fixed amount of accumulated capital. However, Keynes, too, in the stage of the *Treatise on Money*, did not argue about the fluctuation of the national income as a whole. From the second part, where Ishibashi discussed the 'lower limit of fiscal contraction,' we can guess that Ishibashi understood the multiplier effect of public spending. The case in which the reduction of public expenditure automatically results in the increase of C or P is when the economy is in full employment or the full-scale crowding-out is occurring in the fund market.

The economy that Ishibashi (and Keynes) assumed is the economy in underemployment. While Keynes explained the effect of fiscal spending on national income by using the consumption function that combines income and consumption, Ishibashi reached close to it. However, he did not mention Keynes's original idea of liquidity preference in explaining the demand for money. He only discerned the situation of the fund market between the heated situation and not.

Probably, Ishibashi would develop his intuition as an economic journalist under Keynes's influence mixing with the concepts he had learned from his reading of classical and neo-classical economics (D. Ricardo, J. S. Mill, A. Marshall) and Marxian economics. Ishibashi's attachment to the difference between productive and unproductive expenditure is evident compared with Keynes. It is well known that Keynes wrote that even the project that let people dig the jar in the ground could work to counter depression. Ishibashi's conviction was that scarce resources should be used for capital accumulation and the progress in industries while keeping the people's living. Their unproductive use, such as military spending, should be minimized. Probably the difference in the stage of capital accumulation between Britain and Japan was reflected in this contrast.[6]

8.3 Ishibashi's New Liberalism

Ishibashi's *Tōyō Keizai Shimpō* stood firmly for the advance of democracy. Further, since the 1920s, Ishibashi kept sympathy for the labor movement and socialism and admitted the necessity to modify capitalism. Thus, some would include him in the camp of social democrats as Chō (1994) did.[7] However, if we imagine social democrats in Japan before the outbreak of the Second Sino-Japanese War in 1937, the majority were those socialists whose final goal consisted in the socialization of the means of production despite their support of the parliament democracy. Not only the leaders of the legal proletarian parties but also those academicians that studied Marxian economics took this position. Here, we should remember the resolute demarcation that Fukuda Tokuzō made between social democracy and democracy in general. He excluded social democrats from the camp of democrats because the democracy advocated by socialists served a particular class only. If we follow Fukuda, Ishibashi did not belong to the group of social democrats. Instead, we should adopt the label of 'new liberalism' that Ishibashi often used. Together with Fukuda, who integrated class struggles into his concept of social policy, while didn't abandon the initiative of individuals and the freedom of economic activity, Ishibashi stood in the middle position of the reformed capitalism.

According to the chronicle in the final volume of Ishibashi's *Collected Works*, as early as April 14, 1914, Ishibashi contemplated his future entry into politics and decided to build his new philosophy as preparation (ITCW 15: 349). 'New liberalism' as 'the integration of individualism and socialism' was the 'new philosophy' he quested. In the following year, Ishibashi revealed his philosophy in an article titled "Shin Jiyū-shugi no Hattatsu" (Growth of New Liberalism):

> Society is the system in which desires of the self are realized. As there is no society without self, 'I' don't exist apart from society. The thinking that separates the two is no more than a provisional need to discern the desiring self and the contents of desires to modify the society, *i. e.* the realized life of the self.
>
> *(ITCW 2: 476)*

New liberalism emerged in the West in the late 19th century out of the reconsideration of the goods and evils of the industrial organizations grounded on the principle of free competition, which had an advanced hand in hand with the high tide of modern individualism. In Ishibashi's view, the combination of the benefits of the liberal economic order as Adam Smith had argued for and the remedy of the misery and disparity that socialists demanded is the praxis of 'new liberalism.' Ishibashi found the certificates of its advance in the foundations of the corporative ownership and control of the capital in public enterprises, in the development of corporative control of private business such as factory and wage legislations, in the taxation on the automatic increase in income and on the unearned income, and lastly in the progress of the public provision of the goods and services for the inevitable needs of the people.

> From the absolute principle of letting it alone, these must be rejected as interference with the freedom of individuals. However, they are not. They serve to create a genuinely free playing ground for the competition by eliminating the obstacles to the free activities of individuals. [...] Thus, I would call this individualism based on such a new method new liberalism.
>
> *(ITCW 2: 479)*

This manifesto of young Ishibashi corresponded to Keynes's "The End of the *Laissez-faire*" (1926). However, Keynes's repulsion of utilitarianism and money-love from the aesthetic viewpoint is missing totally in Ishibashi's philosophy. For utilitarianism, Ishibashi was affirmative and recommended its perfection by way of the regulation of desires. With the money-love as the driving motivation of the capitalist economy, Ishibashi never took a contemptuous attitude.

In contemplating the 'new liberalism,' Ishibashi acquired a suggestion from Leonard T. Hobhouse's *Liberalism* (1911). This book, together with the writings of John A. Hobson, was a book that led to the reconsideration of the principle of *laissez-faire* and self-responsibility and provided the philosophical foundation for Liberal Reform in Britain in the early 20th century. A representative leader of the Liberal Party was Lloyd George that attracted Kawakami before his devotion to Marxism.

At the beginning of his career as a journalist, Ishibashi was a writer for *Tōyō Jiron*. a short-lived sister magazine of *Tōyō Keizai* that intended to widen the coverage of the readers to the area of politics, society, and culture. It was appropriate to him, who majored in philosophy and ethics at Waseda University. He became an economist from the auto-didactic efforts in economics after his move to the *Tōyō Keizai*. He read E. R. A. Seligman, D. Ricardo, J. St. Mill, A. Marshall, K. Marx, G. Cassel, and at last met Keynes's publication.[8]

His mentor at Waseda was Tanaka Ōdō (1867–1932), who founded his idealistic moral philosophy on John Dewey's pragmatism. Tanaka's advanced individualism and criterion setting in practice influenced Ishibashi's adoption of 'new liberalism' as his fundamental viewpoint of society. Ishibashi could maintain this position in his economic journalism and later in politics.[9]

As we saw already, Ishibashi learned much from Keynes's writings and introduced his view to the Japanese many times. Keynes could be counted in Britain's stream of 'new liberalism'. However, Keynes belonged to the generation rebelling against the vested interests of the rentier class in the hegemonic imperial nation. The element of the aesthetic elitism that Keynes maintained during his whole life was foreign to Ishibashi. It might make Ishibashi impossible to understand one of the essential points of Keynes's theory. However, it means that Ishibashi was an independent contemporary of Keynes, though they lived in a world that kept considerable differences in the maturity of the economy.

Notes

1 For non-Japanese readers, Nolte (1987) and Radtke (1989, 2003) are recommendable to know Ishibashi's position in modern Japanese history. Of the Ishibashi literature in Japan, Masuda (1990, 1995) and Jang (1992, 2014) are recommendable. We refer to Ishibashi's *Collected Works* with [ITCW].

2 In the academic world, the situation was a little different. Because his father, John Nevil Keynes, was well known to Japanese economists, his son Maynard's assumption of the editorship of the prestigious *Economic Journal* (1911) reached Japan as a piece of news among them. Further, a summary translation of the core chapter of Keynes's first book, *Indian Currencies and Finance* (1913), was provided by Takashima Saichirō in 1915. See Hayasaka (1993).

3 A general overview of the situation in Japan on this matter is provided by Metzler (2006).

4 On Takahashi as Minister of Finance in the 1930s, see chaps. 12 and 13 of Smethurst (2007).

5 The first condition was the stability of the US's control policy on its gold reserve. Other countries' governments and central banks could not fix the policy on their currencies without knowing it.
6 The remnant ideas from classical economics in Ishibashi are discussed by Makino (2017) and Fuse (2019).
7 Chō's works (1963, 1974, 1994) contributed much to the reappraisal of Ishibashi in the intellectual history of modern Japan. In his *Shōwa Kyōkō* (Chō 1994), whose original edition appeared in 1973, Chō compared the views of influential Marxian economists and Ishibashi's on economic situation and policies in the early 1930s and suggested the isolated position of Ishibashi's 'new liberalism.' To Chō, this touched on the question of why a coalition that could support the constructive scheme comparable to the New Deal in the United States didn't emerge in Japan.
8 Ishibashi (1994).
9 Nolte (1987) offers a sketch of the intellectual world of Ishibashi's teachers at Waseda in the Taishō era. In her view, Ishibashi kept the ideals of this era, the age of Taishō Democracy, and conveyed them to the post-1945 age.

References

English

Hobhouse, Leonard T. (1911) *Liberalism*. London: Williams and Norgate.

Keynes, John Maynard (1913) *Indian Currencies and Finance*. London: Macmillan. [In JMKCW 1].

———. (1919) *Economic Consequences of the Peace*. London: Macmillan. [In JMKCW 2].

———. (1921) *A Revision of the Treaty: Being a Sequel to the Economic Consequences of the Peace*. London: Macmillan. [In JMKCW 3].

———. (1923) *A Tract on Monetary Reform*. London: Macmillan. [In JMKCW 4].

———. (1930) *A Treatise on Money*. 2 vols. London: Macmillan. [In JMKCW5, 6].

———. (1936) *The General Theory of Employment, Interest and Money*. London: Macmillan. [JMKCW 7].

———. [JMKCW] (1971–1988) *The Collected Writings of John Maynard Keynes*. 30 vol. London: Macmillan.

Makino, Kuniaki (2017) "Japanese Economists on Imperialism and Total War." *Keizai Gakushi Kenkyū*, 59(1), pp. 1–20.

Metzler, Mark (2006) *Lever of Empire: The International Gold Standard and the Crisis of Liberalism in Prewar Japan*. Berkeley: University of California Press.

Nolte, Sharon H. (1987) *Liberalism in Modern Japan: Ishibashi Tanzan and His Teachers, 1905–1960*. Berkeley, Los Angeles, and London: University of California Press.

Radtke, Kurt W. (1989) "Ishibashi Tanzan: a liberal nationalist". *Japan Forum*, 1(1), pp. 83–91.

———. (2003) "Nationalism and internationalism in Japan's economic liberalism: The case of Ishibashi Tanzan." In Dick Stegewernd ed. *Nationalism and Internationalism in Imperial Japan*. London and New York: Routledge Curzon, Chap. 8.

Smethurst, Richard J. (2007) *From Foot Soldier to Finance Minister: Takahashi Korekiyo, Japan's Keynes*. Cambridge, MA: Harvard University Press.

Japanese

Chō Yukio (1963) *Nihon Keizai Shisō-shi Kenkyū* (Studies on the History of Economic Thought in Japan). Tokyo: Mirai-sha.

———. (1974) *Ishibashi Tanzan – Hito to Shisō* (Ishibashi Tanzan: His Person and Ideas). Tokyo: Tōyō Keizai Shimpō-sha.

———. (1994) *Shōwa Kyōkō – Nihon Fascism Zenya* (Shōwa Economic Crisis: Years before Japanese Fascism). Revised edition. 1st ed., 1973. Tokyo: Iwanami Shoten.

Fuse Gōshi (2019) "Ishibashi Tanzan no keizai riron –Kotenha-teki sokumen wo chūshin ni" (Economic theory of Ishibashi Tanzan: Focusing on its classical aspect). *Keizai Gakushi Kenkyū*, 60(2), pp. 1–19.

Hayasaka Tadashi (1993) *Keynes to no Deai* (Encounters with Keynes). Tokyo: Nihon Keizai Hyōron-sha.

Ishibashi Tanzan [ITCW] (1970-1972) Ishibashi Tanzan Zenshū (Collected Works of Ishibashi Tanzan). 15 vols, Tokyo: Tōyō Keizai Shimpō-sha.

———. [ITCW] (1970–1972) *Ishibashi Tanzan Zenshū* (Collected Works of Ishibashi Tanzan). 15 vols. Tokyo: Tōyō-Keizai-Shimpō-sha.

Jang Keshi (1992) *Ishibashi Tanzan no Shisōshi-teki Kenkyū* (Study on Ishibashi Tanzan from the Perspective of Intellectual History). Tokyo: Waseda Daigaku Shuppankai.

———. (2014) *Ishibashi Tanzan*. Tokyo: Yoshikawa Kōbunkan.

Masuda Hiroshi (1990) *Ishibashi Tanzan Kenkyū – Shō-Nihon-shugisha no Kokusai Ninshiki* (Studies on Ishibashi Tanzan: International View of an Advocator of Little-Japanism). Tokyo: Tōyō Keizai Shimpō-sha.

———. (1995) *Ishibashi Tanzan – Liberalisuto no Shinzui* (Ishibashi Tanzan: The Quintessence of a Liberal). Tokyo: Chūō Kōron-sha.

9

INTRODUCING THE SOCIAL INTO ECONOMICS

Power and Communal Elements in Takata Yasuma

9.1 Concept of Society in Modern Japan

As we saw in previous chapters, the Japanese word 'Keizai' 経済, which means 'economy' in English, was derived from the term Keisei Saimin 経世済民 in Chinese Classics, which meant initially the obligation of rulers to maintain the people by a well-managed rule. However, this word's deviated usage near its modern meaning appeared in the late Tokugawa period. Whether early Japanese translators of Western literature knew this usage, their choice of the corresponding Japanese term to 'economy' coincided with the natural evolution of the economy-related concepts in Japan. (See Chapter 1 of this book.)

Contrastingly enough, the term 'Shakai' 社会 that is assigned to 'society' in English was an invention. Under the Shogunate-clan system during the Tokugawa era, goods and money could move beyond the border of clans, and a market mechanism with some degree of adjustment of demand and supply existed. Thus, it was not strange to use 'Keizai' to signify the transactions of goods and services and their interrelation. Persons, however, were firmly constrained to the order of hierarchy, loyalty, obedience, local communities, and kinships. As individuals were integrated into the system of subordination, the concept of interactions of voluntary activities of independent individuals could not emerge.

Of the two meanings of the Western term 'society,' the one that signifies closed communities with some common purpose and rules had several corresponding Japanese words. Both 'Sha' 社 and 'Kai' 会 are such words. The term 'Shakai' was created by combining these two words to signify the second meaning of 'society,' a more general and vague concept of the ensemble of the interactions of individuals with its structure and accumulated results.

Fukuzawa Yukichi at first invented the term 'Jinkan Kōsai'人間交際 (literally, human interaction) to apply to the second meaning of 'society.' But this term

DOI: 10.4324/9781003081319-9

which consists of four Chinese letters, was too long. What survived was 'Shakai' 社会 with two Chinese letters. The term composed of the same two letters in the adverse order, 'Kaisha' 会社, preserved the first meaning of the 'society.' This term is now applied to signify corporations. Shakai, on the other hand, was only an artificial sign for the translation of 'society' at the beginning.[1]

If Fukuzawa had taken the principle of finding an appropriate term from existing Japanese vocabulary, he might have chosen the word 'Seken' 世間. As we saw in Chapter 6, which dealt with Yanagita Kunio, inhabitants of villages (Mura) expressed the life and rules out of their community with this word. But even in this outer world, the criterion of the behavior of the Japanese is not an objective rule. In the economic transaction, its condition and form often vary, depending on the relations and situations of the actors.

Abe Kinya maintains that even now, the world in which the Japanese live is not society but 'Seken.' Even those scholars that eloquently talk about 'society' in public scenes live in 'Seken' when they return to the daily life. Individuals in the Seken follow the implicit rules whose application depends on the particularized situation in human relations. According to Abe: "'Shakai' represents the world in the modernized term with the outer structure whose core lies in the monetary economy. On the other hand, 'Seken' consists of human relations whose main principle is donation and reciprocity" (Abe 1992: 29).

In the Meiji Era, when 'the independence of the nation' was the end and the civilization was the means to attain it, 'society' was behind the 'state' that sought wealth and power. The 'society' appeared first in the late Meiji era as social problems (Shakai Mondai) that were hard to contain with normal administrative controls. Urban poverty, deteriorating health conditions of workers and residents, labor disputes, social unrest, and further 'dangerous thought' such as Shakai Shugi (socialism) belonged to emerging 'social problems.' Under the need to cope with them, new concepts emerged as 'social policy.' Scholars and experts that studied social policy formed Shakai Seisaku Gakkai (Association for the Study of Social Policy) to review social policy under the initial consensus not to adopt socialism. In the initial concept of 'social policy,' the leading actor was the state that intervenes 'society' to control 'social problems.'

The years under Taishō Era, often called Taishō Democracy, were characterized by lively journalism that often led the direction of politics. Not only political scientists (Yoshino Sakuzō, Ōyama Ikuo, and others) and economists (Fukuda Tokuzō, Kawakami Hajime, and others) but also socialists (Sakai Toshihiko, Yamakawa Hitoshi, and others) contributed their views to various papers and journals actively. With the tide towards introducing general suffrage, journalism extended its coverage to contain social movements and social problems. Not only the dissatisfaction of workers and tenant farmers, but women's questions, education problems, mass culture, and leisure of the people also joined the discussion agenda. Ishibashi Tanzan, whom we discussed in the preceding chapter, expressed it as the arrival of "the age in which every problem is socialized." Imagining labor problems and women's questions, he argued that the society progressed from the stage of "emancipation of individuals" and "destruction of old authority" to that of "positive construction" (Ishibashi 1912). The unnoticed death of the Shakai Seisaku Gakkai (Association for the Study of Social Policy) in the 1920s meant the transition from the stage in which 'society' was contained under the state's regulation to that in which society was liberated from the state.[2]

However, how solid was this public liberation of the 'society' from the state? How deep did this liberation root in the mental base of the Japanese? On the opposite side of the society, the non-negligible part of governing elites (absolutist politicians and bureaucrats, military officers) intensified their confidence in the power state from their anxiety over the domestic unrest and international confrontation. The people who rejoiced in the coming parliamentary democracy didn't notice it.

The recognition of the 'society' of intellectuals, including that of Marxists, could not eliminate the translation style, which was foreign to the real sense of the mass. After the 1930s, under the pressure of the special police (Tokkō) that monitored every symptom of the activities of communists and socialists, the term 'society' returned to a term that connoted 'dangerous thought.' In the years after the breakout of the war against China (1937), 'Minzoku' (ethnic nation or group) flourished as the term representing the nation's totality. The two decades from the ending phase of the Taishō democracy to the war years were probably one of the most rapidly changing ages in the intellectual history of Japan.

This chapter will focus on Takata Yasuma (1883–1972) to understand the notion of 'society' of this age's non-Marxian economists in Japan. He studied first sociology, and after publishing *Shakaigaku Genri* (Treatise on Sociology) (Takata 1919) and *Shakaigaku Gairon* (Principles of Sociology) (Takata 1922), turned to economics. He taught principles of economics at Kyoto Imperial University after Kawakami's leave (1928). In economics, around 1930, he introduced general equilibrium theory to Japan and published five volumes *of Keizaigaku Shinkō* (New Lectures on Economics) from 1929 to 1932. He was one of the first economists in Japan that established the system of economics, which is now generally named neo-classical economics.

However, Takata was not content to remain there. In the background of sociology, he would introduce 'Seiryoku' (power) into economics. He would proceed from pure economics to social economics, in which power relations could influence the economic outcome. From today's view, his proposal contained several significant elements that could stimulate contemporary theoretical economists. However, as Takata would not abandon the economic orthodoxy on general equilibrium, his 'power theory' could not form an integrated system in economics. At last, he had to admit that his attempt toward 'power economics' remained fragmented.

What was peculiar about his lifestyle among other scholars was that he had kept the sense of rural community of his home village to the end of his life. He was born in 1883 in a priest's family in a rural village in Northern Kyūshū

(Mikazuki Village, now Ogi City, Saga Pref.). He often returned to his home village whenever he needed rest or quiet life to recover from his chronic stomach disorder. He revealed his conservative sympathy for rural life in the essays or occasional contributions to journals, which he discerned from his academic writings. However, a sociologist, Takata knew well that social scientists could not separate their investigation from their living sentiments. During the war, Takata elevated his lifestyle conservatism to the mission of oriental nations in world history. In 1943 at his retirement from Kyoto University, he assumed the presidency of the newly established Institute of Ethnology, which was disorganized after the defeat of Japan.

In December 1946, Takata was judged as 'illegible for teaching' by a committee composed of his junior ex-colleagues of Kyoto University that investigated his activities during his war years. Takata's appeal to a higher committee was rejected, so he had to live a retired life for several years. In 1951, the then Minister of Education, Amano Teiyū, decided to reverse the verdict. Though Amano had been a critic of Takata's preaching of the 'superiority of the poor' in the war years, he judged Takata 'a liberal' in his essence. Takata returned to academism and founded the Institute of Social and Economic Research at Osaka University. As this contrast in judging Takata in war years tells us, the assessment of Takata's opinions in war years is very delicate. However, it was undoubtedly a variant of Takata's sociology or social economics.[3]

9.2 From Sociology to the Third View of the History

Takata's first academic publication was *Bungyō-ron* (On Division of Labor) (1913), based on his dissertation submitted to the Faculty of Letters of the Kyoto Imperial University. As his mentor Prof. Yoneda Shōtarō had a course for students in economics at the Faculty of Law, Takata kept his interest in economics like his mentor. Thus, Takata's dissertation in sociology appeared first in the publication series of the Faculty of Law *(Takata 1913)*. Takata's first job was also as the lecturer of foreign literature in economics at the Faculty of Law of this university.[4]

As for the division of labor in economics, everyone would recall Adam Smith's view that it developed from the 'propensity to exchange' (Smith 1776). According to Takata, such propensity would emerge only after some degree of social development. Takata replaced this propensity with the 'desire for power' that strived individuals to surpass others. Man has the desire to possess power, demonstrate it, and exert it. At the stage of some degree of the development, with the increased 'social density' due to the population growth, the possibility emerged for individuals to make others dependent on them by engaging in specialized work. Division of labor is pursuing the 'desire for power' by appropriating others' power and creating dependency in the community. Its progress would bring about the separation of dominant groups and subordinated groups. In other words, the division of labor inevitably accompanies the formation of classes.

> The division of labor emerged as the social means to serve the desire for power. Thus, the actor's purpose is nothing but to widen the disparity in power among individuals and to intensify the differentiation of classes.
>
> *(Takata 1927: 206)*

While in Adam Smith's world, the division of labor that emerges from the exchange of equal partners brings about a market economy. In Takata's sociology, pursuing the distinction in power relations would produce a class society with domination–subordination linkages.

In contrast to the Marxian notion of class society in which the conflict of interests and class struggles occupied its central position, what attracted Takata as a sociologist was the aspect of interdependence and attractive elements of class society. At the beginning of his Doctoral thesis on the division of labor, Takata mentioned 'herd instinct,' 'combination by psychological contagion' such as imitation and sympathy, and 'combination on interest base' as the 'three sorts of psychological basis' of the 'social combination of the human race.' According to Takata, division of labor would create substantial dependent relations and reinforce these psychological bases in the group formation process that accompanied the division of labor. The formation of the class itself manifests such subjective and objective combinations.

> The more important result of the division of labor is the cohesion of society. This byproduct increases the sociological significance of the division of labor more and more. The first reason for the cohesion that the division of labor works as the binder of society is that it produces substantial interdependence through transactions of the results of labor. The control of society through psychological contagion and the intensification of the binding of associations are subordinate effects.
>
> *(ibid.: 206)*

Interestingly, the two key concepts that guided him for his entire life, 'desire for power' and 'social density,' appeared in this maiden work. The first, 'desire for power,' grasps the inner motivation of man in the society, not in his simple 'survival' but his pursuit of the advantage in comparison with others. Thus, in Takata's sociology, the factor that brings about social change is not the competition or struggle for survival but the competition or struggle for power. Here, 'survival' meant passive adaptations to the given environment in whichever forms. To Takata, both Adam Smith's 'self-interest' and the 'utility maximization' of neo-classical economists were the theoretical construction of such passive adaptation. The sociological moment i.e. 'power,' is missing in such theorizing. When 'desire for power' should work in the economy, it would form 'Seiryoku' (social power) to support the action to acquire a superior social position beyond the direct and short-termed interest from adaptative activity. Thus, the 'desire for power' was the starting point of Takata's sociology and that of 'power economics' in his later investigation.

However, 'desire for power' remains the inner motivation of human action, and its manifestation varies depending on 'outer conditions.' The second key concept, 'social density,' represents 'outer conditions' in an integrated way. It means "the density of psychological interactions of the members of society" (ibid.: 86) and consists of the population density, numbers of society members, and the effectiveness of the means of communication. Suppose we neglect the geographical distribution and variation in the communication media; the essential element of 'social density' is the absolute number of population and its change, either natural change or social change from immigration, conquest, or integration. The variation of the activity of the members of a society on which division of labor emerges and the capability of utilizing this variation for the 'desire for power' depend on the 'social density.' The division of labor, thus the formation of 'social power' itself, promotes the social density on the one hand, but the former is limited by the latter. As Takata himself was conscious of it, this was the sociological version of Adam Smith's statement, "division of labor is limited by the extent of the market" (Smith 1776:. Book 1, chap. 3).

Takata endeavored for a decade to establish his sociology from his basic view of focusing on the form of 'combination' as the element of social relations. He published *Shakaigaku Genri* (Treatise on Sociology) in 1918 and *Shakaigaku Gairon* (Principles of Sociology)[5] of Takata (1922) in 1950.

When Takata was honored as a Person of Cultural Merit in 1964, its ground was Takata's contribution to sociology (not economics). However, as Takata was entrusted to teach economics besides sociology at the assigned universities in the 1920s (Hiroshima Higher Normal School, Tokyo University of Commerce, Kyūshu Imperial University), he gradually shifted his investigation to economic theory. From 1929, Takata held the course of principles of economics at the Kyoto Imperial University after Kawakami Hajime's leave in the previous year. Takata made his lecture to demonstrate the modern economic theory of non-Marxian orthodoxy. In this stage, Takata endeavored to raise the theoretical level of economics in Japan by assimilating general equilibrium theory in his lectures. In the next section, we discuss Takata's unique attitude to the general equilibrium theory. Here, we should explain his second central theme in this stage, i.e. criticizing the materialistic view of the history of Marxism and establishing his alternative.

In his theory of class in the 1920s, Takata rejected its economic view and defined it as "the group which is based on the affinity of social powers," which were composed of 'forces,' 'wealth,' and 'dignity.' These three sorts of 'social powers' constitute hierarchical stratifications separately or in complexity. (Takata 1924: 3) 'Social class' is at first characterized by the objective affinity of these powers. However, about classes, it can nourish 'sympathy' and develop collaborative action. Various shifts in class relations can occur in such a process. However, the ultimate ground for 'power' is 'the quantitative and qualitative constitution' of the society formed by the population's fluctuation.

This 'quantitative and qualitative constitution' meant nearly the same as 'social density' in his theory on the division of labor. The absolute number of the population and their distribution are the direct result of the change in the independent variable 'population,' which is logically antecedent to the concrete forms of the society. 'Social relations' are the forms in which the pressure of interactions is practically managed. Here, Takata's 'sociological view of the history' traces the following causal relations: <population increase>→<quantitative and qualitative constitution of the society>→<social relations>→<political and juristic institution, economy, ideas> (ibid.: 320).

This is 'the third view of the history' in Takata's words, that would replace the first, idealistic one, and the second, materialistic one. In Takata's view, as the second materialistic view had wholly criticized the first idealistic view, Takata focused his criticism on the second materialistic view of history. He interpreted it as the view that conceived the causal relations from <materialistic productive forces> to <production relations = economic structure of society>, and further to <political and juristic institutions, social forms of consciousness>. Thus, it is a version of the economic view of history. Takata criticized it by questioning the independence of the first factor of materialistic productive forces. The technology and the ways of production that constitute the forces of production depend on the population and its distribution, as well as on the form and structure of the society. Productive forces and social relations are mutually interdependent. Takata knew well the controversies among Marxists on the possible reactions of the superstructure on the substructure. To him, it was only a certificate of the validity of his third view of history.

9.3 General Equilibrium and Power

Takata's style of thinking, drawing the interaction of factors first and then asking about the ultimate determinant behind this interaction, was also apparent in his theoretical investigation of economics.

In the second volume of his *Keizaigaku Shinkō* (New Lectures on Economics), Takata systematically presented price theory from the viewpoint of general equilibrium. Takata wrote in its Preface, looking back on his investigation: "Standing on the theory of general equilibrium means that the author has arrived at the theoretically most superior position." He added, "indeed, the introduction of general equilibrium may be this book's contribution to the economic academism in Japan; it is not the originality of my view." Then, he declared a 'power theory of price' on the ground of general equilibrium as his originality. (Takata 1930: 3) In this stage, he maintained that general equilibrium is needed to determine the price of productive factors (wages in particular) by relations of social powers as its precondition. Against this first consideration of wages, Nakayama Ichirō, who studied general equilibrium theory under Joseph A. Schumpeter in Bonn, presented the objection that the autonomy of economics could not be attained without excluding interference from non-economic factors.[6]

In his reply to Nakayama, Takata declared that he modified his view from the first consideration of wage to the two stages approach to general equilibrium. He admitted that all price variables, including wage, must be determined simultaneously under the general interdependence. However, this is the first stage of investigation in his view. In the second stage of the inquiry, economic theory must admit that the supplier of productive factors were not passive actors in real life. Takata introduced the element of 'resistance' of workers in the labor supply function.

> If we consider the supply price of labor [...], we cannot understand it from the utility of labor to workers. We must admit what rules the resistance of workers is their social power. The social power of the individual worker is determined by his position in the total social construction rather than his effort. Individuals represent their social positions in their resistance in various ways. This resistance makes them demand the supply price of labor according to their economic conditions.
>
> *(Takata 1935: 36)*

Takata would find the effect of social powers in the working of economic laws. In his reply to Nakayama, Takata mentioned five ways social powers could influence the economy's working.

The first is on the institutional arrangement of the economy. "The social organizations - private property, division of labor, and exchange in particular – are supported by social powers" (ibid.: 29).

The second is on the quantities of goods in possession. "The quantities of possession are on the one hand the result of the previous economic process, but on the other hand they are determined by the distribution of social powers" (ibid.: 30).

Third, "Social powers influence the determination of prices by compulsion" (ibid.). The minimum wage, the highest legal price, and compulsory purchase were mentioned under this category. Takata was relatively cool on these coercive measures, saying this category had no theoretical significance so long as the economic theory presupposes free competition. However, he showed considerable interest in the controlled economy in the war years later.

Further, Takata conceived the possibility of the direct effect of social powers on the free actions of individuals. Takata divided this effect into the passive one and the active one from the viewpoint of the degree of economic rationality. The passive effect is the fourth category, and the active effect is the fifth. The passive effect is seen in such cases as both partners of a particular transaction are in a specific social power relation. The one side of the transaction, buyer or seller, might voluntarily diminish his demand as he felt his counterpart's 'dignity.' Takata seemed to have the behavior of tenant farmers to landowners or unskilled workers to employers in his mind. However, this category did not satisfy Takata's theoretical interest because it meant a deviation from the realization of the economic law.

The fifth category, 'the direct and positive effect of the voluntary action,' best fits Takata's criterion of 'the effect of power in the economic law.' Takata considered the behavior of suppliers of productive factors, particularly laborers, who set their supply prices to reflect their social positions. It does not offend the working of the economic law, but it supports this law. "The questing for acquiring maximum from the exchange is the very effect of the economic principle. The passive attitude to refrain from demanding prices that correspond to their social position and to deliver the productive factor at the asking price of the counterpart is nothing other than the violating attitude to the economic principles" (ibid.: 32).

Takata here mentioned the 'dignity' of the better rank that suppresses the individuals in the lower rank and the 'resistance' of the suppliers of productive factor (workers) that came from the awakening of their positions in the economic society. They suggest the relation between Takata's view of Japanese society then and his 'power theory' of economics. In a later article, he made a sociological reflection on his theory. He admitted that the situation in the Japanese economy was the ground on which he conceived the power theory of economics. In his view, it retained 'excessive communal features' in all aspects. The conventional voluntary obedience survived, and the intervention on wages by social powers was so familiar.[7]

Takata wished to develop theories of wages and interests on his power theory of economics. While Takata stressed that in the theory of wages and interest, suppliers could control the quantity of supply, his critics considered it incompatible with general equilibrium. Indeed, it is possible to understand 'power theory' from the hypothesis of the rigid wage or rigid interest rate. But if the rigid rate is supposed to be given as sociological data from outside, it is the same as the wage first theory that invited Nakayama's criticism. Takata quested the logic that the supplier of productive factors could maintain their demand effectively. General equilibrium theory presupposes the well-functioning of the parametric adjustment of the price mechanism. In such a mechanism, every supplier is a passive price-taker. The social element cannot enter this mechanism as such.

However, the actor that Takata's power theory supposed was not an isolated *homo economicus* but *homo sociologicus* that lives in the interaction with others. Fukuzawa Yukichi stressed the mind of independence for the modernization of Japan. It reflected his recognition that unequal relations of dependency were ubiquitous in the actual Japanese society. However, the sense of independence also manifests the state of the interrelations that is supported by certain solidarity and rivalry with others. In Takata's power theory, the 'dignity' of the mighty and the 'resistance' of workers gain significance in an interdependent view of economic activity.

The attitude of employers to the employee affects the work motivation of the latter. Workers may choose the level of their efforts strategically to counter the attitude of the employers and their fellow workers. In case such a direct interdependence should exist, as game theory tells us, the possibility of plural equilibria would emerge. Not every outcome guarantees the social optimum. However, such an interdependent view of the economic action emerged only later. As Takata adopted Walrasian general equilibrium as the orthodox frame of economic theory, he could not proceed beyond replacing the driving force of economic actors from 'utility' to 'power.' However, under the theoretical turn after Takata's death, the view that institutions accompanying norms and conventions represent the rigidities that hinder the working of market mechanism turned to an opposite idea that institutions and other norms can contribute to the stability and smooth working of the market mechanism. As Morishima Michio argues, Takata's power theory contained much for modern economists to challenge.[8]

9.4 From the Crisis of Capitalism to Ethnic Nations

In the previous section, we saw Takata's view of how 'social power' would enter the economic activities of individuals. Then, how did Takata view the reverse direction, i.e. the influence of the economy on society? In this respect, what is interesting is Takata's writings on the economic sociology of contemporary capitalism around 1930 that finally culminated in his view of ethnic nations during the war years.

Takata defined economic activity first as the activity aimed at appropriating material goods and then placed it in the society as the area under the effect of social life. However, in accord with the development of economic activities, the economy tends to dissolve the communal society from which it was born and in which it has developed. Division of labor and the product exchange introduced "the partial combination of specific benefits" into the society and loosened the old communal combination of the community. "Division of labor together with the money accompanying the former has the dissolution effect on the communal societies (Gemeinschaft) and contributed to their transition to interest-oriented societies (Gesellschaft). It has significant effects on the class organization of society as well" (Takata 1934: 181).

According to Takata, capitalism emerged from the progress of 'rationalism' under the loosened social ties and the dissolution of force-centered rank hierarchy. However, Takata argued that capitalism was not "rationalism per se" but "a halfway rationalism." Capitalism emerged from the competition for power in the form of limitless profit-seeking and created the division of classes and their conflict. Takata described it that "capitalism presupposes a sort of irrationality for its existence" (ibid.: 214). Capitalism promotes the progress of rationalism grounded on economic interest. However, harmony in the regional society and production sites would disappear, and an open conflict between classes would emerge.

Here, Takata conceived a "growing rationalism" (ibid.: 217) that would eliminate the growing irrationality from the viewpoint of the organization.

It was not clear what Takata meant by 'growing rationalism.' Probably he suggested various orientations for social reforms, including socialism, by this term. Parallelly to Schumpeter, Takata tried a sociological interpretation of the historical destinations of capitalism. In the case of Schumpeter, who speculated on the trends and futures of capitalism in the United States in the age of the New Deal, the conclusion was that, capitalism was destined to transform itself into socialism due to its success, not due to its failure (Schumpeter 1942). His paradoxical conclusion came from the tendency to decay social support for private property, the growing organization of firms and government, and the diffusion of antipathy toward capitalism among intellectuals. They were the results and manifestations of the rationalism that capitalism nourished by its success. Takata's view on 'growing rationalism' seems to have similar tenets to Schumpeter's. However, Takata could not look over the growing 'irrationality' under capitalism – the class conflicts – avoided to draw any conclusion from his diagnosis of contemporary society.

Instead of the future of capitalism, what caught his attention as a sociologist in the years when Japan entered war step by step was the problem of ethnic nationality of Japanese and Asians. As Kiyono (1987) pointed out, Takata shifted from the cosmopolitan position that regarded the move toward the interest-oriented society (Gesellschaft) as the global tendency to the position of ethnological nationalist that would find the circulation of the dominant ethnic nations in the international conflict after the mid-1930s. Takata stressed the advantage of Asian nations that conserved communal features compared with Western nations that ran forward toward the interest-based society. As ethnic nations had not occupied any central position in the early sociology of Takata, we can interpret Takata's interest in the ethnic nation as his reaction to the surrounding atmosphere.[9] However, it is also true that the theoretical preparation to discuss the problem of the ethnic nation was furnished already in his former investigation in sociology.[10]

The first was the distinction between the ideal–typical communal society (Gemeinshaft) and the 'elements of communal society' that could be compatible with the interest-oriented society (Gesellschaft). By this distinction, it became possible to discuss communal features (race, culture, tradition, ethnic consciousness, etc.) that constituted the ethnic nations or groups in the civilized world and to compare and order different ethnic nations and groups.

The second was 'the law of constant sum of the combination in the society.' Originally this law was the theoretical formulation of trade-off relations between distinct patterns of combination, such that under a strong religious combination, the combination of political organization would be relatively weak. Takata, in war years, applied this law to the trade-off between the 'desire for power' of the class and that of the nation. When the combination of the class, hence its 'desire for power' too, should weaken, the combination of the nation and its 'desire for power' would strengthen instead.

The third was the law of circulation in the class society, presented by Robert Michels and Vilfredo Pareto. Takata applied this law that had been conceived initially to the change of *élites* in the class society to the world society in which many ethnic nations and groups constituted the ladder according to their superiority. The ethnic nations that occupy the dominant position tend to lose their strength due to their favorable position. At the same time, those in unfavorable conditions may keep the vitality and solidarity needed to raise their positions.

Takata's sociology was equipped with several theoretical concepts and statistical apparatus to perform empirical studies of ethnic nations and groups in Asia. Thus, when the government founded Minzoku Kenkyū-sho (Institute of Ethnology) in 1943 to study the ethnic groups and nations in the Greater Asia Co-prosperity Area, Takata assumed its presidency after he retired from the Kyoto Imperial University.[11] However, when he applied his sociological view to the domestic and international situations during the war, Takata's conviction pandered to the situation terribly. We can mention three topics in Takata's publications in the area of his ethnology.

The first was his recommendation for the nation to live in poverty. From the data of agronomics and dietetics, he conceived the change of the staple food of Japanese from rice to potato. It could create the Japanese nation the capacity for further population increase. So long as poverty should not harm the health and vigor of the people, the nation living in poverty could nourish the enterprising spirit. To him, the leveling down of the consumption of all of the nation would contribute to keeping the communal features of Japanese society. It could refrain classes from developing their 'desire for power' and reinforce the 'desire for power' of the ethnic nation.

The second was applying the circulation theory of the class to the worldwide confrontation of nations. Under the view of imperialism as the domination of Western nations over other ethnic nations and groups, Takata regarded the liberation of the subordinated as the main course of world history. The subordination itself nourished the desire for power of the dominated nations. Here Takata supported Japan's confrontation with Western powers as a certificate of his circulation theory and approved Japan's mission as the leading nation of all subordinated nations toward their liberation. The following citation is one of his problematic writings that has been discussed often as the certificates of Takata's support of the war.

> The supremacy of the white itself nourishes among the ethnic nations and groups staying backward the will and power for their liberation. The trend of emergence of their resistance has become apparent in the history of a few centuries. In my view, this is the main direction of world history. Undoubtedly, the Japanese nation occupies the vanguard position destined

> to be its leader. Thinking so, the Chinese nation that Japan is fighting at present is not the enemy but the mightiest friend. She is a comrade in the liberation movement. The present military action aims to make her desert the anti-Japan policy and shake hands with our nation.
>
> *(Takata 1940: 247f.)*

The third was his dream of building an "East Asian ethnic nation" from economic collaboration and cultural exchange under the Great East Asian Co-prosperity ceiling. While in Japan's policy statement in the war years, the partnership of the ethnic nations or groups in Asia was often stressed, Takata proposed the future vision to form a united ethnic nation of East Asia in the broader sense of the nation. Takata argued that by strengthening the combination of various ethnic nations in East Asia, the formation of a new nation in the broader sense would emerge. So long as various elements nourish the communal features in their daily lives, an ethnic nation in the broader sense is possible, at least in principle. In Takata's view, what could ultimately support the new order in East Asia was neither military hegemony nor block economy but the formation of the collective attachment to the same East Asian nation. It was the motivation that made Takata assume the presidency of the Institute of Ethnological Studies in 1943 after he retired from the chair at the Kyoto Imperial University.

9.5 Neglect of Civil Society

Takata was a giant scholar that led Japanese academics both in sociology and economics. He assimilated the newest theories in both areas from overseas literature and had never fallen into Japanese provincialism, at least in his academic investigations. During the war years, when both streams of loyalist economics on Japanese spirit and totalitarian mobilization economics flourished, he kept a critical stance on both. He continued a theoretical examination of the orthodoxy of economics in the West.[12] Then, why did such an eminent scholar advocate those naïve ideas about the ethnic nations that were very hard to discern from war propaganda? To conclude this chapter, we will add three remarks on Takata's vision of society and his concept of social economics.

The first is that his adaptation to the politics in war years occurred not in the direction of the command economy of the mighty state but in the direction of strengthening the communal element of the nation. Without joining the camp of 'political economists' that expected social reform from the state intervention in the war economy, Takata quested for the solution of interest theory, reading J. R. Hicks and J. M. Keynes. Thus, he had no such illusion that the 'new order' and the war economy could overcome capitalism. However, his antipathy to 'political economy' seems to have prevented him from analyzing the relations between classes and states in the war years. Instead, he applied his 'law of constant sum of combination' directly to the society of Japan. He acquired 'ethnic nationality' as the entity of combination that filled the place where 'class' had occupied once.

The legitimation of the war from the circulation theory of ethnic nations was its result.

The second is that the elements of 'equality' and 'mutual recognition' are missing in his sociology, while 'superiority' and 'power' are dominant there. It was also the case in his theory of ethnic nations. Takata inherited the dichotomy of communal society (Gemeinshaft) and interest-oriented society (Gesellschaft) from F. Tönnies. However, he was disillusioned by the latter, representing society's weakened cohesion and disruption. What sociologist Takata quested for in the war years were the communal elements of the society. In his ethnic theory in the war years, the aspect of the quest for superiority emerged in his argument for the circulation of ethnic nations. In contrast, the element of communal aspect appeared in the idea of the fusion to bear the East-Asian ethnic nation. However, the principle of self-determination and mutual recognition was blurred.

Third, all in all, we are obliged to raise the question of whether Takata had the idea of the modern civil society with universal norms and open-minded morals and the individuals corresponding to it. Indeed, individuals who are conscious of others and quest for 'power' over them have a broader sociological perspective than the homo economicus that only recognize prices and their wants. However, as 'superiority' or 'advantage' emerges only with the presupposition of others as fellow persons, there must be a sympathetic relation beforehand. Without it, the quest for 'superiority' would proceed beyond the superiority within a society and result in absolute domination over enslaved people and herds.

Takata rejected the Smithian concept of 'inclination to exchange' and replaced it with 'desire for power.' As we can see from the *Theory of Moral Sentiments* (Smith 1759), Smith presupposed the actor who can understand the personality and the interest of others empathetically and have a viewpoint of others inside him. Thus, before performing an economic exchange, there is an imaginary exchange of the positions of each other. According to Smith, the judgment of the 'impartial spectator,' whether he can approve or not in his empathic imagination, is the ground of every norm of the society. Most ordinary persons have such 'impartial spectator' in their minds.

Or we can take the theory of social contract. Before the real economic exchange takes place, there must be universal recognition of each other personalities and possessions. Mutual recognition of personalities and their right is the fundament of the ideas of modern civil society.

In Takata's case, however, the element corresponding to the recognition of the fellow personality was given only in the combining ties that reflect the communal nature of the society. The path of refinement and universalization of mutual recognition was not open. Even if the development of the division of labor and the exchange guided by the 'desire for power' can accompany the mutual recognition, so long as it is a part of the quest for superiority, it would reflect the difference in the hierarchical structure of class society only. Such an exchange, either in the real or in the imaginary exchange, would not create the rights and norms that are indifferent to the peculiar positions and interests of the actors.

The reason for Takata's disarray in war years may have the origin in the absence of the basic concepts of civil society in his understanding of the 'society' itself.

Notes

1 See Yanabu (1982: 1–22).
2 See Ishida (1984: chap. 2).
3 Takata was a prolific author. His publication list is in Takata Yasuma Hakushi Tsuisōroku Kankō-Iinkai ed. (1981). See Daidō (1953) and Tominaga (1972) on Takata's sociology. Takata (1989), together with Tominaga's introduction, is a helpful guide to Takata's sociology for the English language world. On Takata's power theory in economics, see Hayasaka (1973), Nakanishi (1987, 1988), Tanaka (1998), Makino (2005), and Negishi (1998, 2004). Morishima Michio showed his gratitude to his mentor by editing Takata (1995) with his Preface. As a critical examination of Takata's sociology, see Kiyono (1987).
4 It was just before the separation of the Economics Faculty from that of Law (1917). Sociology then was a far minor study area in the department of philosophy of the Faculty of Letters.
5 Takata (1989) is the English translation from its revised version of 1950. See also its Preface added by Tominaga Ken'ichi.
6 Nakayama (1932). Nakayama published his summary of general equilibrium theory with the title of *Junsui Keizaigaku* (Pure Economics) (Nakayama 1933). On the introduction and the development of modern economics in Japan, see Ikeo (2014: chapter 4).
7 Takata (1938) included in Takata (1949).
8 See Morishima's Preface to Takata (1995) and Morishima (1994). Bowles and Gintis (2001) recently introduced the power relations and conflicts in economics with their concept of 'contested exchange.'
9 In his recollections that Takata contributed to Weekly *Economist* in 1957–1958 (Takata 2022), he admitted the influence of the atmosphere of the age over him and his concession to nationalism (ibid.: 157, 194).
10 In the Preface of Takata (1942), Takata declared that he applied principles of his sociological theory to the structure and trends of ethnic nations (p. 2).
11 On this Institute and its relation to Takata, see Nakao (1997).
12 Takata engaged in these years in the critical examination of J. M. Keynes's theory on unemployment and J. R. Hicks's theory of interest from the viewpoint of his power theory.

References

English

Bowles, Samuel and Gintis, Herbert (2001) "Contested exchange: A new microeconomics of capitalism."" In G. M. Hodgson, M. Itoh, and N. Yokokawa eds. *Capitalism in Evolution: Global Contentions – East and West*. Cheltenham: Edward Elgar , pp. 21–35.

Ikeo, Aiko (2014) *A History of Economic Science in Japan: The internationalization of Economics in the Twentieth Century*. London and New York: Routledge.

Negishi, Takashi (1998) ""General equilibrium theory and beyond: Yasuma Takata and Kei Shibata." In Sugihara Shirō and Tanaka Toshihiro eds. *Economic Thought and Modernization in Japan*. Cheltenham: Edward Elgar, pp. 97–116.

———. (2004) "Kyoto school of modern economic theory." *Kyoto Economic Review*, 73(1), pp. 1–10.

Schumpeter, Joseph A. (1942) *Capitalism, Socialism, and Democracy*. New York: Harper & Brothers.
Smith, Adam (1759) *Theory of Moral Sentiments*. London: A. Millar, and Edinburgh: Alexander Kincade and J. Bell.
———. (1776) *An Inquiry into the Nature and Causes of the Wealth of Nations*. London: T. Cadell and W. Strahan.
Takata, Yasuma (1989) *Principles of Sociology*. Introduction by Ken'ichi Tominaga. Tokyo: University of Tokyo Press.
———. (1995) *Power Theory of Economics*, tr. by Douglas W. Anthony. Foreword by Morishima, Michio. New York: St. Martin's Press.

Japanese

Abe Kin'ya (1992) *Seiyō Chūsei no Ai to Jinkaku – Seken-ron Josetsu* (Love and Personality in Medieval Europe: Prelude to the Theory of Seken). Tokyo: Asahi Shimbun-sha.
Daidō Yasujirō (1953) *Takata Shakaigaku* (Takata Sociology). Tokyo: Yūhikaku.
Hayasaka Tadashi (1973) "Nihon Keizai-gakushi ni okeru Takata Yasuma Hakushi" (Dr. Takata Yasuma in the history of economics in Japan). *Kikan Riron Keizaigaku*, 24(2), pp. 46–60.
Ishibashi Tanzan (1912) "Mondai no shakai-ka" (Socialization of problems). *Tōyō Jiron*, April 1912 issue, pp. 101–106. Tokyo: Tōyō Keizai Shimpō-sha.
Ishida Takeshi (1984) *Nihon no Shakai-Kagaku* (Social Sciences in Japan). Tokyo: Tokyo Daigaku Shuppankai.
Kiyono Masayoshi (1987) "Takata Yasuma ron" (On Takata Yasuma). *Ritsumeikan Sangyō-Shakai Ronshū*, 23(1), pp. 99–124.
Makino Kuniaki (2005) "Takata Yasuma no kakaku-ron to seiryoku-ron" (Takata Yasuma's price theory and power theory). *Keizai Ronsō* (Kyoto University), 176(4), pp. 514–539.
Morishima Michio (1994) *Shisō to shiteno Kindai Keizaigaku* (Thoughts in Modern Economics). Tokyo: Iwanami Shoten.
Nakanishi Yasuyuki (1987) "Takata Yasuma no jinkō-ron to keizaigaku" (Population theory and economics of Takata Yasuma). *Keizai Ronsō* (Kyoto University), 140(5/6), pp. 273–292.
———. (1988) "Takata Yasuma – Ippan kinkō riron to kōchoku chingin" (General equilibrium and rigidity of wages). *Keizai Ronsō* (Kyoto University), 141(4/5), pp. 236–53.
Nakao Katsumi (1997) "Minzoku Kenkyū-sho no soshiki to katsudō" (The organization and activities of the Institute of Ethnology). *Minzokugaku Kenkyū*, 62(1), pp. 47–65.
Nakayama Ichirō (1932) "Keizai kinkō riron no honshitsu to kakaku seiryoku gakusetsu" (General economic equilibrium and power theory of prices). Included in *Nakayama Ichirō Zenshū* (Collected Works of Nakayama Ichirō). Vol. 1. Tokyo: Kōdan-sha, 1972.
———. (1933) *Junsui Keizaigaku* (Pure Economics). Tokyo: Iwanami Shoten.
Takata Yasuma (1913) *Bungyō-ron* (On the Division of Class). *Hōritsugaku-Keizaigaku Kenkyū Sōsho* (Series of Studies in Law and Economics), no. 13. Kyoto Hōgakkai (Academic Society of Faculty of Law, Kyoto Imperial University).
———. (1919) *Shakaigaku Genri* (Treatise on Sociology). Tokyo: Iwanami Shoten.
———. (1922) *Shakaigaku Gairon* (Principles of Sociology). Tokyo: Iwanami Shoten.
———. (1924) *Kaikyū oyobi Daisan Shikan* (Classes and the Third View of the History). Tokyo: Kaizō-sha.

———. (1927) *Bungyō-ron* (On the Division of Labor). Revised ed. Takata (1913). Tokyo: Tōkō Shoin.

———. (1930) *Keizaigaku Shinkō*, vol. 2, *Kakaku Riron* (New Lectures on Economics, vol. 2, Theory of Price). Tokyo: Iwanami Shoten.

———. (1934) *Kokka to Kaikyū* (State and Class). Tokyo: Iwanami Shoten.

———. (1935) *Rishi-ron Kenkyū* (Studies on Interest Theory). Tokyo: Iwanami Shoten.

———. (1938) "Seiryoku-setu ni okeru sonzai hikōsoku-sei" (Restraint of being in the power theory). *Keizai Ronsō*, 47 (59), pp. 601–613. Included in Takata (1949).

———. (1940) *Minzoku to Keizai* (Ethnic Nation and Economy). Tokyo: Yūhikaku.

———. (1942) *Minzoku-ron* (On Ethnic Nations). Tokyo: Iwanami Shoten.

———. (1949) *Seiryoku-setsu Ron-shū* (Studies on Power Theory). Tokyo: Junshin-dō.

———. (2022) *Takata Yasuma Jiden: Watashi no Tsuioku* (Autobiography of Takata Yasuma: My Recollections). Edited by Yoshino Kōji and Makino Kuniaki. Saga Shimbunsha.

Takata Yasuma Hakushi Tsuisōroku Kankōkai ed. (1981) *Takata Yasuma Hakushi no Shōgai to Gakusetsu* (Life and Academic View of Dr. Takata Yasuma). Tokyo: Sōbun-sha.

Tanaka Hidetomi (1998) "Takata Yasuma no seiryoku keizaigaku ronsō (Controversies on Takata Yasuma's power theory)". *Jōbu-Daigaku Shōgakubu Kiyō*, 10(1), pp. 23–40.

Tominaga Ken'ichi (1972) "Takata Yasuma no seiryoku riron" (Power theory of Takata Yasuma). *Shakaigaku Hyōron*, 23(2), pp. 28–46.

Yanabu Akira (1982) *Hon'yaku-go Seiritsu Jijō* (The Making of the Translation Equivalent Terms). Tokyo: Iwanami Shoten.

10

MARXIAN ECONOMICS AND JAPANESE CAPITALISM

Reproduction with Semi-feudal Agriculture

10.1 Beyond the Stage of Introduction

It was around 1900 that the name Karl Marx was known to the Japanese. In 1902 Nishikawa Mitsujirō, one of the founders of Shakai Minshu-tō (see Chapter 4), published an introduction to him. However, this small book did not deal with Marx's economic theory. Both Kōtoku Shūsui's *Shakaishugi Shinzui* (Essence of Socialism) (1903) and Katayama Sen's *Waga Shakaishugi* (My Socialism) (1903) showed the influence of Marxism clearly. Further, *Heimin Shimbun*, a weekly paper founded by Kōtoku and Sakai Toshihiko, carried the translation of the *Communist Manifesto* and received the ban promptly in November 1904. While Kōtoku turned to anarchistic radicalism after the closing of this paper, Sakai continued the activity of the propagation of Marxism. However, to have a reliable translation of Marx's *Capital* (Marx 1867–1894) as Abe Isoo could not continue his first attempt in 1909, the Japanese public had to wait till the mid of 1920s to see its completion by Takabatake Motoyuki.

Marx and Marxism's early introduction was generally carried out by a small circle of socialists and journalists. However, after World War I, economists and other social scientists in academism joined it. The discussion around the Marxian theory emerged in such well-sold journals as *Kaizō* and *Chuō Kōron*. As we saw in the preceding chapter, Kawakami started his journal *Shakai Mondai Kenkyū* in 1919, intending to propagate Marxism. At the Faculty of Economics of the Imperial University of Tokyo, a group of young scholars began to investigate Marxian economics. In Osaka, the newly founded Ōhara Shakai Mondai Kenkyūsho (Ohara Institute for Social Research) provided ambitious researchers with the best academic citadel to examine social problems from a Marxian viewpoint. Its president was Takano Iwasaburō, who had left Tokyo University due to the trouble around Japan's delegate to ILO in 1920. A group of young

DOI: 10.4324/9781003081319-10

scholars that had the chance to stay in the early years of the Weimar Republic of Germany witnessed the political and ideological competition between Social Democrats and Communists. They returned to Japan, convinced that Marxism represented the new science grounded on the emerging working class. In such a situation, Takabatake Motoyuki completed his translation of *Capital* in 1924, and the *Collected Works of Marx and Engels* (*Marx Zenshū*) began to appear in 1928. In the intellectual world of Japan, the so-called 'Marx boom' prevailed.[1]

The early disputes on Marxian economics occurred from Marx's criticism of non-Marxian scholars like Fukuda Tokuzō and Koizumi Shinzō, that knew the literature of the controversies on Marxian economics well.[2] The topics covered include capital accumulation under capitalism, the contradiction between value and production price, and the theory of absolute rent. Defenders were, at first, those of the early generation of Marxian scholars, Kawakami Hajime, Yamakawa Hitoshi, Kushida Tamizō, and Inomata Tsunao. Before the third decade of the 20th century, the level of understanding of Marxian economics in Japan remained such level of popular introductory literature of socialism in the West or that of Karl Kautsky's summary of Marx's *Capital* (Kautsky 1887) at its best. In a decade, its level reached the level comparable to Marxian scholars in the West, including Russians, both in the literature background and its theoretical level.

The publication project of *Keizaigaku Zenshū* (Complete Works on Economics) that Kaizō-sha launched in 1928 arranged not only its first volume to Kawakami's *Keizaigaku Taikō* (General Outline of Economics) but also three volumes (vols. 10–12) to the theoretical commentary of Marx's *Capital*. At first, the part of the second volume of *Capital*, The Circulation Process of Capital, was entrusted to Uno Kozō (1897–1977). However, under the eager request of Yamada Moritarō, (1897–1980) Uno transferred its third part, 'Reproduction and Circulation of Total Social Capital,' to Yamada and confined himself to its first and second parts. Thus, this volume was published in 1932 by the coauthor of the two.[3] By the way, the author of vols. 10 and 12 that dealt with vols. 1 and 3 of *Capital* was Sakisaka Itsurō (1897–1985). All three were representative figures of the new generation of Marxian economists. Interestingly, Yamada's investigation into the reproduction scheme of capital (Yamada 1932) prepared his application of the reproduction view of Japanese capitalism in his later work. In contrast, Uno's investigation into capital circulation and its rotation contributed to his idea of the circulation view of Marxian economics. Thus, in these years of the early 1930s, Marxian economics in Japan reached the stage of creative struggle beyond the stage of introduction and assimilation.

10.2 From Value to Reproduction

Yamada Moritarō was born in the Kisogawa town in Aichi Pref. He knew Marx by reading the first issue of Kawakami's journal *Shakai Mondai Kenkyū* that he bought at the bookshop in Nagoya when he was a high-school student. He entered Tokyo University to study economics, worrying about the effects of the purge of promising scholars after the Morito Incident in 1920.[4] But this crisis was managed by the deliberate behavior of the figures concerned. Yamada could remain a research staff of the Faculty of Economics after graduation and be appointed an associate professor in 1925. He chose the theory of reproduction of capital as the subject of his seminar in 1929. The following year, he was arrested in charge of the financial aid to illegal Japanese Communist Party and left the University. Contributing *Saiseisan Katei Hyōshiki Bunseki Joron* (Analytical Introduction of the Scheme of Reproduction Process) to Volume 10 of the *Keizaigaku Zenshū* was Yamada's first job after he became an independent scholar.

> I first majored in the basic theory of economics and studied the value theory of various schools. i.e. Adam Smith and Ricardo's classical school, the utility value theory of Menger and Böhm-Bawerk, and Marx's value theory. I acquired the conclusion that the value is an essential category in Marx that regulates the whole system of economic categories on the one hand; still, on the other hand, it is determined by the latter. Since then, my research interest has moved to the problem of reproduction. [...] The reproduction theory also became the base of my thinking of economic issues in later years.
>
> *(YMCW 1: 55)*

'The conclusion' in this recollection meant his article "Kachiron ni okeru Mujun to Shiyō" (Contradiction and solution in the value theory, Yamada 1925) that Yamada published in the *Keizaigaku Ronshū* (The Journal of Economics) in 1925. Yamada dealt with the problem of the incompatibility between labor value and the price with average profit, which Koizumi Shinzō had raised from the comparison between Ricardo and Marx (Koizumi 1922). In Yamada's view, Ricardo modified labor value from his finding of the effect of the difference in the composition and the rotation of capital. At the same time, Marx constructed the production price from the relation of the total sum of the capital value and surplus-value. Thus, in Yamada's view, Marx's value realizes itself by constructing the second stage law of the production price under the total picture.

The reproduction scheme in the third part of volume 2 of *Capital* certainly fits Yamada's criterion of 'integrative, total, and general analysis.' It presents how the capitalistic social construction of production and classes continues from the viewpoint of the circulation and reproduction of total social capital. Here, we probably need some explanation.

Assume a textile factory that employs many workers. For this factory to continue production, three conditions must be filled. The first is that the materials for tomorrow's production and the machinery to be replaced must be produced in other places today. The second is that the workers can work tomorrow, i.e. they can refresh their labor power by consuming necessary goods on their wages. It means other consumer goods must be produced elsewhere by other producers.

The third is that the product of this factory sells for the price with which the factory owner can pay the purchased materials and machinery and the wage for workers of today or tomorrow. If the product of this factory is cotton cloth, it is purchased by other factories to produce clothes and others. If the products are final products, such as clothes, they are purchased by workers' wages and by non-workers' revenues, which are the derivatives of the surplus value acquired from the production. The demand for the product comes from the wages paid to workers and the profit and other derivative revenues from the production in the whole society. Thus, the third condition is nothing other than the reflection of the total society-wide coexisting relations of production to the price of the product.

If we move our eyes from individual capital to whole social capital, we can draw a model of two sectors and two classes. Adopting sectors I and II for the production of the means of production, and that of the means of consumption, respectively, and W, C, V, and M for the value of the total output, means of production consumed, wages, and surplus value (raw profit including interest and rent payment) respectively, we acquire Marx's reproduction scheme.

Sector I: $W1 = C1+V1+M1$

Sector II: $W2 = C2+V2+M2$

In this model, the condition for the reproduction of the same scale is $W1=C1+C2$, thus $V1+M1=C2$. The condition for the enlarged reproduction is $W1=C1+C2+\Delta C1+\Delta C2$, thus $V1+M1=C2+\Delta C1+\Delta C2$.

However, the reproduction scheme is only an abstract model of the reproduction of capitalist production. How does it relate to the social and historical view of Japanese capitalism? Without answering this question, we cannot truly understand the meaning of the phrase "substantiation of the reproduction theory to the analysis of Japanese capitalism." It contains two problems. One is whether it is possible to acquire such a historical view of capitalism's emergence, development, and collapse. Another is the kind of significance the reproduction theory can have for the economy in which capitalist production does not prevail in the whole sector.

In the history of Marxian economics, several attempts, such as Lenin's theory of market formation and Henryk Grossmann's collapse law (Grossmann 1929), exist that applied reproduction schemes to the construction of the historical model of capitalism. However, Yamada was very cautious and argued for the significance and limitation of the analysis of the reproduction scheme.

> Reproduction theory deals with the forms of the movement of capital. As such, i. e. the problem of capital, in general, remains an abstract concept. Not recognizing this well, some tried to acquire conclusions favorable to them. For example, Tugan would have the eternality of capitalism, and Rosa would acquire the economic grounds of imperialism from the difficulty of the realization of I m(c)+m(v) and II m(c)+m(v) [market for the

> products corresponding to the capital accumulation: YK]. Both were mistaken, as we saw before. Reproduction theory is no more than a problem at the general abstract level. However, so far as it emerges as the general conclusion of the moving form of the whole social capital, it has definitive significance.
>
> *(ibid.: 254)*

Using the reproduction scheme of enlarged production, Tugan-Baranovsky (1901) argued that under the assumption of the rapid increase of the demand for the means of production, capitalism could grow despite the decrease in consumption. In contrast, Rosa Luxemburg (1913) grounded her theory of imperialism on the missing market for the means of consumption due to the investment for the enlarged production. In Japan, Fukuda rejected capitalism's failure using Tugan's argument, while Kawakami argued for the 'deadlock' of capitalism, referring to Rosa Luxemburg. That was the so-called dispute on capital accumulation and reproduction.

Yamada was very loyal to Marx in his commentary on the reproduction theory. The contradiction and conflict of capital and labor was described as "the countervailing contradiction that is inherent even under the assumption of ideal correspondence" (ibid.: 55). More precisely, that means the countervailing relation between wage (consumption) and profit(accumulation). If we reduced the grade of abstraction to introduce the dependency of labor productivity on the worker's skill and the level of technology and further consider the material difference of the product, reproduction theory would develop into the structural theory of social reproduction that could integrate the interindustry analysis. In this scheme, we can incorporate the incomes of social classes and their expenditure. The path of the reproduction of social capital is formed when the factors of international trade, taxation, fiscal expenditure, and financial institutions are integrated. The abstract reproduction theory itself can be substantialized in such a way and become applicable to the analysis of the national economy and its crisis. The imamate existence of the countervailing contradiction itself is not the sufficient reason for the real crisis of capitalism. The emergence of the economic crisis and its form is determined by the concrete conditions and the structure of the reproduction of capital.

The above is the provisory answer to the first problem. Let's move to the second problem. To Yamada, that knew Francois Quesnay's *Tableau économique* (Quesnay 1758, 1759) well; reproduction theory was not confined to that of capitalist production. In the Marxian reproduction theory, ground rent is only a derivative revenue from the 'surplus value.' In contrast, in Quesnay, the revenue of the landowners absorbs the whole surplus of the society. It is worth noticing that the price's nature is different between Marx and Quesnay. In Marx's case, the labor theory of value and its adaptation to capitalist production (production price) are valid. However, in Quesnay's *Tableau*, while the price of corn contains the surplus, the price of manufactured goods does not bring profit to artisans. In Japan, while capitalist production prevailed in the manufacturing sector, the agriculture sector was not; non-capitalist ownership of land lasted, and enormously high rent in kind was imposed on tenant farmers. As Yamada saw it, the Japanese economy before 1945 was characterized by the coexistence of Marx's reproduction scheme and Quesnay's *Tableau économique*.

In Yamada's view, the agriculture of pre-1945 Japan is the small-scale family farming that had developed from the Tokugawa period to the Meiji Era. The concentration of land ownership after the liberation of the land transaction resulted in the landowner–tenant farmer relations that didn't touch the small-scale farming inherited from the feudal period. It was called 'Kisei Jinushi Sei' (parasite landownership) because landowners charged a high-level rent mostly in natural form without exerting any productive effect on production. In his view, the essential nature of this landownership was feudal or semi-feudal as it inherited the high rate of exploitation from the feudal lords, using every coercing element (non-economic coercion) to keep tenant farmers in the semi-serfdom situation.

Yamada's description of Japanese agriculture with such term 'semi-feudal' or 'semi-serfdom' may sound odd to the reader today. However, even if we disregard such non-economic elements as the natural form of the rent, various non-economic coercion, and feeble right of tenants, we cannot deny the continuity of the small plot's cultivation and high rent rate that showed the commonality to the feudal era. Further, this non-capitalistic sector of agriculture played a decisive role in providing materials, labor forces, and funds to the capitalistic sector of the industry, together with its contribution to supporting the government with high-rate land tax. Thus, even in investigating the structure of the reproduction of the capitalist sector of manufacturing, the introduction of the relationship with the sizeable non-capitalistic sector becomes inevitable. This relationship determines the specific features of the national economy and the distinctive 'form' of the capitalism of the country concerned. The famous phrase in the *Nihon Shihon-shugi Bunseki* (Yamada 1934), 'the reciprocal determination of the small-scale cultivation with semi-serfdom and capitalism,' meant this.

10.3 Analysis of Japanese Capitalism

It was in the same year, 1929, with his seminar on reproduction theory, that Yamada began to be interested in the empirical study. An ex-student came to his room with a pile of statistics materials. He asked Yamada to guide his study on the situation of working youth under the pressure of the rationalization of industries. He also requested some contributions to the *Musansha Shimbun* (Press of Proletariat). The following year, Yamada was indicted in charge of financial aid to the illegal Japanese Communist Party (JCP).

After his detention for a few months, he finished writing his study on reproduction theory. Then he joined the team of authors of *Nihon Shihonshugi Hattatu-shi Kōza* (Lectures on the Historical Development of Japanese Capitalism), which Noro Eitarō (1900–1934) led. In this series, Yamada was allotted to three parts: "Early forms of the capitalist industry, manufactures, and house industry" of the first distribution (May 1932), "Development of factory manufacturing" of the fifth distribution (February 1933), and "Reforms in Agriculture in the age of Meiji Restoration" of the seventh distribution (August 1933). Together with his fragmentary reflections that he wrote for this lecture series (*Kōza*), Yamada integrated them into a book entitled *Nihon Shihonshugi Bunseki – Nihon Shihonshugi ni okeru Saiseisan Katei Haaku* (Analysis of Japanese Capitalism: A grasp of the reproduction process in Japanese capitalism) that appeared in February 1934. In this book version, the first contribution was renamed 'Turn of production=Reformulation: Forms of manufactures and house-industries,' and the second 'Axes of turning =Construction of the combination of military organization and key industry,' and the third 'Base, semi-feudal land ownership=small scale cultivation with semi serfdom.' Each of renamed titles suggested the constitution of this work.

Despite its origination from the separate contributions to *Kōza*, this book impresses us with its clear-cut consistency.[5] In the first part, the emergence of two lines of consumer goods industry – silk and cotton manufacturing that had the ground in the household industry and the outflowed labor forces from rural areas – was described. If we allow us to say without paying attention to the level of abstraction, this part dealt with Sector II in Marx's reproduction scheme. In the second part, the formation and the structure of key industries: machinery and metal industry, the sector of basic materials like coal and iron ore, and transportation and communication. This part corresponds to the analysis of Sector I in Marx's scheme. These key industries were created under the state's need to build up the military organization to compete with the overseas powers. Thus, they kept considerable dependency on the military apparatus of the state. Still, they could exert a binding effect over the light industries oriented to the overseas market.

If the Japanese economy before 1945 should have been a fully capitalistic one, the analysis of the book should end here. However, it was not the capitalistic sector but the non-capitalist agricultural sector that supplied the labor force to the developing capitalist industries. The non-capitalist agricultural sector had provided funds for industrialization and supported the government by offering land tax. In this sense, non-capitalist agriculture was regarded as the 'base' of the whole structure of Japanese capitalism. In this sector, the semi-feudal landowners prospered over the small farmers imposing the high rent that absorbs the whole surplus and degenerates the living standard of the tenants at the lowest level.

Such complex of the light industry depending on cheap labor, the heavy industry integrated with the state's military apparatus, and semi-feudal agriculture and their relations are the 'reproduction structure' of Japanese capitalism with the adjective 'militaristic and semi-feudal.' However, to understand Yamada's view in the *Bunseki* (*Analysis*), we should not overlook his view of the stages of Japanese capitalism and the world economy. The following is my relatively free translation that may hopefully deliver the readers its contents and Yamada's unique style together.

> In the case of Japanese capitalism that stands on the definitive mutual relations with the mini-sized cultivation on the semi-serfdom in agriculture, the founding process of the industrial capital with its dominant feature of the epoch is given as the prospect of the domestic production of the means of labor on the precondition of the qualitative and quantitative development of the clothes production. It emerged as the process occurred around the 30th and 40th years of the Meiji Era. It was the process that formed dual relations between high ground rent on semi-serfdom and the low, semi-slave-like wages. It also emerged as the process that determined the dual relations of the foundation of industrial capital in Japan and her transformation into imperialism. Upon this fundamental determination, the formation process of financial capital, which consists of two stages, continued. Its first stage emerged in its early forms around the Russo-Japanese War years and was represented in the railway nationalization (1906). The second stage, with its full-fledged form of financial capital, occurred during the years under the World War and was represented by the Mobilization Law of Munition Industry (1918). Along with consolidating the military and semi-serfdom financial capital, a general crisis emerges on this criterion.
>
> *(YMCW 2: 154)*

As this citation reads, *Bunseki* regarded the years when the cotton and silk industry as representative consumption goods-producing sectors were established, and the prospect of domestic production of the machinery for them emerged as the foundation age of the industrial capital in Japan. The cotton and silk industries dissolved the traditional ties of agriculture and rural handicrafts. They were replaced by the production hierarchy, from sericulture and wage weaving to the modern factory spinning and weaving, based on the low-wage labor force. The metal industry and machinery production were obliged to be founded from above in an integrated form with the state's military apparatus. On the other hand, Yamada noticed that the height of the rent of the prevailing tenant system was comparable with that of the tribute in the feudal age. Yamada regarded Japanese agriculture as 'semi-feudal' and the situation of small farmers under the tenant system as 'semi-serf.' Here comes the peculiar term for Japanese capitalism, 'military and semi-serfdom capitalism.'

The low wage of workers determined by the living standard of small farmers under the 'semi-feudal' tenant system limited the growth of the domestic market. Thus, the light industries of Japan had to rely on the overseas market. The Asian market, particularly China, had a decisive significance to the cotton industry. Thus, the transition to Japanese capitalism's imperialism followed soon after its industry capital's foundation. However, as the heavy industry of Japan that depended heavily on the state's military spending was not sufficiently equipped with the technology and productivity to supply the high-quality means of production, its dependency on Western industries continued. In addition to the foreign dependence of such materials as raw cotton and silk export on the fragile luxury demand of Western nations, this deficiency in the productivity of the key industry reinforced the risk of the imperialistic advance of Japanese capitalism.

Financial capital (concerns) that dominated the light and heavy industries represented the typical structure of militaristic and semi-feudal capitalism. However, the base of the labor force that had sustained the reorganization to capitalist production was beginning to decay; together with the growing tensions in the overseas markets and international relations, it became the origin of the general crisis of Japanese capitalism. In the mid of the critical situation, the movement of rationalization, i.e. industrial restructuring, began. It strengthened the contradiction in the existing structure of reproduction and gave rise to many labor disputes. Thus, industrial rationalization meant not only the reorganization of capital but also the formation of the 'basic series structure of the proletariat,' whom 'the basic line' of the movement of 'the semi-serf tenant farmers' was going to meet. Such was the perspective that Yamada's *Bunseki* presented as the 'shaking of the total structure' in the coming future.

> Japanese capitalism was obliged to construct the gigantic system of militaristic key industries with the government's aid upon the vast base of semi-serf lilliput cultivation. It formed the structure of Japanese capitalism and determined the track of reproduction. In this case, the form of its militaristic and semi-serfdom features constituted the archetype of Japanese capitalism. It formed a typical pattern that added 'civilized fetters of excess labor' to the 'barbarism of serfdom.' This form appears as the purely Japanese archetype, different from the British capitalism that emerged in the home nation of free competition, [...] This form of double fetters now becomes the constraint against developing productive forces. It is illuminated by the determining factor of the productive forces, i. e., the proletariat.
>
> *(ibid.: 150f.)*

10.4 Semi-Feudal Agriculture

The image of Japanese capitalism with its militaristic and semi-feudal form that Yamada described in his *Bunseki* with his unique style and invented terms penetrated profoundly and widely into the intellectuals of Japan. It coincided with the appearance of Comintern's so-called *'32 Theses* that appealed to the fight against the absolutistic emperor system (Tennō-sei). The preceding *'27 Theses* took the view that the state of Japan, with its all relics and remaining nature of feudalism, had performed 'the transformation to a bourgeois state.' The new Theses warned of the undervaluation of the absolutistic emperor system that occupied the center of Japan's military and policing apparatus. In its view, the absolutistic power of

Japan had the main base in the semi-feudal landowner and integrated 'greedy bourgeoisie' under its hegemony. (Ishidō and Yamabe eds. 1961) This view of *the '32 Theses* fit well with Yamada's argument that the complex semi-feudal domination in agriculture and militaristic state apparatus molded the 'form' of Japanese capitalism, which couldn't disappear by its development. As Yamada's *Bunseki* (Analysis) was the representative work of the Kōza group, their works were generally interpreted as the substantiation of the *'32 Theses*. Here, the name of the 'Kōza faction' and its political implication emerged. But the actual editorial process of *Kōza* had been more delicate, and not all of its contributors were in accord in this respect.

Under the situation where the discussion on the emperor system was prohibited, it was natural that the debate concentrated on the agriculture problem. The group that opposed the views of *Kōza*-faction was named '*Rōnō* faction'[6] from the title of the journal *Rōnō* (Laborer and Farmer), they published from 1927 to 1932. Politically this group had its origin in the elder generation of Marxists such as Sakai Toshihiko, Yamakawa Hitoshi, and Inomata Tsunao, that had participated in the first foundation of the Japanese Communist Party in 1922 but had not participated in its second foundation at the end of 1926. Thus, they were independent of the authority of the Comintern. Later several academic economists joined this group. The long-continued debate between the two factions that produced an enormous amount of controversial literature was called the debate on Japanese capitalism.[7]

To this group, the modernization of land ownership by the legislation in the Meiji era was taken for granted. The extraordinarily high land rent, too, must be explained not by the pressure of semi-feudal coercion over tenant farmers but by the competition among small farmers. As early as 1931, Kushida Tamizō gave this group's basic view on the high rent imposed on the tenant farmers. Though he admitted the pre-capitalistic nature of the land rent in Japan, he argued that its height was due to the fierce competition of small farmers for cultivating the land. To the economists of the *Rōnō*-faction, the argument of the *Kōza*-faction that would attribute this height to the non-economic cohesions of the semi-feudal nature of the tenant system was a suicidal attempt for the theory itself.

Sakisaka Itsurō's following words expressed the fundamental stance of this group best: "Examining particularity is nothing but to find its tendency to dissolve into the general tendency. Without this perspective, one cannot grasp the development of capitalism" (Sakisaka 1935). Against such a view, Yamada would reply that without the total picture of Japanese capitalism, the 'decay of the form' itself would be interpreted as 'the progress.' Economists of *Rōnō*-faction endeavored to demonstrate the certificates of the capitalistic development in various fields. Tsuchiya Takao's investigation into the 'manufacture' in the Tokugawa period and Suzuki Mosaburō's study of the finance capital in Japan are examples.[8] However, from the works of this faction, no impressive image of Japanese capitalism could replace that of Yamada. It is known from the praising words by Arisawa Hiromi, who was usually counted in *Rōnō*-faction: "As the investigation of Japanese capitalism, this *Analysis* was the boring that dug through the hard bedrock and reached the untrodden depth" (Arisawa 1989: 210f.).

However, in our view, two problems remain to wait for the answer. The first is how to explain the survival of the 'semi-feudal' features of agriculture under the highly developed capitalism from the viewpoint of economic theory. The second is how to grasp the development of the productivity in agriculture and the small family farming that embodied this development even though they did not have the capitalistic traits. As for the first, Yamada seemed to have told nothing more than the continuity of the specific form that had emerged in the stage of the formation of Japanese capitalism. Probably he might have been convinced himself by the continuity view of the forms of Japanese capitalism from the foundation stage of industrial capital to that of finance capital and imperialism. It is the notorious 'invariability thesis of the form.' The second was the problem that caught Yamada's attention in his agriculture research at the Tōa Research Institute, to which Yamada, after his second arrest/detention in 1936, belonged.

At a research meeting in 1946 that the Ministry of Foreign Affairs arranged to prepare the economic reconstruction plan, Yamada revealed the conclusion of his investigation in the nearly one decade of the forced silence.[9] At the beginning of his report, Yamada showed the superiority of Japanese farming in its technology and management to the agriculture of Chinese and Southern nations and attributed this superiority to the independence of the farmer's household as 'Ko' 戸 at least in principle. This productivity had been the base that supported the capitalist development in the economy and made the liberation of the small family from the large kinship family in the society. However, compared with Western farming, the disparity was so significant that it was impossible to contain them in the same category. Yamada attributed this disparity to the prevalence of the 'basic form' that emerged from the mutual relation of the pressure of tenant exploitation and the smallness of farming.

> Assume now an owner of two Chōs [ca. 2 ha.] paddy fields would lease them. In the case of Japan, then, two tenant farmers borrow each one Chō and deliver the rent at the rate of one Koku [ca. 180 l.] brown rice per Tan [ca. 10 a.] to this owner. In total, the owner acquires 20 Koku brown rice. This amount of rice equals the two tenant farmers' total income and the harvest of a farmer that owns one Chō land. It means that even a tiny ground owner can enjoy the life standard of an ordinary farmer by the land lease. It promotes the transition of small landholders to inactive landowners. [...] Pressures of the tenant relationship and the smallness of the farming determine each other. Without breaking this basic form, the structural advance in Japanese agriculture is hard to proceed with.
>
> *(YMCW 3: 172)*

As was stated in this citation, the negative effect of the tenant system in Japan did not consist in the existence of large-scale landlords that exerted harsh exploitation using various pressures. Such might exist partly. But in essence, the reason lay in the advantage of rent acquisition surpassing that of the expansion of farming. In the agricultural sector, where the benefit of becoming a parasite landowner prevailed, chronic stagnation, in general, occurred instead of the positive expansion of farming. Thinking so, Yamada argued for the necessity of the post-war land reform.

What remains is, however, the question of why such a high land rent emerged that enabled small landowners of merely two Chōs could live as a parasite living in the countryside. If we neglect the non-economic coercion, we come to the question of why so many landless or land-deficit small farmers exist in the rural society of Japan. It cannot be answered with the definition of the 'form' of Japanese capitalism. It is a synonym for the first question that we saw just before.

Uno Kozō would explain this question not from the inside of the agricultural sector but from the outside, i.e. from the absorption of labor forces by the growing capitalist industry. In his article "Shihon-shugi no Seiritsu to Nōson Bunkai no Katei" (Foundation of capitalism and the process of the dissolution of rural villages), published in 1935, Uno compared the labor absorption effect of capitalist industry in the advanced capitalist countries and the latecomers such as Japan. He argued that in the latecomers that could introduce technologies of high productivity from the beginning, the dissolution of farmers tended to be milder than in their forerunners. While teaching the course of economic policy at Tohoku University after his research abroad in Germany, he found in the historical development of economic policies in Germany the emergence of policies that would countervail the dissolution of rural society. From this finding, Uno concluded that the form of the accumulation of capital and the policies that corresponded to it differ in each stage of the development of capitalism. The development of capitalism does not necessarily bring forth such a thoroughgoing dissolution of farmers that had once occurred in Britain, as described by Marx in his *Capital.*

> To capital, generally, the foundation of its reproduction process in a country remains in the range of conditions it needs. Its completion itself is not the aim. […] Also, in the latecomer countries, the growth and investment of capital promote the dissolution of agricultural society through the domestic reproduction process. But it does not necessarily work for the development of large-scale capitalist farming. Particularly, the agricultural sector that remains the supply sector of corns and other direct consuming materials receives the intrusion of capitalism, often keeping its old form. Naturally, in this process, the proletarianization of farmers gradually proceeds, not necessarily in the typical form.
>
> *(Uno 1965: 51f.)*

Indeed, this view is free from the simplicity of Sakisaka's of seeing the primacy of general tendency everywhere. In this article, Uno gave only the feature that latecomer capitalism is apt to have compared to the preceding capitalism. Later, Uno elaborated this idea into his 'stage theory' and established his original version of Marxian economics with three layers structure; elementary theory (principles) – stage theory – contemporary analysis.[10]

Uno viewed the agricultural sector of the latecomer countries from the viewpoint of growing capitalist industries with stage-specific features. It contrasts Yamada's view, which stressed the influence of the vast agricultural sector over the growing capitalist industry. However, we don't think that both are incompatible. They are rather complementary to each other.

10.5 From the *Tableau* Économique to Reproduction Scheme

Marxian economists generally adopt a history-dependent view on the nature of the theory. Their relativistic attitude originates from their belief in materialism which regards every intellectual conception as the result or reflection of the existing social relations. In Yamada's case, the recognition that theories are 'no more than social products' was the conviction on which he began his investigation. Indeed, as his caution on the reproduction scheme suggested, Yamada admitted the difference in the level of abstraction between the theoretical model and empirical research. However, all the concepts and their linkages were considered to have their origin in real social relations. The substantiation of theory was nothing but a way to make historical analysis possible. In this respect, Uno, that regarded his elementary theory as ahistorical theorizing, was unique among Marxian economists.

We mentioned already that Yamada grasped the structure of Japanese capitalism as the coexistence of Marx's reproduction scheme and Quesnay's *Tableau Économique*. Thus, it would be no surprise when we read the following statement in which he regarded the mission of the post-war land reform in the dissolution of Quesnay's *Tableau* into the reproduction scheme.

> A historical age covering the industrial revolution and French Revolution lies between Quesnay's *Tableau Économique*, in which rent absorbs the whole surplus, and Marx's Reproduction Scheme, in which rent is a branch of surplus-value, as is the same with industrial profit and capital interest. In the agriculture of Japan, however, such a relation exists that admits, like Quesnay's *Tableau*, the subsumption of total surplus under rent, while in the industrial sector, a highly developed capitalism that makes Marx's reproduction scheme the dominating relation exists. Figuratively saying, Quesnay's *Tableau* and Marx's Scheme coexist. The coming land reform aims to dissolve Quesnay's *Tableau* into Marx's Scheme.
>
> *(YMCW 4: 49)*

However, the dissolution of the parasite land ownership does not directly mean the reform of the small farming itself. Thus, Yamada continued that to enter the relation of the Marxian Scheme, Japanese agriculture must advance into the construction of the 'technological base of sound agriculture' that can provide profit, rent, and interest. A pseudonym review ridiculed its similarity with the reform plan of the Ministry of Agriculture. As Yamada was collaborative with the land reform of 1947 and organized the documentation of this reform on his initiative, this view sounds plausible. However, three decades after this review, Ōshima Yūichi dared to guess Yamada's true vision of developing Japanese agriculture.[11] Following Ōshima's conjecture, Yamada conceived in the depth of his mind of the transition to the socialist collective farming on the nationalized land ownership. It was the direction that the US occupation would strictly oppose. Ōshima cited the following sentences that came directly after the above-cited sentences.

> We should pay attention to the fact that between Marx's scheme and the present land reform, another historical age spanned from Lenin's scheme to the Russian revolution exists. Here, we know the position of the current land reform and its limitation at this stage of world history.
>
> *(ibid.)*

Lenin's scheme means Lenin's early articles demonstrated the possibility of market expansion to develop capitalist farming in Russia. The Russian Revolution was a revolution that reorganized the Russian economy into a socialist economy. 'Position' and 'limitation' in world history meant probably the destination of Japanese agriculture that had to restart the market-oriented development under the political limitation that prohibited the revolution toward socialism.

From today's view, it is clear that both Yamada's hidden aim (in Ōshima's guess) of the socialist collective farming and his recognition of the 'position' in the world history is erred. However, it is also confirmed that the post-war land reform that reinforced the small landholding exclusively without the structural change of agriculture and the collaborative relations with manufacturing industries left the problem of the construction of the sound and independent agriculture as an industry afterward.

Notes

1 See Chapters 4 and 6 to know the author's view on the intellectual situation of the early stage of the introduction of Marxism in Japan. Moriya (1967) provided the story from the viewpoint of orthodox Marxism close to that of JCP, while Hidaka, Hayashi, Sakurai, Watanabe, Furihata, Suzuki (1967–1968) represented the view close to the Uno school. For non-Japanese readers, chap. 2 of Hoston (1986) and chap. 3 of Morris-Suzuki (1989) are recommendable.
2 Fukuda (1921), Koizumi (1922).
3 Uno (1970: 328–330).
4 In 1920, an article on P. A. Kropotkin that associate professor Morito Tatsuo published in the starting issue of Economic Faculty's house journal, *Keizaigaku Ronshū*, became the target of ultra-nationalists that regarded it as a propaganda of anarchism.

The author and the responsible editor Ōuchi Hyōe were judged guilty and obliged to leave the Faculty. Morito and Ōuchi found their shelter in the Ohara Institute of Social Research, headed by Takano Iwasaburō.

5 However, not everyone agreed on the integrity of this book. See Nagaoka (1980).

6 Ishiko (2008) gives a historical overview of Rōnō-faction. Ishiko provided biographies of Sakisaka (Ishiko 2014), Yamakawa (Ishiko 2018), and Kushida (2021), too.

7 There are several historical commentaries on this long-continued controversy. Probably the most detailed is Koyama and Yamazaki (2014). Hidaka, Hayashi et al. (1967–1968) provided the view from the Rōnō and Uno group. Nagaoka (1984) is also readable. Andō (1998) is a concise guide to this debate for English language readers. However, we cannot miss the masterpiece of Hoston (1986) in this area, though she didn't set her focus on Yamada. Terade (2008) interpreted Yamada's *Analysis* from the viewpoint of modernist architecture. The echo of this controversy in post-1945 social sciences of Japan can be heard from Barshay (2004), whose chaps. 3 and 4 dealt with Yamada and Uno, respectively.

8 This debate was so attractive that it made a non-Marxian development economist look for the theoretical constellation that could ground the view of *the Kōza* faction. Yasuba (1975) offers a labor market model with disguised unemployment in the agricultural sector.

9 In August 1945, Yamada joined the Special Research Committee of the Ministry of Foreign Affairs, which was founded soon after Japan's capitulation, to discuss the plan of recovery and reconstruction of Japan. From October 1946 to March 1948, he was a member of the Councils for Land Reform.

10 On the significance of Uno's findings in agricultural problems for the formation of his economic system, see Ōuchi, Kamakura, Hayashi, and Saeki (1979: chaps. 2 and 3).

11 Ōshima (1982), p. 18. See also NNN (1948).

References

Western Languages

Andō, Takaho (1998) "The debate on Japanese capitalism: The Kōza faction and its perception of society." In Sugihara, Shirō and Tanaka, Toshihiro eds, *Economic Thought and Modernization in Japan*. Cheltenham: Edward Elgar, pp. 78–96.

Barshay, Andrew (2004) *The Social Sciences in Modern Japan: The Marxian and Modernist Traditions*. Berkeley: University of California Press.

Grossmann, Henryk (1929) *Das Akkumulations- und Zusammenbruchsgesetz des kapitalistischen Systems (Zugleich eine Krisentheorie)*. Jena: C. C. Hirschfeld.

Hoston, Germaine A. (1986) *Marxism and the Crisis of Development in Prewar Japan*. Princeton, NJ: Princeton University Press.

Kautsky, Karl (1887) *Karl Marx' ökonomische Lehren*. Stuttgart: Dietz.

Luxemburg, Rosa (1913) *Die Akkumulation des Kapitals: Ein Beitrag zur ökonomischen Erklärung des Imperialismus*. Berlin: Vorwärts.

Marx, Karl (1867–1894) *Das Kapital: Ktitik der politischen Oekonomie*. (Bd. 1. *Der Produktionsprocess des Kapitals*. 1867; Bd. 2. *Der Zirkulationsprocess des Kapitals*. Herausgegeben von Friedrich Engels. 1885; Bd. 3. *Der Gesamtprocess der kapitalistischen Produktion*, Herausgegeben von Friedrich Engels. 2 Theile. 1894). Hamburg: Otto Meisnner.

Morris-Suzuki, Tessa (1989) *A History of Japanese Economic Thought*. London and New York: Routledge.

Quesnay, Francois (1758, 1759) Tableau économique. Versailles [See Kuczinski, M. and Meek, R. (1972) *Quesnay's Tableau Économique*. London: Royal Economic Society].

Tugan-Baranowsky, Michael V. (1901) *Studien zur Theorie und Geschichte der Handelskrisen in England*. Jena: G. Fischer.
Yasuba, Yasukichi (1975) "Anatomy of the debate on Japanese capitalism." *The Journal of Japanese Studies*, 2(1), pp. 63–82.

Japanese

Arisawa Hiromi no Shōwa-shi Hensan Iinkai (1989) *Gakumon to Shisō to Ningen to* (Science, Thought and People). Tokyo: Tokyo Daigaku Shuppankai.
Fukuda Tokuzō (1921) "Shihon zōshoku no rihō to shihon-shugi no hōkai" (Logic of capital accumulation and collapse of capitalism). *Kaizō*, (October pp. 15–76 and November pp. 29–52).
Hidaka Hiroshi, Hayashi Takehisa, Sakurai Tsuyoshi, Furihata Setsuo, Suzuki Hiroshi (1967–1968) *Nihon no Marx Keizaigaku* (Marxian Economics in Japan). 2 vols. Tokyo: Aoki Shoten.
Ishidō Kiyotomo and Yamabe Kentarō eds. (1961) *COMINTERN, Nihon ni kansuru These-shū* (Collection of the Comintern's Theses on Japan). Tokyo: Aoki Shoten.
Ishiko Yasukuni (2008) *Rōnō-ha Marx-shugi*. 2 vols. Tokyo: Shakai Hyōron-sha.
———. (2014) *Marx wo Nihon de sodateta Hito: Hyōden Yamakawa Hitoshi* (The Man that Fed Marx in Japan: Biography Yamakawa Hitoshi). Tokyo: Shakai Hyōron-sha.
———. (2018) *Sakisaka Itsurō Hyōden* (Biography of Sakisaka Itsurō). Tokyo: Shakai Hyōron-sha.
Katayama Sen (1903) *Waga Shakaishugi* (My Socialism). Tokyo: Shakaishugi Tosho-bu.
Koizumi Shinzō (1922) "Rōdō kachi-setsu to heikin rijun no mondai" (The problem of the labor theory of value and average profit). *Kaizō* (February, pp. 43–63).
Kōtoku Shūsui (1903) *Shakaishugi Shinzui* (Essence of Socialism). Tokyo: Chōhō-sha.
Koyama Hirotake and Yamazaki Ryūji (2014) *Nihon Shihonshugi Ronsō-shi* (History of the Controversy on Japanese Capitalism). Tokyo: Kobushi Shobō.
Kushida Tamizō (1931) "Wagakuni kosaku-ryō no tokushitsu" (Special features of the land rent in Japan). *Ohara Shakai Mondai Kenkyū-sho* Zassi, 8(1), pp.63–103.
Moriya Fumio (1967) *Nihon Marx-shugi Riron no Keisei to Hatten* (Formation and Development of Marxian Theory in Japan). Tokyo: Aoki Shoten.
Nagaoka Shinkichi (1980) "*Nihon Shihonshugi Bunseki* no rekishi to ronri" (History and logic of the analysis of Japanese capitalism). *Keizaigaku Hihan*, 8, pp.32–46.
———. (1984) *Nihon Shihonshugi Ronsō no Gunzō* (Figures of the Controversy on Japanese Capitalism). Kyoto: Minerva Shobō.
Nishikawa Mitsujirō (1902) *Karl Marx*. Tokyo: Chūyō-dō.
N.N.N. (1949) "Shijō no riron to chidai hanchū no kiki" (Theory of market and the crisis of the category of rent). *Keizai Hyōron*. (March pp. 29–35, April pp. 43–49, and May pp. 35–40). Vo. 24 (2), pp. 1–19.
Ōshima Yūichi (1982) "*Nihon Shihonshugi Bunseki* no kiseki" (Path of the *Analysis of Japanese Capitalism*). *Tochi Seido Shigaku*, whole no. 94: 24(2), pp. 1–19.
Ōuchi Hideaki, Kamakura Takao, Hayashi Tekehisa, and Saeki Naomi (1979) *Uno Kōzō – Chosaku to Shisō* (Uno Kōzō: Works and Thoughts). Tokyo: Yūhikaku.
Sakisaka Itsurō (1935) "*Nihon Shihonshugi Bunseki* ni okeru hōhōron" (Methodology of *Analysis of Japanese Capitalism*). *Kaizō* (October), pp.65–83.
Terade Michio (2008) *Yamada Moritarō*. Tokyo: Nihon Keizai Hyōron-sha.
Uno, Kōzō (1935) "Shihonshugi no seiritsu to nōson bunkai no katei" (Foundation of capitalism and the dissolution process of rural society). *Chuō Kōron*, whole no.

576, vol. 50 (11), pp. 2–22. [Included in Uno Kōzō (1965)] *Zōho Nōgyō Mondai Joron* (Enlarged ed. Introduction to Agrarian Problems). Tokyo: Aoki Shoten.

———. (1970) *Shihonron 50 nen* (50 Years with Marx's *Capital*). Tokyo: Hosei Daigaku Shuppan-kyoku.

Yamada Moritarō (1925) "Kachi-ron ni okeru mujun to shiyō" (Contradiction and solution in the value theory). *Keizaigaku Ron-Shū*, 4(2), pp. 183–212 [YMCW 1].

———. (1932) *Saiseisan Katei Hyōshiki Bunseki Joron* (Introduction of the Analysis of the Scheme of Reproduction Process). Tokyo: Kaizō-sha. [YMCW 1].

———. (1934) *Nihon Shihonshugi Bunseki* (Analysis of Japanese Capitalism). Tokyo: Iwanami Shoten. [YMCW 2].

———. (1947) "Saiseisan hyōshiki to chidai hanchū" (Schema of reproduction and category of rent). *Jinbun* 1, pp. 2–42. [YMCW Sequel].

———. [YMCW] (1983–1985) *Yamada Moritarō Chosaku-shū* (Collected Works of Yamada Moritarō). 5+1 vols. Tokyo: Iwanami Shoten.

11

COLLABORATION AND REFORM UNDER WAR ECONOMY

Ryū Shintarō and Shibata Kei[1]

11.1 War Economy as the Challenge for Economists

The second decade of the Shōwa Era (1936–1945) was one of the most challenging ages for intellectuals and journalism in the history of Japan. As the late Taishō Era and early Shōwa Era were the heydays of scholars and journalism, the contrast is very conspicuous. In the early years of this decade, liberalists and leftists could openly discuss current events in Japan and the world in the media. However, left authors first retreated from the scene due to the series of repression, the 'Communist academy' incident (July 1936), 'popular front' incident (December 1937 and February 1938), and others. Then the figures of liberalist diminished also from the repression and attacks led by ultra-nationalists. The blank was filled preliminary by the policy lectures of bureaucrats and military officers. Entering the Pacific War (December 1941), journalism was pressed both by media control on the one hand and by the tightened distribution of paper on the other hand. Journals became thinner and thinner in 1941 and 1942, and at last, some journals were obliged to suspend.

Japan entered a full-scale war in July 1937 from the so-called China Incident.[2] However, after the Manchuria Incident in 1931, Japan headed toward militaristic expansionism under the growing dissatisfaction of the people. Even in these years of quasi-war and war age, those intellectuals who were not robbed of the space for their activity struggled to live, think, and act. They did so under the given situation, which meant their every move was related to the collaboration with the war in a certain sense. As is easy to see, making some general evaluation of the activities of intellectuals in these years is complicated. Without collaboration, even under its disguise, no resistance was possible. Some would discover the way of renovation of Japan during the critical years of the war. They would see in the challenge of the war economy the way to overcome capitalism, which they thought was the ground of imperialism that caused the war.

DOI: 10.4324/9781003081319-11

In this chapter, we will see the commitment of two economists, Ryū Shintarō (1900–1967)[3] and Shibata Kei (1902–1986),[4] to the economic reform during the war years.[5] Ryū was an editorial staff of the influential paper *Asahi Shimbun*, whose background was a Marxian economist of the Ohara Institute of Social Research. He joined Shōwa Kenkyū-kai (Shōwa Research Association) in 1938 and led its economic section. His *Nihon Keizai no Saihensei* (Reorganization of Japanese Economy), which appeared in December 1939, had wide repercussions. The following year, Ryū was sent to Europe by the *Asahi*, which anticipated his risk of arrest. Thus, he stayed in Berlin and then in Bern during the years of the Pacific War. Shibata Kei was the hope of modern equilibrium economics at Kyoto University. After his research abroad from 1936 to 1938, he returned to Japan with a will to rescue Japan. He devoted himself to the quest of 'communal totalitarianism' that should ground the New Order Economy. He published *Nihon Keizai Kakushin-an Taikō* (Outlines of the Reform of Japanese Economy) in October 1940 and volunteered for Premier Konoe's New Order Movement. He believed that the new order collaborative economy no longer dominated by the interest of capital could be the base on which the co-prosperity of Asian nations could be attained. Shibata made his policy proposal both in economic administration and the cease-fire in China. After the war, Shibata was purged by GHQ (General Headquarters of Supreme Commander of the Allied Powers) directly as an 'advocator of militarism and ultra-nationalism.' While Ryū, after his return to Japan, became an opinion leader of post-war democracy and pacifism as the chief editorial writer of the *Asahi*, Shibata had to live a bitter life till the cancellation of the purge.

One of the reasons that estranged Japanese researchers from the intellectual situations in war years is shown in this contrast between Ryū and Shibata after the war. Indeed, we can discern the difference between Ryū's and Shibata's concepts: Ryū's *Reorganization* stressed the autonomous control of management while Shibata's *Reform Plan* relied more on the power from the viewpoint of totality. However, we cannot draw such a clear line between the two as that divides critics and supporters of the war economy. One year's difference in their publication might be influential if the progress in politics wouldn't outstrip authors. The two were the same in their hope that non-capitalistic reform of the economy could open the way to save Japan and other Asian nations from the crisis.

11.2 Significance of the Sino-Japanese War in the World History

The outbreak of the Sino-Japanese War in July 1937 (the China Incident) profoundly affected the attitudes of Japanese intellectuals toward politics. Most of them were grown up in the liberal years called Taishō Democracy (1911–1925) and were more or less influenced by the dominant wave of Marxism in the first decade of the Shōwa Era (1926–1935). But most intellectuals shared dissatisfaction with the deprived with ultra-nationalists as they felt opposed to the existing systems. Though general suffrage was introduced in 1925, the strives of bourgeois parties and schisms in proletarian parties estranged the mass. The cooperative diplomatic policy represented by Shidehara Kijyūrō was conceived as a concession to the Western hegemony. Intellectuals in Japan naturally had sympathy for the new China that endeavored to recover China's national integrity. However, except for rare cases, Japanese scholars didn't show a definite attitude to Japan's vested interests in the China Continent, to say nothing of its overseas territories.

Manchuria Incident in September 1931 that the Kwantung Army executed without Tokyo's order shocked the Japanese. However, as the fire ceased in several months and the 'Manchukuo' gradually shaped its system, the people's anxiety about 'Manchukuo' seemed to be mitigated. The advance to Northeast China seemed to have opened a new horizon of various possibilities for the military, the government, and the mass Japanese.

The Army wanted to establish a great industrial base to supply provisions for Japan's next war. To economic bureaucrats, the 'Manchukuo' should guarantee the material base for the survival of Japan's economy in the world that tended toward the formation of bloc economies. A new industrial system that relied on planning and administrative control was introduced to build the economy's industrial base. Though the construction of the industrial base had not been completed when a fire at the Marco-Polo Bridge near Beijing (July 1937) opened the China Incident (the Second Sino-Japanese War), several bureaucrats and military officers brought their experience in 'Manchukuo' back to Japan in arranging the war mobilization system of Japan.

In the making of 'Manchukuo' by positioning the last Qing's Emperor Puyi as its Emperor, the cooperation of five ethnic groups - the Manchus, the Japanese, the Han Chinese, the Mongols, and the Koreans – was advocated by the slogan Gozoku Kyōwa (Five Races Under One Union).[6] When Japan extended military operations to Mongolia and Northern China, this idea of trans-racial cooperation developed into the 'Cooperative Community of East Asia' that legitimized the leading position of the Japanese over other Asian nations.

By 1937, Japanese intellectuals were caught in a dilemma between their convictions and national loyalty. The commitment to the war was necessary to exert any influence over public matters. One might save one's conscience by keeping silent, but to do so was tantamount to harboring a laissez-faire attitude toward the national fate. In addition, community control at the grassroots level made it virtually impossible for intellectuals to hide their convictions. Again, they were affected by the patriotic fervor during massive military inductions.

A leading philosopher Miki Kiyoshi (1897–1945)[7] wrote, "fortunately or unfortunately, matters have come to a head. In what direction to push them is the problem" (Miki 1938). He appealed to intellectuals to leave their studies and to change themselves to the men of action. He was a member of Shōwa Kenkyūkai (Shōwa Research Association),[8] which was duly recognized as the think tank of Prince Konoe Fumimaro.[9] He also assumed a responsible post in this Association by becoming the head of its cultural section. At about the same time, in the philosophical sphere, Miki formulated a doctrine of the Kōsōryoku (the logic of design), which was conceived to overcome the traditional dualism between idealism and materialism. Miki further believed that his method of resolving philosophical dilemmas could also be applied to Japan's domestic or international difficulties. He argued that the 'Western' principle of Gesellschaft (association based on instrumental interest) and the 'Asiatic' principle of Gemeinschaft (association based on communal ties) were antithetical principles that required synthesis in the form of Kyōdō-shugi (Cooperativism). Therefore, Miki concluded that joining such a cooperative order of Asian nations could circumvent 'the false and destructive dichotomy of communism vs. liberalism.'

In a lecture of 1938 (Sakai 1992: 161ff.) as well as in Booklet No.1 of the Shōwa Kenkyūkai, *Shin Nihon no Shisō Genri* (Basic Ideal Principles of New Japan), 1939, Miki asked whether the 'China Incident' could have any 'epoch-making significance in the world history.' He answered his question under two headings: 'The unification of East Asia' and 'The elimination of capitalism.' Although nowadays one tends to look at any Japanese intellectual who dares utter a phrase such as 'unification of East Asia,' Miki intended to tame fanatical Japanese nationalism. He maintained that the new order in East Asia must have a universal principle whereby the individual character of each component was promoted, and the nationalist fanaticism was avoided. Moreover, he insisted on institutionalizing a genuine guarantee so that Asian 'cooperation' should not become a mask of imperialism. Following regnant views of imperialism, Miki regarded capitalism as the economic basis for imperialism. Thus, he concluded that establishing a peaceful, cooperative order in Asia presupposed the domestic reform of Asia's leading nation, Japan, to the extent of eliminating the egoistic nature of capitalism. Consequently, if systematic domestic reform was successful, the war might give birth to the ideal Asian order, which would have a decisive impact on world history, one that had hitherto been Eurocentric.

11.3 Ryū Shintarō on the Reorganization of the Japanese Economy

At about the same time that Miki became a leading member of the Shōwa Research Association, Ryū Shintarō became the new head of its economic policy section. His predecessor, Takahashi Kamekichi (1894–1977), had advocated the reform of capitalism along the lines of the US's New Deal policy but was reluctant to eliminate the profit-oriented engine of the capitalist economy.[10] Compared with the self-made economist Takahashi who had grown up at the liberal weekly economic journal *Tōyō Keizai Shimpō*, Ryū's background was Marxian economics. After leaving the Tokyo University of Commerce in 1926, Ryū joined the Ohara Institute of Social Research and became known as one of the leading investigators of the problems of money and inflation. However, a few years before Ryū participated in the Shōwa Research Association, Ryū had to move to the editorial board of the *Asahi Shimbun* because of budget reductions at the Ohara Institute. As such, he changed his style from the detached stance of a Marxian critic to that of a realistic journalist who attentively looked for more favorable policy alternatives from the national point of view. Nevertheless, he continued to criticize the capitalist economic order.

He joined the Shōwa Kenkyūkai together with a few colleagues in the *Asahi* under the approval of its chief editor, Ogata Taketora. In this Association, Ryū assumed the responsibility for devising a policy that would lead to the 'Overcoming of Capitalism.' The collaboration of Miki and Ryū was shown in Booklet No.3 of Shōwa Research Association, *Economic Ethics of Cooperativism* (1940), written immediately after hearing Ryū's views on this connection.[11]

A year after the outbreak of the Sino-Japanese War, the Japanese government began to stress the urgent need to develop a sustainable wartime economy under the slogan of 'Long-term Construction.' Inspired by the idea of 'total war,' the military pressed the Diet to approve the National Mobilization Law, while the government organized a mass campaign called 'National Spiritual Mobilization Movement.' But nowhere was there to be found a systematic concept of wartime economy applied to Japan. Ryū's main task in the Shōwa Research Association was to fill this blank as the chief of its section for the 'Provisory Plan of the Reorganization of the Japanese Economy.'[12] Its popular version that was published under Ryū's name, *Nihon Keizai no Saihensei* (Reorganization of Japanese Economy) (Ryū 1939) became one of the bestsellers then.

Ryū quested for the reorganization that would make Japan's wartime economy compatible with the required accumulation of productive capital. Being familiar with the Marxian reproduction scheme, he recognized clearly that the only way out of the crisis of reduced reproduction was to build up the heavy industry to a high level as the basis for supplying weapons and capital goods. But this implies that it would be concomitantly necessary to reduce the nation's general level of consumption. To maintain national consensus under the stress of a difficult period of reorganization, profit inflation should be carefully avoided at the expense of the masses. Inflation would also make it difficult for Japan to balance the increasing import of raw materials and production equipment. The export industry needed to further replace its outmoded equipment to keep competitive in the world market.

Ryū maintained that the problem of wartime economy was not only one of properly organizing price control and distribution systems but also of increasing productivity and rationally reducing production costs. Accordingly, Ryū emphasized the need to develop a system of 'control from inside' whereby the producers would actively participate in rationalizing their production process. At the core of this proposal was the disclosure of corporate accounting, which would enable the control of profits and production costs. Together with limiting gains and eliminating monopoly control of technology, this public disclosure would change Japanese firms' character from 'profit-oriented' to 'production-oriented,' even though the basic ownership pattern would remain intact. A more significant proportion of profits would be retained by firms to reinvest in new productive capital. The everyday use of improved technologies in each industry would enhance quality and productivity. Further, Ryū's proposal for control of production involved the coordination of production capacity and actual production volumes in national planning, rationalizing work organization, and conserving and developing the workforce.

> New moving forces will naturally result from the subsequent extension of the control of the business. This is because the original purpose of economic activity will become transparent in tandem with eliminating the liberal attributes of a capitalist economy by controlling profit. That is to say, 'production' will be manifested in its pure form. Business management's national and social 'function' will take the pure form of productive activity. A new institutional structure emerges in which 'production' becomes the principle, and 'function' becomes the basis for industrial activity, albeit still within the framework of a capitalist economy. Accordingly, despite the control element, this kind of capitalist economy is unfettered because what we would now have would merely be a new institutional setting. In this setting, the entrepreneurial activity could develop adequately without coercion. In this sense, one can even say that this form of control is actually an autonomous control system. However, in another sense, the terms 'autonomous' and 'control' seem inappropriate because this institutional setting is a homeostatic system.
>
> *(RSCW 2: 638)*

Ryū's proposal for reorganizing the Japanese economy inspired several 'reform bureaucrats' to search for ideas conducive to implementing a controlled economy. They integrated such concepts as the separation of ownership and management, profit control, and public status of management into the New Economic Order of the Cabinet Planning Board (Kikaku-in) plan. However, in alliance with the traditional right, conservative business interests resisted the policy of the institutionalization of a controlled economy. The Shōwa Research Association was accused of covert pro-communist activity.[13] If Asahi had not sent Ryū to Europe in late 1940, he would have been arrested in April 1941, together with 'red' bureaucrats of the Cabinet Planning Board.[14]

11.4 Shibata Kei's Communal Totalitarianism

The task of Ryū and Miki was to formulate a historical justification for the controlled economy, which had been introduced pragmatically from the necessity of supplying the war. They maintained as follows:

> It would be incorrect to think that the former liberal economic order would be reconstituted after the termination of the war in China. *Au fond* it was historically necessary for the older economic order to evolve into

> the new economic system due to the former's internal contradictions. One should think that even the China Incident is based on this necessity and will promote this transformation.
>
> *(Shōwa Kenkyūkai 1941b: 119)*

Thus, unless a controlled economy were to be taken as a temporary expedient, 'it would need a fundamental principle to guide controllers toward proper ends and indicate the means to achieve these ends.' Such a regulating principle would manifest 'the internal structure of the controlled economy.' As mentioned, Miki (and Ryū) used the term 'cooperative economy' to refer to the controlled economy they envisaged. This type of economy 'stands for totality and is guided by the principle of public benefit.'

Miki's 'Cooperativism' demanded exposure to the 'internal unity of business and ethics.' Lest economic control degenerates into merely external coercion of business, ethics which works as 'an internal element of the economy' or one which works as 'an internal element of the economy' or one which in itself belongs to the 'logic of the economy,' would have to be developed. Its seemingly utopian character notwithstanding, he thought a system characterized by this unity was not only possible but also objective and necessary. For he believed it could come about as a consequence of a rational reorganization of the economy on the principle of 'production orientation.' By transforming the nature of the firm from 'profit-oriented' to 'production-oriented,' the consciousness of workers would have to be improved in that they would have a definite awareness of their 'function' in the social production system. Thus, according to Miki (and Ryū), the elimination of the dominance of the profit motives over the 'production principle' was the precondition for the rational reorganization of an economy that would make the efficient production (logic) and the social fairness (ethics) compatible. This line of thinking was further succeeded by the 'wartime productivity theory' among labor economists.[15] (Ōkouchi Kazuo and Kazahaya Yasoji)

Shibata Kei used the term 'Kyōdō-teki Zentai-shugi' (communal totalitarianism) to designate a similar concept of economic reform. He studied economics at Kyoto Imperial University, where Marxian economics taught by Kawakami Hajime first influenced him. Later he encountered Walrasian general equilibrium theory under the tutelage of Takata Yasuma, a Kawakami's rival. When J. A. Schumpeter visited Kyoto in 1931, he came to praise Shibata's eagerness in theoretical inquiry. Shibata's mathematical examination of Marx's theory, published in English in the *Kyoto University Economic Review* (Shibata 1933), stimulated Oskar Lange to write his famous article on the relationship between modern economics and Marxian economics (Lange 1935).

At the time of the outbreak of the war in China, Shibata found himself on tour as one of the last researchers abroad that Japan's Ministry of Education sent to Europe and the United States before World War II. Lange mistakenly took Shibata for a socialist and invited him to join the 'university of refugees.' which was to be established in New York. Shibata, who was a patriot, did not take this proposal seriously. However, on his way back to Japan to remain a loyal citizen of a nation that became criticized as the 'aggressor' by most Western nations, Shibata had to ponder the cause of the war and the policy to save his nation.

According to his autobiography, Shibata hit on the idea that 'monopolization in a capitalist economy' was at the root of the world crisis and concluded that "the only way to save Japan lies in the eliminating the system of monopolistic capitalism which engendered war profiteering and instead establishing an economic order in which every Japanese would be free to participate in dealing with the difficulties of the nation" (Shibata 1987: 78ff.).

At the end of 1939, Shibata wrote the draft of 'Outlines of a Reform for the Japanese Economy' (Shibata 1940). He urged his Reform Plan onto Prince Konoe, who was expected to embark on the nationwide New Order Movement then. The fundamental idea behind this plan was that capitalist firms were to be restructured as "semipublic corporations composed of persons as providers of the productive services." The owners of capital would be deprived of the power to place managers. Managers would not be evaluated by their capacity to generate profits for the owners but rather by their ability to provide industrial support to the nation. In Kyoto, Shibata organized a workshop for the New Order Movement. But its influence on business circles in the Kansai area was blocked by conservative politicians. After two years of activity, this workshop was dissolved due to the arrest of its core members. Shibata's New Order Movement, too, had been suspected of a disguised communist/socialist activity by the highly sensitive Tokkō (Special Higher Police).

According to Shibata's plan, each industry would set up a control organ to supervise constituent firms. The control organs would be vested with the power to hire and fire managerial personnel upon the recommendation of the supervisorial boards for individual firms. Owners of capital would be reimbursed by interest payment but were not allowed to exert any influence over management; Profits are to be allocated to workers as a whole, including management personnel, provided a National Board Audit approved such allocations. While the firms of each industry would be controlled horizontally by industry-wide control organs, it would also be the case that there would be coordination organs constituted at the local level. A reorganized central government would establish a United Ministry of the Economy.

Shibata supplemented his economic reform plan by drawing up a plan of reform for the political sphere. He advocated "a total, organic unification of the government and the nation" (Shibata 1940b: 75). This unified structure would go beyond any system of representative democracy. Compared with Ryū's stress on the initiative of business people, Shibata favored bureaucratic leadership. Indeed, this difference may have reflected the rapid shift of the situation between the conception of the two reform plans, Shibata's naïveté, even compared with Ryū, in not recognizing the evil consequences of the bureaucratic control of the economy cannot be denied.

In demanding 'an organic unification of the state and the nation,' Shibata did not recommend a party-driven type of totalitarianism such as Nazi Germany or Soviet Russia. He maintained that Japan already had a solid basis for spontaneous unification and advocated the mutation of bureaucrats and the government, which had thus far governed the people from above. This vision of political reform corresponded to the internal structure of Shibata's 'communal totalitarianism.' 'Communal totality' was neither the 'ensemble of atomized individuals' nor the collectivistic 'totality' that would deny individuality. The 'totality' would give life to the 'plurality' of distinct individuals constituting the whole (Shibata 1942: 12). Guided by a ghostly vision taken from the Kyoto School of Philosophy, Shibata was striving to produce the principle of organization which had to replace the individualistic one, based on the private property system. According to Shibata (1943a: 274), the economic aim of communal totalitarianism was "to maximize the production of real income for society as a whole," in contrast to capitalism, whose purpose was "to maximize the benefit accruing to a particular class." In this type of economy, the individualistic utilitarianism of a capitalist economy would be replaced by a conscious synthesis of totalitarianism and individualism. Shibata devoted his wartime investigation to establish the superiority of 'communal totalitarianism' to the capitalist economy.

Though Shibata was not successful in his campaign for the New Economic Order, he still conducted highly productive research during the war years. In *Fundamental Theory of Capitalism* (1941) which he published first in English as a private print, he rebutted Marx's arguments for the law of the falling rate of profit. He derived this tendency from the basis of the monopolization of capital. He further criticized J. M. Keynes too, to be blind to this primary cause of the instability of modern capitalism. In *Shin Keizai Ronri* (The New Logic of Economy) (1942), *Keizai Genron* (Principles of Economics) (1943a), and *Shin Keizai-gaku Hihan* (New Criticism on Economics) (1943b), Shibata would demonstrate the superiority of his 'communal totalitarian economy' to the capitalist economy.[16] Shibata argued that active intervention in determining factors prices (interest, rent, and wages) could produce a larger net social product than in a capitalist market economy.

> Suppose the elasticity of the supply of some productive factor (e. g., service of real capital) is zero and that of other factors (e. g., labor) is more significant than zero. In that case, the latter's supply should be increased by setting its factor price higher than its marginal productivity with the fund acquired by setting the factor price of the former under its marginal productivity. As long as the marginal productivity of the latter (in this case, labor) is not zero, the net produce as a whole would be thus increased. [...] Differences exist between elasticities of the supply of productive factors, [...] a similar result would be obtained.
>
> *(Shibata 1943a: 273)*

The Japanese economy then suffered from an absolute shortage of capital, while it kept a large reserve of labor in agriculture and small business sectors. This condition would reflect the contrast of a high level of enumeration to capital and a miserably low standard of wages. Based on Shibata's theory, one might recommend the policy of limiting the profit (or interest) accruing to capital owners while utilizing potential labor resources by setting the wage level higher than its market rate. However, the low elasticity of capital supply, the precondition of the application of Shibata's theory, in this case, would be guaranteed only by an introduction of effective control over capital which could prevent capital exodus or its influx to the speculative markets. Further, raising the real wage would be impossible to face the overall reduction of consumption under the pressure of the war; in other words, the conditions for the effective use of the controlled factor prices as posed by Shibata were missing under the actual economic situation of Japan then. The targets of wartime production were more directly achieved by direct conscription and mobilization of productive resources and whole working forces together with the profit remuneration as the complementary principle.

Shibata knew the so-called 'economic calculation debate' well. Shibata's quest for the superiority of the economy of 'communal totalitarianism' could be counted as an achievement in this genre. However, Shibata was unsatisfied with the static nature of this debate's literature and his work. The dynamic efficiency of communal totalitarianism depends on combining wartime enthusiasm with the rationally grounded activities of production and innovation. When Shibata turned his inquiry into the dynamics, his inquiry was interrupted by his induction into the military in the summer of 1944.

11.5 Productionism and Economic Man

In this closing section, we will attempt to answer the question about the nature of the legacy passed on to post-1945 Japanese economic thought from the war economy and the discussions on the economic reforms, including Ryū's and Shibata's in war years.

The first would be that the function and the ethics of the 'economic man' in the modern industrial society were discussed seriously. The 'egoism' of the economic man had been the 'original sin of economics,' which had annoyed such Japanese economists as Kawakami Hajime. Both Ryū and Shibata denied the validity of the concept of an egoistic economic man and correspondingly demanded the unification of economics and ethics. In contrast to Kawakami, who quested for pure altruism, both economists looked for an ideal economic man who would fulfill the task of developing productive forces, not the economic man who would seek monopoly profit, intermediary exploitation, or speculative gains. It was not coincidental that the academic interest in the so-called 'Adam Smith problem' was aroused amid wartime controlled economy.

In the post-war writings of both Ryū and Shibata, the categorical distinction between ethical, economic man and the egoistic economic man disappeared.

In his widely read *Mono no Mikata ni tsuite* (On Ways of Thinking) (1950), Ryū recommended the sensible British way of thinking, which would not separate thought and practice to the younger generation of Japanese. This naturally contained a revaluation of the Smithian concept of economic man upon which rational economic society would have to be based. Just two months after Japan's surrender, Shibata admitted that the Japanese had disregarded the peculiarly Western idea of 'public morality,' which was a consequence of Western liberal individualism. In denigrating this individualism and materialism, wartime Japan had forgotten the need for 'public morality', which guarantees mutual fairness on the part of citizens. In wartime Japan, under the surface, where only what claimed to be 'public' were allowed to emerge, the favoritism and the egoistic use of privileges diffused widely. As was the case of both Ryū and Shibata, it was upon reflections such as these that post-war Japanese social scientists developed the idea of 'modern economic man.'

Second, from the present viewpoint, attention should be directed to the significance of the 'new order of firms' in the wartime economy. It is now commonly recognized that integrating private firms into the wartime mobilization system promoted the separation of ownership and management of Japanese firms. In his discussion on Ryū's *Reorganization* in the *Chuō Kōron*, Tōbata Seiichi interpreted Ryū's concept of the function of production leaders by reference to Schumpeter's analysis of entrepreneurship. He argued that the task of the economic reform was nothing more than 'the greatest possible purification of the element of entrepreneurship' by reducing its capitalistic element (Ryū, Tōbata, et al. 1940). However, in the opposing camp were those who held the 'new bureaucrats' position and advocated state control of private firms. The reorganization of firms as public corporations or the idea of 'state control of private ownership' represented this position. The real wartime economy did not follow the path of free entrepreneurship but rather that of increasing bureaucratic control.

Ryū's idea of profit control and Shibata's concept of the "active determination of factor prices corresponded to the debate concerning the enforcement of article 11 (the limitation of dividend) of the National Mobilization Law in November 1938. Aided by the Ministry of Commerce and Industry and using both overt and covert means, business interests rolled back the penetration of 'progressive' ideas of 'Economic New Order' around the circle of the Cabinet Planning Board in implementing the controlled economy of wartime. Indeed, the Japanese wartime economy could not eliminate the profit engine of private enterprise" (Okazaki 1987). However, the control of funding under the mobilization system was constructed without severe opposition and became the basis for post-war Japan's controlled financial market system. The style and idea of economic control under the wartime economy were handed to the policy-makers during the period of economic recovery after 1945.[17]

The separation of ownership and management and intervention in determining the factor prices were introduced as elements of wartime economic mobilization. But they were also essential features of the post-war Japanese economy up to the age of high-speed economic growth. The 'production ethics' that had been imposed on both managers and workers of the wartime munitions industry were also carried over by both sides in the industrial relations in response to the demand for the promotion of production in the post-war economic recovery period.[18] Industrial and financial policy focused on the mobilization of resources for the promotion of production. In other words, both theory and praxis of economic reforms under the wartime economy served as preparation for the 'production-oriented' structure of the economic system of post-war Japan.[19]

Lastly, we will close this chapter by noting the strange negligence of the Asian dimension in the post-1945 reflections of Japanese intellectuals, as seen in both cases of Ryū and Shibata. The agenda of economic reforms during the war years of Japan was raised initially in combination with the solution to the ever-expanding military conflict in China and further with the desire for harmonic unification of Asian nations. However, in both cases of Ryū and Shibata, their conversion from 'cooperativism' and 'communal totalitarianism' occurred by their reassessment of Western sciences, ideas, and public morals, not from their concern over Asian nations that the Japanese Empire invaded.

Apart from the soldiers that returned from the battlefield in China, most Japanese believed that the massive attacks of US forces defeated Japan. However, even before the opening of the Pacific War, the failure of Japan's military operation in China was apparent. Why wouldn't the Japanese admit the plain fact that Japan was defeated because they were imperialistic invaders in other foreign countries? It would seem probable that this attitude stems from a combination of Eurocentrism (including American influence) and a peculiar view of the Second Sino-Japanese War that the true enemies of Japan should be the United States and Britain (and eventually also Soviet Russia) that steadfastly supported China. These two manifest a peculiar worldview of the Japanese that originated in the civilization/industrialization of Japan in the Meiji Era. According to this view, Japan was destined to be the leader of other Asian nations from its advanced position in the progress of civilization. In other words, the proper focus was not directed to Asia but to Western powers. The view that Japan was defeated by the science and rationalism of the Western civilization was only an atavistic resurrection of the forced opening of ports before the Meiji Restoration. This is self-deception that forgets the whole historical process of the modernization of Japan. Japan was defeated because it was an invader to neighboring nations.

Notes

1 This chapter is a revised version of my article on the same topic (Yagi 1997).
2 The war that broke out in July 1937 and continued to August 1945 had no official name in Japan because Japan did not declare war from the concern to maintain trade with the United States intact. It was simply called the China Incident and then joined into Daitōa Sensō (Greater East Asia War) in December 1941.
3 Ryū's Collected Works (RSCW) was published by Asahi Shimbunsha in 8 volumes (Ryū 1968–1969) together with recollections of him (Ebata ed. 1969).

4 See his autobiography (Shibata 2009) and new biography (Makino 2015b). On Shibata's position in the economic academism of Japan, see Negishi (1998).

5 Makino (2010) provides an overview of economics and economists in Japan during the war years. Yanagisawa (2008, 2015) investigated the economic policy discussions in Japan from 1930 to 1945 from their relations to German Nazism.

6 For the intellectual climate of 'Manchukuo' and its repercussions on mainland Japan, see Yamamuro (1995), and Kobayashi et al. (1995).

7 Miki started first as a disciple of Nishida Kitarō. Miki learned the hermeneutical approach similar to the early phase of Martin Heidegger in his study abroad and applied it first to Blaise Pascal and then to Karl Marx. His approach to Marxism in the late 1920s was interrupted by his arrest in 1930. After his expulsion from the Marxists group, Miki concentrated on creating his own philosophy of history. His engagement in wartime problems was grounded on his philosophy. See Yagi (2019).

8 Shōwa Kenkyūkai was organized first in 1933 as a private study circle surrounding Konoe Fumimaro by Konoe's schoolmate Gotō Ryūnosuke. When the expectation of Konoe's premiership rose in 1936, Shōwa Kenkyūkai moved to institutionalization and expansion. Miki was invited to join this Association on the ground of his journal article (Miki 1937), in which Miki stressed the need for the 'grounding idea' for the 'legitimation' of Japan's action. In 1938, it had over a dozen specialized research groups that covered almost all areas of policy issues. Though it had considerable influence on wartime reforms and New Order Movement, due to the attack from patriotic nationalists and the criticism from business circles, it dissolved in November 1940 by joining Taisei Yokusan-kai (Imperial Rule Assistance Association). See Shōwa Dōjinkai (1968), Sakai (1992), Fletcher III (1982), Makino (2015a).

9 Konoe Fumimaro (1891–1945) was the only politician who could maintain his position as a national leader during the war years (1935–1945). This position came from his lineage, Konoe, the family of the highest nobility. He formed his cabinet three times. In his first term as Prime Minister (June 1937–January 1939), his cabinet could not settle the military collision in July 1937, which gave way to the full-scale war. A year after his resignation, his expectations rose again, and Konoe himself advocated the mass movement (New Order Movement) to renovate Japan. In the second term of his cabinet (July 1940–July 1941), he concluded the alliance treaty with Germany and Italy. He established the wartime fascist state with a mass organization Taisei Yokusan-kai (Imperial Rule Assistance Association). In the third term (July 1941–October 1941), he would avoid the war against the US but could not prevent the army from adopting the 'southward' advance. Anticipating the war in the Pacific Ocean, he resigned in October 1941. Army General, Tōjō Hideki, succeeded him. See Makino (2015a), too.

10 Matsuura (1995) argues that Takahashi supported the position on economic policy maintained by Ikeda Shigeaki, the head of Mitsui concern, who served as the Minister of Finance in Konoe's first cabinet. Matsuura argues that Ikeda's policy reflected the willingness of big businesses to adapt to the conditions of a controlled wartime economy. Finally, Matsuura regarded Ryū as an opponent of Ikeda's policy from the left.

11 Intellectuals that participated in Shōwa Kenkyūkai had to fix their attitude toward Marxism before starting their quest for the 'ideological principle of New Japan.' Miki chaired the discussion on 'the materialistic view of history' and approved Ryū's negative judgment on it (Ryū 1967).

12 The first draft of this *Provisory Plan* was written by Arisawa Hiromi, a Marxian economist of the Rōnō-faction being tried then. Ryū managed the section of the Association, hearing from Arisawa on his draft to finalize the Association's *Provisory Plan* (Shōwa Kenkyūkai 1940). See Sakai 1992: 139.

13 Apart from the attack of the fanatical right, conservative business circles made the most of Yamamoto's anti-interventionist criticism of Ryū (Yamamoto 1941). As for

the debates around the Economic New Order, see Nakamura and Hara (1973) and Makino (2015a).

14 Chō interprets Ryū's transformation from a Marxian critic to the policy designer of the wartime nation rather sympathetically as being akin to going through "a mental purgatory which is not to be reduced to the invisible surrender to the militaristic pressure to journalism" (Chō 1994: 300), that is a process through which Ryū purified from the Marxian partisanship and acquired the style of national thinker. However, W. M. Fletcher (1982)'s judgment is very cool that he regarded Ryu as seeking prestige and influence since his move to the *Asahi*.

15 Ōkouchi Kazuo and Kazahaya Yasoji studied labor policies within Shōwa Research Association and advocated rationalizing labor relations and improving working conditions as the prerequisite of the production promotion pressed by the war.

16 Shibata's demonstration of the superiority of 'communal totalitarianism' was not successful mathematically. Negishi (2008) gave proof for it.

17 Noguchi (1995) maintained that the system of administration of the industry in Japan had its origin in the wartime-controlled economy and named it the '1941 Regime.' In a more academic style, see Okazaki and Okuno eds, (1993). On this issue, see further Gao (1997).

18 Production promotion policy during the war reached the bottom of the firm. To control the workforce, branches of Sangyō Hōkoku-kai (Industry Patriotic Movement) that covered most blue colors and clerks were organized in most factories and offices. The resurgence of labor unions in the post-war years emerged from the heritage of this wartime collaboration movement. See Gordon (1985: chap. 8).

19 The extensive mobilization of the wartime economy could not sustain itself under peaceful conditions. The transformation of the extensive mobilization to intensive mobilization was necessary to start the post-war economic growth. See also my sketch on this problem in Yagi (1995).

References

English

Fletcher III, Williams Miles (1982) *The Search for a New Order: Intellectuals and Fascism in Prewar Japan*. Chapel Hill: University of North Carolina Press.

Gao, Bay (1997) *Economic Ideology and Japanese Industrial Policy: Developmentalism from 1931 to 1965*. Cambridge and New York: Cambridge University Press.

Gordon, Andrew (1985) *The Evolution of Labor Relations in Japan: Heavy Industry*. Cambridge, MA: Harvard University Press.

Lange, Oskar (1935) "Marxian economics and modern economic theory." *Review of Economic Studies*, 2(3), pp. 189–201.

Makino, Kuniaki (2015a) "The New Konoe Order and reform bureaucrats." In Tsutsui Kiyotada ed. *Fifteen Lectures on Shōwa Japan: Road to the Pacific War in the Recent Historiography*. Tokyo: Japan Publishing Industry Foundation for Culture, pp. 217–235.

Negishi, Takashi (1998) "General equilibrium theory and beyond: Yasuma Takata and Kei Shibata." In Sugihara, Shiro, and Tanaka, Toshihiro eds., *Economic Thought and Modernization in Japan*. Cheltenham: Edward Elgar, pp. 97–116.

Shibata, Kei (1933) "Marx's analysis of capitalism and the general equilibrium theory of the Lausanne School." *Kyoto University Economic Review*, 8(1), pp. 107–136.

———. (1941) *Fundamental Theory of Capitalism*. Private print.

Yagi, Kiichiro (1997) "Economic reform plans in the Japanese wartime economy." In Ikeo Aiko ed. *Economic Development in Twentieth Century East Asia*. London and New York: Routledge, pp. 100–115.

———. (2019) "Quest for the consciousness of historicity by Kiyoshi Miki." *Revue de Philosophie Economique*, 20(1), pp. 159–174.

Yanagisawa, Osamu (2015) *European Reformism, Nazism and Traditionalism: Economic Thought in Imperial Japan, 1930–1945*. Frankfurt a.M.: Peter Lang.

Japanese

Chō Yukio (1994) *Shōwa Kyōkō* (Economic Crisis of Shōwa). Tokyo: Iwanami Shoten.

Ebata Kiyoshi ed. (1969) *Kaisō: Ryū Shintarō* (Ryū Shintarō in Recollections). Tokyo: Asahi Shimbun-sha.

Kobayashi Hideo, Okazaki Tetsuji, Yonekura Seiichirō, NHK Team (1995) *Nihon Kabushiki Gaisha no Shōwa-shi* (The Shōwa History of Japan Inc.). Tokyo: Sōgensha.

Makino Kuniaki (2010) *Senji-ka no Keizai Gakusha* (Economists under the War). Tokyo: Chuō Kōron Shin-sha.

———. (2015b) *Hyōden Shibata Kei* (Biography Shibata Kei). Tokyo: Nihon Keizai Hyōron-sha.

Matsuura Masataka (1995) *Ni'chū Sensō-ki ni okeru Keizai to Seiji* (Economy and Politics during the Sino-Japanese War). Tokyo: Tokyo Daigaku Shuppankai.

Miki Kiyoshi (1937) "Nihon no genjitsu" (Reality of Japan). *Chuō Kōron*, 52(12), pp. 4–20.

———. (1938) "Chishiki-kaikyū ni atau" (To the intellectuals). *Chuō Kōron*, 53(6), pp. 52–56.

———. [MKCW] (1966–1986) *Miki Kiyoshi Zenshū* (Miki Kiyoshi Collected Works). 20 vols. Tokyo: Iwanami Shoten.

Nakamura Takafusa and Hara Akira (1972) "Keizai shin-taisei" (New Economic Order). *Nempō Seijii-gaku*, 23, pp. 71–133.

Negishi Takashi (2008) "Shibata Kei hakushi to shin keizai ronri" (Dr. Kei Shibata and his economics of planning). *Nihon Gakushi-in Kiyō*, 63(3), pp. 197–213.

Noguchi Yukio (1995) *1940 nen Taisei* (1940 Regime). Tokyo: Tōyō Keizai Shimpō-sha.

Okazaki Tetsuji (1987) "Senji keikaku keizai to kakaku tōsei" (Wartime planned economy and price control). *Nenpō Nihon Kindai Kenkyū*, 9, pp. 175–198.

Okazaki Tetsuji and Okuno Masahiro eds. (1993) *Gendai Nihon Keizai System no Genryū* (Origins of Modern Japanese Economic System), Tokyo: Nihon Keizai Shimbun-sha.

Ryū Shintarō (1939) *Nihon Keizai no Sai-hensei* (Reorganization of Japanese Economy). Tokyo: Chūō kōron-sha. (Included in RSCW vol. 2 (1969)).

———. (1967) "Zunō to jōnetsu no hito" (Man of brain and enthusiasm). In Geppō attached to [MKCW 3].

———. [RSCW] (1968–1969) *Ryū Shintarō Zenshū* (Collected Works Ryū Shintarō). 8 vol. Tokyo: Asahi Shimbun-sha.

Ryū Shintarō, Tōbata Seiichi, Nagata Kiyoshi, Kishimoto Seijirō, Tsurushima Mizuo, Yamamoto Masao. (1940) "*Nihon Keizai no Sai-hensei* tōron-kai" (Discussion on Reorganization of Japanese Economy). *Chuō Kōron* 55(5), pp. 226–255.

Sakai Saburō (1992) *Shōwa Kenkyū-kai* (Shōwa Research Association), original ed., 1979. Tokyo: Chuō Kōron-sha.

Shibata Kei (1940) *Nihon Keizai Kakushin-an Taikō*, 2nd ed. (Outlines of a Reform Plan for Japanese Economy). Tokyo: Yūhikaku.

———. (1942) *Shin Keizai Ronri* (New Logic of the Economy). Tokyo: Kōbun-do.

———. (1943a) *Keizai Genron* (Principles of Economy). Tokyo: Kōbun-dō.

———. (1943b) *Shin Keizaigaku Hihan* (New Economic Criticism). Tokyo: Yamaguchi Shoten.

———. (1987) *Zōho Keizai no Hōsoku wo motomete* (In Search for the Laws of Economy, enlarged ed.). Tokyo: Nihon Keizai Hyōron-sha.

Shōwa Dōjin-kai ed. (1968) *Shōwa Kenkyūkai*. Tokyo: Keizai Ōrai-sha.

Shōwa Kenkyūkai (1940) *Nihon Keizai Saihensei Shian* (Provisory Plan of the Reorganization of Japanese Economy). Tokyo: Shōwa Kenkyūkai.

———. (1941a) *Shin Nihon no Shisō Genri*, Gappon-ban (Ideological Principles of New Japan, enlarged. ed.). Tokyo: Seikatsu-sha.

———. (1941b) *Kyōdō-shugi no Keizai Rinri*, Gappon-ban (Economic Ethics of Cooperativism, enlarged ed.) Tokyo: Seikatsu-sha.

Yagi Kiichirō (1995) "Seido no keizai-gaku to dōin-gata keizai" (Institutional economics and mobilization-type economy). *Hikaku Keizai Taisei Kenkyū*, 2, pp. 25–44.

Yamamoto Katsuichi (1941) *Ryū Shintarō "Nihon Keizai no Saihensei" Hihan* (Criticism on Ryū Shintarō's Reorganization of Japanese Economy). Tokyo: Genri Nihon Sha.

Yamamuro Shin'ichi (2004) *Chimera: Manshukoku no Shōzō*, Zōho-ban (Chimera: Portrait of Manchukuo, enlarged ed.). Tokyo: Chuō Kōron Shin-sha.

Yanagisawa Osamu (2008) *Senzen Senji Nihon no Keizai Shisō to Nazism* (Japanese Economic Thoughts in pre-war and war years Japan and Nazism). Tokyo: Iwanami Shoten.

12

EPILOGUE

Revolving Door for Economists 1945–1950

12.1 Variety of the August 15

On August 15, 1945, Emperor Hirohito told the nation the acceptance of the Potsdam Declaration by broadcasting his recorded relict. [1]

Yanagita Kunio lived in Tokyo, making his family evacuate. From the previous year, while trying charcoal making using garden trees expecting its coming necessities, he began to realize his post-war task from the request of writing a textbook on the rural life for the evacuated pupil. He had anticipated Japan's surrender on the information from his friend a few days ago and roused himself for the post-war work. His diary on August 15 recorded simply: "At noon the Imperial Relict announced. Could not refrain excitement. Got cold in the afternoon. Temperature 38.2°C" (YKCW Suppl. V. 4: 237).

He imposed on him and his learning (Minzoku-gaku: folklore studies): "At this very time, we must conceive a new social organization sufficiently reliable that should never become the sacrifice under the reactionaries once more, and that suit well to the nature of the folk" (YKCW 10: 4). He added a new Preface to the manuscript of *Senzo no Hanashi* (Stories of Ancestors)[2] that he had completed at the end of May and published as his first book after the War. He maintained that the *Ie* community that consists of the communicative relations between ancestors and descendants could form the sound base of cooperation in the countryside and the nation. In this explanation, he implicitly criticized the state cult for war heroes and the patriarchal family system founded by the Meiji state.

Kawakami Hajime, that had been released from prison in June 1937, lived in Kyoto. Despite the cease of the long-continued probation in February 1944, his condition was rapidly declining. Still, as soon as he received the notice of the Emperor's broadcast, he correctly foresaw in the conversation with his wife that

DOI: 10.4324/9781003081319-12

it should be that of surrender. On September 1, he could acquire the vigor to take his pen and write an essay with the title "Shōkoku Kamin" (A small country with a small population), whose phrase had its origin in Laozi.

> With the goal of a large country with a large population and a prosperous nation with strong forces, Japan has so far pushed forward the path of militarism and invasion. As it failed in the large-scale gambling of the great, Japan will sign the treaty of unconditional surrender with the Allied Nations of United States, Britain, USSR, China, and others on September 2, tomorrow. All the people are in the mid of grieving, chagrining, regretting, and enraged by the defeat. Soon, as details of the capitulation become known step by step, their resentment will be heightened more and more. However, I think the Japanese people would become happier if the Japanese could recognize the significance of Laozi's teaching in a small country with a small population on this occasion. Generally, those states that use military forces to conquer foreign people exert a violent and militaristic suppression domestically over the nation (and subordinated classes). Those that acquire benefits from the invasion are limited to a small circle of the ruling and powered class, while the ordinary people were obliged to receive only the remainder. They experienced suffocation under oppressive rule for over a hundred years. They couldn't be happy. Now from the defeat of the war, Japan is obliged to abandon the aggressive invasion policy, while the nation's freedom is expanding rapidly. It is very fortunate. If we could take one step further and move into a Soviet organization widely in a few years, we could recover the living standard of the prewar years in several years. After that, the general people's welfare would continue to rise rapidly.
>
> *(KHCW Seq. 4: 431f.)*

These sentences tell us that Kawakami reached the position on the opposite end of his starting point of moralistic nationalism in the last days of his life. It is now easy to laugh at him because of his naïve admiration for the Soviet Union and its leader. However, irrespectively to the difference in the evaluation of Kawakami's recognition, it is worth memorizing him in awe in respect to holding his conviction under repression for over a dozen years.

Ishibashi Tanzan listened to the imperial relict in Yokota, Akita Pref., where the whole Toyo Keizai Shimpo-sha evacuated. He explained the policies of the allied forces to a group surrounding him and recommended they engage themselves in ordinary works. On the next day, he wrote the editorial "The start of Japan's rehabilitation: A bright future" and added the next August 25 issue of the *Tōyō Keizai Shimpō*, which was just before its final proofreading.

> When the news of the Soviet Union's declaration of war against Japan on August 8 was reported in Tokyo on the following day without modification, the editor believed the war's end was very close. … However, despite

> this belief, the editor still had anxiety……… Fortunately, however, this anxiety was groundless. Japan differed from Germany in its constitution fundamentally. Awfully the decision of the highest calmed every dispute and closed the war. August 14, Showa 20, was the starting day of the new Japan for all the Japanese nation to celebrate eternally.
>
> *(ITCW 13: 3f.)*

In the series of nine editorials, *Tōyō Keizai Shimpō* argued the basic viewpoint after the surrender: The purpose of the allied forces consisted in the democratization of Japan; the reduction of the territory was not disadvantageous; the industrial reconstruction was possible; the critical factor of the economic reconstruction lay in the development of human intelligence. The defeat gave the chance to realize the years-long opinion of the *Tōyō Keizai Shimpō*, Small Japanism. Ishibashi himself intimately wrote on August 18 in his diary: "Thinking it from today, in a sense, I have fought against the vices in Japan together with the US and Britain. This is the reason why this defeat did not cause sorrows to me" (Ishibashi 1974: 47).

Ryū Shintarō received the news of Japan's surrender in Bern. In vain, he had participated in the secret peace operation with diplomats in Switzerland. The belayed final acceptance of the Potsdam Declaration had so irritated him that he had thought to send the recommendation of surrender to Japan via journalist telegram. On the post-war government, he thought: "it would not go so far (Prime Minister Ōyama Ikuo). But Minister of Finance Ōuchi Hyōe is possible."[3] This forecasting was near to reality when we consider that Yoshida Shigeru requested Ōuchi to assume this position in his first cabinet in May 1946 or that this cabinet was replaced by the coalition under the socialist Prime Minister Katayama Tetsu in the next year. However, due to the difficulty for journalists of the defeated nation to acquire the returning route, he could not observe the post-war politics with his own eyes.

As we mentioned in Chapter 8, Yamada Moritarō, who had participated in the comparative study of Asian agriculture under a government-affiliated institute, was invited to the Ministry of Foreign Affairs special committee. Then, he became the advisory councilor of the Ministry of Agriculture, performing the land reform.

Takano Iwasaburō and other members of the Ohara Institute of Social Research were in Tokyo since it moved to Tokyo in March 1937. Though the Institute managed to survive without a patron during the war years, the office and library were burnt down by the air raid. The reconstruction of the Institute accompanied heavy obstacles, whose solution was only attained later in 1949 to become an institute of Hosei University. On the other hand, the activities of its members under the tide of democratization were remarkable. Takano appealed for the resurgence of a socialist party with Abe Isoo and Kagawa Toyohiko and drafted his version of the democratic constitution of Japan.[4]

Shibata Kei was at the Tokyo office of the Ministry of Munition after his several months' stay in Shanghai and Nanjing as a conscripted accountant officer. The official reason for his return to Japan's mainland was to nationalize a private airplane maker; in reality, he was involved in designing a partial withdrawal plan of troops from China. He listened to the radios from Sidney and Honolulu on August 11th or 12th and "couldn't sleep in that night due to thousands of emotions in the heart" (Shibata 2009: 94). Demobilized Shibata returned to Kyoto University and wrote an essay titled "My view on the Causes of the Defeat."[5] He attributed the ultimate reason for Japan's defeat to the prevailing underestimation of the individualistic liberalism of the West. In his view, it missed the existence of rationalism and public morals at the core. Thus, Shibata admitted the defeat of his communal totalitarianism.

12.2 Reshuffling in Academism

The previous ruling system was still working for several weeks immediately after August 15. Contrary to releasing political prisoners, it strengthened the public control to suppress the uprisings of Koreans and communists using the confusion accompanied by the surrender. The Direction of Education for the Construction of New Japan that the Ministry of Education distributed on September 15 still lined up the preservation of the fundamental constitution of the state together with the construction of a peaceful state and the promotion of the scientific spirit.[6] In this stage, the government and the ruling elites of Japan believed that the previous control and education system could serve the allied forces under the hegemony of capitalist countries (the United States and Britain), so far as this system discharged the elements of militarism.

Allied forces began the occupation at the end of August. After the signing of the treaty of surrender on the battleship Missouri, the United States decided to rule Japan by her hand solely. When GHQ (General Headquarters, the Supreme Commander for the Allied Powers) ordered the Japanese Government to release political prisoners, abolish of thought police, and permit free discussion on the Emperor system, the cabinet that Kuninomiya, an Emperor's family, headed, collapsed to be replaced by a new cabinet headed by a pro-US and Britain diplomat Shidehara Kijyūrō. GHQ ordered Shidehara on October 11 further the liberation of women, promotion of unionization, liberalization of school education, the prohibition of the secret civil procedures, and the five basic policies for the democratization of the economy. The preparation for the dissolution of the concerns (Zaibatsu Kaitai) and the land reform began.

As the firm will of GHQ to start the democratization of Japanese society became clear, responses emerged soon. Presidents and deans of most universities and faculties resigned, and most of the research centers and academic chairs that had been created or enriched during the war years were reorganized or renamed if they were not abolished. At the same time, a general move appeared to pursue the responsibility of the collaboration in war.

Takano's contribution to the November 11 issue of the *Teikoku Daigaku Shimbun* (Paper of Imperial University) "Gakunai Seisō no Dankō wo Nozomu – Tokyo Teikoku Daigaku no Sasshin Saiken no Hōkō" (Wishing the Cleaning of the University – Direction of the Renovation/ Reconstruction of the Imperial University of Tokyo)[7] canalized the critical opinions in academism, whose impact was beyond the range of Tokyo University. In this article, Takano lined up the topics of the abolition of the name of 'Imperial University,' revision of the University Ordinance, open-door for women, encouragement of the democratic spirit of students, promotion of international scientific activity, course of the history of social thoughts, promotion of competitive lecture courses, open-access to university lectures, and so on. He demanded further the return of the purged professors and elimination of the militarists and war collaborators by founding a special investigation committee. The new dean of the Economics Faculty of Tokyo University, Maiide Chōgorō, declared his will to follow the directives of GHQ loyally. He visited Ōuchi Hyōe soon after his inauguration and showed Ōuchi the reshuffling plan, according to which seven professors should return while six should leave.[8] Maiide realized this reshuffling plan with a milder form of voluntary leaves and transfers to other universities in the case of the purging. This reshuffling was the starting point of the reconstructed economics faculty of the University of Tokyo.

Opening the course of the history of social thought as a standard course and providing students with the knowledge of social problems and socialism, and further encouraging students' participation in labor movements, social and educational woks were typically proposals that Takano, a social-liberal, likely to recommend. After ten days, the same campus paper printed another contribution that was quite different from Takano's: Yasui Takuma "Gakumon Suijun no Rakusa wo Umeyo – Keizaigaku no Shin-Dōkō ni tsuite" (Erase the Distance in the Scientific Standard – On new trends of economics).

As Yasui saw it, even after the retreat of Marxism, "Japanese economics could not advance in its due course and continued fruitless rotation and stagnation." "Since the outbreak of the Sino-Japanese war, under the dominance of patriotism and the war economy, the understanding and the interest in the advancing modern economics gradually diminished. What emerged instead as the mainstream of the academism, or at least its vogue, were a variety of political economies, Gottl [F. Gottl-Ottlilienfeld] 's economy, Japanese economics and so on. … If economics should be caught by such impressive but superficial changes and be engaged in a philosophy-like idealism, in most cases, it showed the decadency of economics. Much more in such cases that this idealism could bring forth neither 'light' nor 'fruit' to the reality and only follow the surface with various flags, we must conclude that this is the death of economics" (Yasui 1979: 170).

What Yasui proposed was not limited to acquiring the core of the 'mainstream of modern economics with its center of the equilibrium theory.'[9] He raised two further suggestions; one was to learn from American institutionalism's sociological, statistical, and inductive attitude. Another was raising the level of academic interaction with Marxian economics concerning the reappraisal of Marxian theory by modern economists such as O. Lange, W. Leontief, and J. Robinson. These seem to be valuable advice from today's eye. However, as for the second, most Marxian economists, whose number increased considerably, did not follow it. Because most of them were dazzled by the illusion of post-war democratic revolution and were caught by the holy trinity of Marx, Lenin, and Stalin. The interaction between modern economics and Marxian economics was tried by such economists as Tsuru Shigeto and Sugimoto Eiichi, usually considered to belong to the camp of modern economics.

After the first purge of the officials of the police department and of the Ministry of Interiors and those of the Special Higher Police (Tokkō Purge) in early October 1945, GHQ ordered the purge in the education sector. GHQ issued the first directive on education reform on October 22 and suggested the principle to eliminate 'exponents of militarism and ultranationalism' and return those who had been expelled due to liberal or anti-military ideas. The second educational directive showed the concrete procedure of the eligibility investigation of the educational staff. Japanese government brought it into legislation (Imperial Edict No. 263) in May 1946. Following this legislation, the eligibility investigation of teachers started at every educational institution in Japan, from elementary schools to universities, and ca. 7,000 teachers were purged (Yamamoto 1994).

GHQ issued the directive for a general public purge on January 4, 1946. Its list of those 'unfavorable persons' to be expelled contained the item of 'those other militarists and ultranationalists,' in addition to those whose involvement in the war was objectively certified. This item (item G) covered those journalists and authors, including economists, whose writings advocated militaristic nationalism and supported the invasion. This item of judging the opinion *per se* was absent in the denazification in post-war Germany. In the case of the occupation of Japan, this item was added to give flexibility in the application's range of the purge for the allied forces' convenience (Masuda 1998: 50). The typical case in which this term was used for political reasons was Ishibashi's purge by GHQ in the mid of his work as the Finance Minister of the Yoshida Shigeru's cabinet in May 1947.

The eligibility examination in universities was nearly completed at the end of 1946. Though the number of those judged ineligible in total, 86 persons, seems relatively small. However, cases of direct nomination by GHQ, such as Shibata's case, also existed. Further, those dismissed without investigation due to their career as military officers or policemen amounted to 326. In addition, many teachers chose early retirement to evade the investigation. Thus, the effect of this purge on post-1945 academism was not negligible.

Let's see the case of Kyoto University. The voice of pursuing the attitude of the Economics Faculty emerged first at the vigil of Kawakami, who died on January 30, 1946. The growing critical voice made the Faculty hold a special meeting on February 19 in which full professors, associate professors, and lecturers had an equal say. At this meeting, the Faculty decided to show its 'general repentance' by submitting all teachers' resignations to the new dean Prof. Shizuta Hitoshi.

Out of the collected resignations Shizuta sent those of six professors (Kojima Shōtarō, Shiomi Saburō, Taniguchi Yoshihiko, Ninagawa Torazō, Shibata Kei, Nakagawa Yonosuke) and made them leave. Though remaining were expected to work on the reconstruction of the Faculty, one associate professor, one lecturer, and two assistants left Kyoto University without recalling their resignations.[10]

This so-called total resignation was only a prelude. GHQ, eagerly searching for the ideologues that legitimized the war, focused its attention on the activity of scholars of Kyoto University (so-called Kyoto School) and began the investigation of nine professors. Not only three philosophers – Takayama Iwao, Kōsaka Masaaki, Suzuki Shigetaka – six economics professors – Ishikawa Kōji, Matsuoka Kōji, Nakagawa Yonosuke, Ninagawa Torazō, Shibata Kei, Taniguchi Yoshihiko – were on the target. Of the latter, Ishikawa, on May 2, Shibata and Taniguchi, on May 15, were dismissed as 'active advocators of militarism and ultranationalism' directly by GHQ (Memorandum cases of SCAPIN).[11] Later, Nakagawa's dismissal on the same charge and Matsuoka's on his capacity as an army officer followed. Prof. Tokunaga Kiyoyuki was also dismissed on his part-time service to military police. Further, Sakuta Sōichi, Shibata's mentor that had served Kenkoku Daigaku in 'Manchu-kuo' as its president, was also purged.

Including newcomers, those that underwent the eligibility screening at Economics Faculty were 20. Out of them, Ōtsuka Ichirō and Takata Yasuma were judged illegible in November 1946. As the Faculty organized the screening committee, they were judged illegible by their colleagues.[12] As we wrote in Chapter 9, Takata had to wait for the denial of this verdict till June 1951, when the then Minister of Education denied this verdict. At last, the remained professors were only three: Shizuta, Horie Yasuzō, and Hozumi Fumio. For the reconstruction, Economics Faculty promoted three associate professors (Aoyama Hideo, Nakatani Minoru, and Sawa Senpei) to full professors and invited Kishimoto Seijirō and Toyosaki Minroru to maintain the list of full professors. A similar scale reshuffling occurred at the Osaka University of Commerce (later Osaka City University), where a large-scale suppression covering teachers and students occurred from 1943 to 1945. Here, too, the post-war reconstruction started with the unanimous resignation of professors.

12.3 Participation in Post-war Economic Reform

Participation of economists in the post-war economic reform began with a committee named Nihon Hondo Jikatsu Hōsaku Kenkyūkai (Research Committee of the Provision of Necessities of Japan Mainland). The Ministry of Greater East Asia organized it just before the surrender. Its first meeting was held on August 16, 1945, under the changed name Sengo Mondai Kenkyūkai (Research Committee of Postwar Problems) and was transferred to the Ministry of Foreign Affairs in November. This committee organized a subcommittee that aimed at a "theoretical understanding of Japanese economy from the viewpoint of diplomatic relations in the new postwar situations and the basic economic policies grounded on the former." It gathered economists widely whose contribution to the post-war economic policy-making was expected. It contained not only Arisawa Hiromi, Tōbata Seiichi, and Nakayama Ichirō. They were later called 'the trio' of the post-war advisors on economic policies and Marxian economists such as Uno Kōzō and Yamada Moritarō. After several months of discussion, this committee was dissolved with its publication *Nihon Keizai Saiken no Kihon-mondai* (Basic Problems of the Reconstruction of Japanese Economy)[13] in March 1946. In Chapter 9, we saw already that Yamada further participated in the land reform as a council and committee member collaborating with the Ministry of Agriculture.

A substantial commitment to policy-making began with the first Yoshida's Cabinet in May 1946. Yoshida Shigeru had the fortune to assume Prime Minister thanks to the purge of Hatoyama Ichirō, the head of Jiyū-tō (Liberal Party), which acquired the most significant mandate in the first general election, would invite several scholars into his cabinet. He would have Ōuchi Hyōe as Minister of Finance, Tōbata Seiich as Minister of Agriculture, and Arisawa Hiromi as the Director of the Headquarters for Economic Stabilization (HES). Although this plan failed due to the refusal of the three, weekly lunch meetings around Yoshida were held at the Ministry of Foreign Affairs, whose Minister too Yoshida assumed. In addition to the named three, other scholars and experts joined this meeting, to which the Minister of Agriculture Wada Hiroo[14] served as the secretary, and Ōkita Saburō worked on recording the discussion. At this lunch meeting, Arisawa talked about his plan for the recovery of the Japanese economy by prioritizing coal and steel production for the first time. After this presentation, Arisawa accepted the request to assume the head of the special committee on coal production, which served Yoshida privately.

On the other hand, in this first Yoshida cabinet, Ishibashi served as its Finance Minister on Hatoyama's recommendation. Ishibashi believed that his new liberalism that introduced Keynesian policies was effective in the post-war economic reconstruction of Japan. Ishibashi pushed forward an active fiscal policy that promoted production recovery by using Fukkō Kinyū Kinko (Reconstruction Finance Corporation) and subventions for the price difference replenishment. He was convinced that the fiscal injection would not cause inflation so far as the economy had the unemployed productive resources. Yoshida sympathized with Ishibashi in respect of the conviction of liberalism. However, Ishibashi became a burden to him when Ishibashi entered into a conflict with GHQ on the halt of the war repartition and the expenditure for the occupation. Besides Yoshida's suspicion of the rapid growth of Ishibashi's influence in the Liberal Party, Ishibashi was in the power structure then surrounded by the antipathy of left New Dealers in GHQ and interventionist scholars attending the Yoshida's lunch meeting. At the level of mass politics, though Ishibashi's stubborn attitude to various demands of GHQ acquired some popularity on the one hand, under the post-war inflation and the scarcity of necessaries, it was difficult for Ishibashi to reject the image of 'inflationist' on the side of big business. GHQ that aimed to eliminate Ishibashi intentionally modified the criteria of the purge of journalists and enforced his purge against all objections of the investigation committee of the Japanese side on May 16, 1947. Yoshida did not act against this purge of his Finance Minister.[15]

When the three parties' coalition – Shakai tō (Socialist Party), Minshu-tō (Democratic Party), Kokumin Kyōdo-tō (National Cooperation Party) – cabinet formed under Katayama Tetsu, a Christian socialist, started in June 1947, the primary responsibility of economic policies was transferred to HES. HES was a provisory office that was created to cope with the economic crisis with the mighty support of GHQ. In the area of economic policies, its authority excelled over that of other ministries. Further, it had autonomy in its personnel recruitment without the government's intervention. In the period of the first Yoshida Cabinet, HES did not start its substantial activity. The Katayama Cabinet allowed HES to work on a full-scale by appointing ex-Minister of Agriculture Wada, that had performed the agrarian land reform. Among economists that supported Wada, Tsuru Shigeto (Subchief of the general coordination committee), that had studied at Harvard University, and Inaba Hidezō (vice chief secretary), that had experienced imprisonment by the Kikakuin (Planning Board) incident, were conspicuous.

Soon after its start, Katayama Cabinet determined the Emergent Economic Program and asked the nation for 'endurance, collaboration, and efforts with blood and sweat.' The Program covered the securing of food and other necessities for the rationing, stability of prices and wages, promotion of coal production, sound fiscal budget, financing with priority, employment and other labor policies, export promotion, to guidelines for small- and medium-sized firms including the formation of cooperatives. In July, the first *Keizai Jissō Hōkokusho* (White Paper on Real Situation of Economy), whose principal author was Tsuru, was published. In this white paper, the government explained the present economic conditions and policies to the citizen for the first time, beginning with the reality that all the three sectors of a national economy, government, private firms, and households, were in deficit. This white paper applied the frame of national accounting and described the critical situation of the national economy in plain words. It further quested for a way of the departure from it. In conclusion, it appealed to establish the "system that makes it possible for the people to increase the fruit of their industry and ensures them to use it to enrich their well-being" (Keizai Antei Honbu 1947: 7). In economic policies, HES succeeded not only the priority production but also stressed: "the elimination of the black profit based on the monopoly in distribution" (ibid.). Without this elimination, wages and prices couldn't attain the situation in which all the working nations could be in accord. In other words, the first white paper wished to construct an economic system grounded on the nation's industry, avoiding profit inflation.

While Tsuru's viewpoint focused on the consensus-building on the base of the working nation, that of Inaba, who had worked on a plan of mobilization of materials in the Kikakuin, centered on the supply of goods by production promotion policies. He adopted Arisawa's proposal of priority production and worked for its substantiation in the HES. Miyazaki Yoshikazu, who reviewed the economic thoughts of HES, saw the cohabitation of two views; the one that "prioritized the equilibrium of prices and wages by the elimination of black profits" and then another that "prioritized the equilibrium of production and consumption by way of priority production" (Miyazaki 1971: 343). This constellation reminds us of the relation between Ryū's plan for the reorganization of the Japanese economy, focusing on the control of profit by making the firm's accounting open, and the attitude of Kikakuin's bureaucrats that received Ryu's proposal of the reorganization in the frame of the controlled economy from above and conceived the New Order Economy.

The collapse of the Katayama Cabinet in March 1948 occurred from a disaccord in the cabinet about financing the subvention to the public servants. GHQ rejected HES's plan that considered the position of the left-wing Socialist and adopted the Ministry of Finance's plan that implied the hike of passenger fares, which offended the consensus of the Socialist Party. The new Prime Minister Ashida Hitoshi (Minshu-tō) made the Minister of Finance Kurusu Takeo take the direction of HES additionally, against the will of HES. From this process, Tsuru judged that the future of HES was lost. He resigned from HES and moved to the Institute of Economic Research, Hitotsubashi University.[16] Inaba, too, left HES and returned to the think tank he had founded in 1945 and later became the director of The Sankei Shimbun, a mass paper with an anti-communist direction. Wada, one of the independent parliamentarians of the House of Councilors, joined the Socialist Party in 1949 and changed to the House of Representatives in 1951. He belonged to the Left Socialists in the split of the Socialist Party but kept the stance of a non-dogmatic social democrat.

In October 1948, Yoshida's Liberal Party won the election, and his second cabinet started. It was renovated to the third in February 1949. During this period, stabilization of the economy and consolidation of public finance became the main agenda. Under the nine points directions that American banker Joseph Dodge suggested in February 1949 (so-called Dodge Lines), nearly all of the subvention and industrial financing using public funds were abolished, and the government adopted an austerity policy. It naturally caused severe depression. Most firms adopted rationalization in production and curtailed employment, even if they didn't go into bankruptcy. Labor disputes occurred in all areas of Japan. It was the special procurement demand of the Korean War (1950–1952) that released Japan from this depression. Though HES survived up to 1952, the ministerial bureaucracy restored their policy-making initiative perfectly, and no room remained for the activity of non-bureaucrat economists.

12.4 Reverse Course

In the latter half of 1949, the items of the public purge were applied to Communists and other activists. As the victory of Communists over Nationalists in Mainland

China became apparent, the anxiety against the spread of communism in the Pacific and Asian regions strengthened. Within GHQ, the initiative moved from the hand of GS's New Dealers to the hand of G2's anti-communists. In July, W. C. Eelles, a councilor of GHQ's Educational Section, made a lecture tour at Japanese universities and demanded the elimination of communist professors from universities, which caused protests against his visit to many universities. The victims of the red purge at universities were not so many, but in Japanese schools, ca. 1,700 teachers were purged in total. On June 6 and 7, 1950, GHQ purged members of the central committee of the Japan Communist Party (JCP) and editors of JCP's paper *Akahata* (Red Flag). Further, on July 24, GHQ ordered newspapers to purge communists and sympathizers from their offices. On September 1, the Japanese government decided the direction of purging Communists from its office. The number of the purged was said to amount to over 22,000 in total, adding those purged in private firms.[17] On the other hand, the cancelation of the purge of the war collaborators proceeded. It was called the age of 'reverse course.'

In the third section (economics and commercial science) of the Science Council of Japan (SCJ), in which many Marxian economists were elected, Moriya Fumio lost his membership on the grounds of his participation in the editing of JCP's *organ, Akahata*. Yamada Katsujirō, an economist of the Kōza faction in the 1930s, was refused to be nominated to be a member of the Conference on the Administration of Science and Technology.[18] SCJ, whose members were elected in each academic section by the vote of registered scientists, was initially founded by GHQ as the model case for the democratization of science and learning in Japan. However, not only Section 3, SCJ itself often went into conflict with the government. The government avoided SCJ to acquire the advice and created other routes to mobilize scientists to achieve national policies, such as the use of atomic energy. From then to the present, SCJ has been under pressure from the government and conservative politicians. The age when scholars were expected to participate in the democratization of society did not continue long.[19]

Notes

1 To acquire a general view of Japan after the War, see Dower (1999). See Yagi (2000) on the economics academism after 1945 and Yagi (2016) on the Marxian economics after 1945.
2 In English translation Yanagita (1988).
3 Sasamoto (1969) and Shimamoto (1969) in Ebata ed. (1969: 168, 171).
4 Ōhara Shakai Mondai Kenkyū-sho ed. (1971) Section V. See also Takano's biography, Ōshima (1968).
5 Shibata (1945). Shibata dated its completion on October 10.
6 Even a half year after August 15, the draft of the Kenpō Mondai Chōsakai under the government (February 1946) presupposed continuity from the old Imperial Constitution.
7 Included in Takano (1961).
8 Arisawa (1989: 41). Those who should return were Ōuchi Hyōe, Yanaihara Tadao, Tsuchiya Takao, Arisawa Hiromi, Yamada Moritarō, Wakimura Yoshitarō, and

Kimura Takeyasu. At the same time, those who should leave were Hashizume Akio, Naniwada Haruo, Araki Mitsutarō, Yumoto Toyokichi, Nakagawa Tomonaga, and Watanabe Shinichi.

9 In this aspect of the 'internationalization' of Japanese economics, see Ikeo (2014). Makino (2010) provides another view on the economics during the war years.

10 Kyoto Daigaku (1997), Section of Economics Faculty.

11 Ishikawa was a fanatic patriotist. Taniguchi collaborated with Shōwa Kenkyū-kai and Konoe's New Order Movement. Yamamoto (1994: 44–50) cited from GHQ's memorandums on Ishikawa, Shibata, and Taniguchi.

12 Most official histories of Japanese universities spare only a limited space for this investigation. See Hitotsubashi Daigaku Gakuen-shi Kankō Iinkai (1995: 175–178). In the case of a private university, see Sugimoto (1996).

13 Included in Arisawa gen. ed. (1990). Following names were mentioned as main members of the committee: Arisawa Hiromi, Aki Kōichi, Inaba Hidezō, Ishikawa Ichirō, Inoue Harumaru, Uno Kōzō, Ōuchi Hyōe, Ōno Kazuo, Kameyama Naoto, Kishimoto Seijirō, Kondō Yasuo, Taira Teizō, Tsuchiya Kiyoshi, Tōbata Seiichi, Tomooka Hisao, Nakayama Ichirō, Yamanaka Tokutarō, Yamada Moritarō, Wakimura Yoshitarō. Those staff that concluded the discussion and wrote the report were Ōkita Saburō, Gotō Yonosuke, Oda Hiroshi, and Namiki Masayoshi.

14 Originally Wada had been one of the most-expected young officials in the Ministry of Agriculture. He was arrested in 1941 while he was transferred to the Kikaku-in (Planning Board). Though Wada's appointment as the Minister of Agriculture was an alternative to Tōbata Seiichi, he accomplished the land reform within a year of his service as Minister. We'll see his service as the Director of HES soon.

15 On Ishibashi's purge, see Masuda (1996: chap. 2).

16 Tsuru (1912–2006) was one of the keypersons in the history of economic thought of post-1945 Japan. See Odaka and Nishizawa eds. (2010).

17 As an investigation into the 'red purge,' see Hirata (2002).

18 Nihon Gakujutsu Kaigi (1977: 307). In September 2021, Prime Minister Suga Yoshihide did not nominate six scholars out of the candidate list that SCJ submitted in due process. Though Suga didn't give a clear explanation for this omission, most watchers are in accord that they were refused in charge of joining critical proclamations against policies of the LDP government.

19 On the economics and social sciences in Japan after 1950, see Barshay (2004), Ikeo ed. (2000), Ikeo (2014), and Morris-Suzuki (1989).

References

English

Barshay, Andrew E. (2004) *The Social Sciences in Modern Japan: The Marxian and Modernist Traditions*. Berkeley: University of California Press.

Dower, John W. (1999) *Embracing Defeat: Japan in the Wake of World War II*. New York: W. W. Norton.

Ikeo, Aiko ed. (2000) *Japanese Economics and Economists since 1945*. London and New York: Routledge.

———. (2014) *A History of Economic Science in Japan: The Internationalization of Economics in the Twentieth Century*. London and New York: Routledge.

Morris-Suzuki, Tessa (1989) *A History of Japanese Economic Thought*. London and New York: Routledge.

Yagi, Kiichiro (2000) "Economics in the academic institutions after 1945." In Ikeo Aiko ed. *Japanese Economics and Economists since 1945*. London and New York: Routledge, pp.50–92.

———. (2016) "Marxian economics in Japan after 1945: Between heritage and innovation." Yokokawa Nobuharu, Yagi, Kiichiro, Uemura, Hiroyasu, and Westra, Richard eds. *The Rejuvenation of Political Economy.* New York and London: Routledge, pp. 11–29.

Yanagita, Kunio (1988) *About our Ancestors: The Japanese Family System*, tr. by Fanny Hagin Mayer and Ishikura Yasuyo. Tokyo: Yūsho-dō and New York: Greenwood Press.

Japanese

Arisawa Hiromi (1989) *Arisawa Hiromi no Shōwa-shi* (Arisawa Hiromi's History of Shōwa Era). Tokyo: Tokyo Daigaku Shuppankai.

———. (gen. ed.) (1990) *Shiryō: Sengo Nihon no Keizai Seisaku Kōsō.* (Documents: Concepts of Post-War Economic Policies). 3 vols. Tokyo: Tokyo Daigaku Shuppankai.

Ebata Kiyoshi ed. (1969) *Kaisō: Ryū Shintarō* (Ryū Shintarō in Recollection). Tokyo: Asahi Shimbun-sha.

Hirata Tetsuo (2002) *Red Purge no Shiteki Kyūmei* (Historical Research of the Red Purge). Tokyo: Shin Nihon Shuppan-sha.

Hitotsubashi Daigaku Gakuen-shi Kankō Iinkai (1995) *Hitotsubashi Daigaku Hyaku-Nijyū Nen-Shi* (120 Years History of Hitotsubashi University). Kunitachi: Hitotsubashi University.

[ITCW] Ishibashi Tanzan (1970–1972) *Ishibashi Tanzan Zenshū* (Complete Works of Ishibashi Tanzan). Tokyo: Tōyō Keizai Shimpō-sha.

———. (1974) *Tanzan Nikki: Shōwa 20–22.* (Tanzan's Diary 1945–1947). Tokyo: Ishibashi Tanzan Kinen Zaidan.

[KHCW] Kawakami Hajime (1982–1986) *Kawakami Hajime Zenshū* (Complete Works of Kawakami Hajime). 28 v. + 7 seq, + 1sp. v. Tokyo: Iwanami Shoten.

Keizai Antei Honbu (1947) *Keizai Jissō Hōkokusho* (White Paper on Real Situation of Economy). Tokyo: Keizai Antei Honbu.

Kyoto Daigaku (1997) *Kyoto Daigaku Hyakunen-shi, Bukyoku-shi I.* Kyoto: Kyoto Daigaku.

Makino Kuniaki (2010) *Senji-ka no Keizai Gakusha* (Economists under the War). Tokyo: Chuō Kōron-sha.

Masuda Hiroshi (1996) *Kōshoku Tsuihō: 3-dai Seiji Purge no Kenkyu* (Purge of Public Officials: Investigations into Three Political Purges). Tokyo: Tokyō Daigaku Shuppankai.

———. (1998) *Kōshoku Tsuihō Ron* (On the Purge of Public Officials). Tokyo: Iwanami Shoten.

Miyazaki Yoshikazu (1971) ""Keizai Antei Honbu no shisō" (Ideas of Headquarters of Economic Stabilization). In Chō, Yukio and Sumiya, Kazuhiko eds. *Kindai Nihon Keizai Shisō-shi II.* Tokyo: Yūhikaku, pp. 321–356.

Nihon Gakujyutsu Kaigi (1974) *Nihon Gakujutsu Kaigi 25 Nen-shi* (25 Years History of the Science Council of Japan). Tokyo: Nihon Gakujyutsu Kaigi.

Odaka Kōnosuke and Nishizawa Tamotsu eds. (2010) *Kaisō no Tsuru Shigeto* (Tsuru Shigeto in Recollections). Tokyo: Keisō Shobō.

Ōshima Kiyoshi (1968) *Takano Iwasaburō-den* (Takano Iwasaburō Biography). Tokyo: Iwanami-Shoten.

Sasamoto Shunji (1969) "Ryū san no taiō 7 nen" (Mr. Ryu's seven years in Europe). In Ebata ed. Ebata Kiyoshi ed. *Kaisō: Ryū Shintarō* (Ryū Shintarō in Recollection). Tokyo: Asahi Shimbun-sha, pp. 163–170.

Shibata Kei (1945) "Haiin kanken" (My view on the causes of the defeat). *Keizai Ronsō*, 60(4/5/6), pp. 25–31.

———. (2009) *Shinban Zōho, Keizai no Hōsoku wo Motomete* (In Search of Rules of Economy, enlarged and revised ed.). Tokyo: Nihon Keizai Hyōron-sha.
Shimamoto Tōru (1969) "Bern 8 gatsu 13 nichi" (Bern on August 13). In Ebata Kiyoshi ed. (1969) *Kaisō: Ryū Shintarō* (Ryū Shintarō in Recollection). Tokyo: Asahi Shimbun-sha, pp. 170–171.
Sugimoto Takashi (1996) "Daigaku kyōiku to 'sensō sekinin'" (University education and accountability for the War). In Shirai, Atsushi ed. *Daigaku to Asia Taiheiyō Sensō* (University and Asia-Pacific War). Tokyo: Nihon Keizai Hyōron-sha, pp.300–331.
Takano Iwasaburō (1961) *Kappa no He – Ikō-shū* (Farts of Kappa: Collection of Manuscripts), ed, by Suzuki Kōichirō. Tokyo: Hosei Daigaku Shuppan-kyoku.
Yamamoto Reiko (1994) *Senryō-ka ni okeru Kyōshoku Tsuihō* (Purge of Teachers under Occupation) Meisei Daigaku Shuppanbu.
[YKCW] Yanagita Kunio (1968–1971) *Teihon Yanagita Kunio-shū* (Authorized Collection of Yanagita Kunio). 31+ supple. 5 vols. Tokyo: Chikuma Shobō.
Yasui Takuma (1979) *Keizai-gaku to sono Shūhen* (Economics and Its Surroundings). Tokyo: Bokutaku-sha.

INDEX

Note: Page numbers followed by "n" denote endnotes.